'WE AIN'T GOING AWAY!'

THE BATTLE FOR LONGBRIDGE

'WE AIN'T GOING AWAY!'

THE BATTLE FOR LONGBRIDGE

Carl Chinn and Stephen Dyson

First Published by Brewin Books Ltd
Studley, Warwickshire, B80 7LG
in 2000

The moral right of the authors has been asserted.

British Library Cataloguing – in – Publication Data
A Catalogue record for this book is available from
The British Library

ISBN 1 85858 174 5

Made and printed in Great Britain by
Warwick Printing Co. Ltd., Theatre Street, Warwick CV34 4DR.

Front cover picture Thousands of protesters set off on the march on 1 April. Near the front is the huge *Evening Mail* banner 'Don't Let Rover Die'. Carrying it on the left is Stephen Dyson, co-author of this book and the paper's head of news, and editor Ian Dowell, pictured at the centre. *Picture by Steve Murphy*

DEDICATIONS

In tribute to Lord Herbert Austin and all the men and women of Longbridge: 'Most everything worthwhile is born of some dreamer's dream.' **Carl Chinn**

****

In memory of my grandad, Frank Ward, who in his time with Middleton & Johnson made many tools for The Austin. **Stephen Dyson**

ACKNOWLEDGMENTS

The authors would like to thank the following individuals: John Towers, for agreeing to write the foreword; Ian Dowell, editor of the *Evening Mail*, for his support; Phil Addis and Steve King, of The Birmingham Post & Mail, for their help with preparing the photographs; and Colin Whittock, for his permission to use two of his brilliant cartoons

   Last but not least, both authors are grateful to their families for putting up with the disruption caused by the Rover crisis and by the quick production of this book. They are: Kay, Richard, Tara, Catríona and Rochelle Chinn, and Ruth, Thomas, Ben and Daniel Dyson.

CONTENTS

FOREWORD

John Towers

Chairman, MG Rover Group

It was a very emotional moment when I drove through Q Gate at Longbridge just after 2pm on 9 May, hours after signing the deal to buy Rover. Hundreds of people milled around the car that carried myself, business partner Nick Stephenson and union leader Tony Woodley, and none of us will ever forget the reception we received. It took quite an effort to squeeze through the handshakes and cheers, and it was all any of us could do to hold back our own flood of emotion.

It was never clearer to me than then just how many people had been willing the Phoenix bid to succeed. The Rover workers were perhaps the most important in this process, because without their readiness to accept what Phoenix had to offer there would not have been much point in going on. And yes, there were the consortium members themselves, various bankers, unions, some politicians and even one of two in the media who backed us, and I'm sure they all deserve and will receive a mention in this book. BMW too have received very little credit for the flexibility and support which they ultimately showed in making this deal happen. But the reason why I am more than happy to write the foreword for this book is because it concentrates on the people, the workers, the families and the general public who stood up and were counted.

Whilst I've never been much of a 'marcher' myself, at least not in public, I'm glad that the man who triggered that great march for Longbridge, Carl Chinn, has jointly written this account with the journalist who became perhaps the closest observer of the Rover crisis, Stephen Dyson. I feel their involvement makes them better equipped than most to produce an accurate recording of this particular chapter of our industrial history.

There is, of course, a long way to go for Rover, an enormous amount of things to do and a lot of hard work for all involved. But it will hurt none of us to sit back for a few hours, to thumb through these pages and to remember those 56 turbulent days, and equally turbulent nights, when what started as a grim scenario for so many people turned round into a very real chance of saving something worthwhile for the future.

"Whatever you do don't drive to Cannon Hill Park in your BMW...!"

INTRODUCTION

Carl Chinn is the popular broadcaster, historian and writer who became personally involved in the Rover crisis. Born in 1956 in Birmingham, he is well known as a defender of the city and for his passionate belief that history belongs to everyone. This ardour saw him call for the great march for Longbridge that eventually involved more than 80,000 people. He then got to know many workers from the shopfloor, in particular forging a powerful bond with shop stewards Carl Lanchester and Ian Robinson, amongst others. They worked unstintingly until the day when the factory was saved. In

Carl Chinn on the 1 April march. *Picture by Steve Murphy*

this book's first chapter, he emphasises that the fervent fight for Longbridge by the workers and people of Birmingham and the West Midlands can be understood only by appreciating the history of the factory and its prominent place within a city which is proud of its manufacturing prowess.

Stephen Dyson is the head of news at the *Evening Mail* in Birmingham, and led the team of journalists who reported on the Rover crisis. He was born in West Heath in 1968 and brought up there and in Kings Norton – both parts of south Birmingham that feel reverberations from the nearby Longbridge car plant. Schooled at West Heath Junior and what was then Primrose Hill Secondary, Dyson attended Matthew Boulton Technical College and Lancaster University before entering journalism. He started as a reporter at the Birmingham-based Caters News Agency in 1991,

Stephen Dyson on the 1 April march. *Picture by Alan Williams*

moving to the city's *Metro News* before working for the *Sunday Mercury*. He joined the *Evening Mail* in 1994 as industrial correspondent, and was named Midland Business Journalist of the Year in 1995. Dyson has headed the paper's newsroom since 1998. Although this job is mainly deskbound, he still loves reporting and hit the road again during the Rover crisis. Using his old industry contacts and local knowledge, he quickly gained the trust of Phoenix insiders and, through the pages of the *Evening Mail,* helped to keep the Midlands appraised of all developments as the final deal reached its climax.

The authors first met in 1992 when, as historian and journalist, they worked together to save the emotive 'Archway of Tears' landmark at a former workhouse in Birmingham. They have since become good friends and when they both found themselves involved in the Rover crisis they agreed to write this book. From different disciplines, the authors' writing styles obviously vary, and so their individual contributions are clearly acknowledged within the text.

Unless otherwise indicated, quotes used in the book are either from the Birmingham *Evening Mail* or from the authors' own notes of the dates in question. Similarly, the majority of photographs are courtesy of The Birmingham Post & Mail, unless acknowledged to another source.

CHAPTER ONE

The Austin: A Dreamer's Dream
By Carl Chinn

Birmingham is founded upon dreams. A manufacturing centre of the first order, a place of practical people, a city marked out by its overwhelming desire to get things done, still it exists solely because its folk have reached out to grasp their hopes and visions. Acting upon imagination, realising possibilities and bringing into being expectations are the characteristics which bond the folk of Brum whoever they are, wherever they are from and whatever may be their class, creed or colour. And like a wire which is finely and expertly drawn, these characteristics run throughout Birmingham's history.

Of course, each village, town and city is the result of the endeavours of its people, but unlike most great urban centres, Birmingham is overwhelmingly the product of those who have come here – for it has no physical, natural or geographical features which can explain its success. It is not at the crossing point of a wide river; it is no port looking out to the seas; it has no defensive advantages and cannot boast a castle on a crag; and it has no treasures beneath the earth such as coal, iron ore, limestone or fire clay. The most that can be said of Birmingham's location is that it was the crossing point of a number of important routes locally. In itself, this factor was never enough to thrust Birmingham onto the international stage as the workshop of the world. Only its people could gain for it this title. And they could do this only because they were both hopers and doers.

The place itself was founded in the Dark Ages by an Anglian peasant called Beorma. Searching for a spot where he and his 'ingas', his people, could make a 'ham', a home, where they would be beholden to no man or woman, he settled close to the modern Bull Ring sometime in the late 500s or early 600s. Half a millennium later, the lord of the manor, Peter de Bermingham, sought to make something of a holding which agriculturally was poor and in 1166 he bought from the king the rights to hold a weekly market. That date jumps out from the history of Brum as the cause for its evolutionary growth and from its beginning, this new town of Birmingham was marked out not only by its traders but also by its fashioners of metal.

Growing slowly but surely for over 500 years, at the dawn of the Industrial Revolution, Birmingham leaped like Prometheus unbound to the notice of nations across the globe. It did so because in the eighteenth century men of ingenuity and inventiveness made happen their ideas. Foremost amongst them was Matthew Boulton, a Brummie born and bred who was a man for all parts. A craftsman, entrepreneur, marketer, thinker and achiever, he owned the largest factory in the world at the Soho Works. A pivotal figure in the renowned and influential Lunar Society, he allowed others to develop their own talents. Amongst them were two Scots who exemplified the fact that Birmingham owed its success as much to those who were pulled from elsewhere as to those who were crafted in its own smithies and workshops. They were James Watt and William Murdock. Through his development of the steam engine, Watt was an essential figure in pumping Britain forward into industrial supremacy; whilst Murdock was responsible for the discovery of coal-gas lighting and was a pioneer of steam-driven transport.

These heroes of industry were not alone. There were others from Birmingham who helped to make the modern world. They included John Taylor, the Brummagem button king, whose genius lay in designing and making gilt buttons; John Baskerville from Worcestershire, who revolutionised japanning (a form of varnishing) and then went on to devise an incomparable form of type which yet carries his name; and Henry Clay, who brought out wonderful goods made of papier mâché. Industrial inspiration did not die with these princes of manufacturing. During the nineteenth century, new generations of folk emerged whose swiftness of mind was bonded to a cunning in their hands. Amongst their number were Josiah Mason from Kidderminster and Joseph Gillott from Sheffield, two men who democratised the art of writing through the mass production of low-priced yet good quality steel pens. Then there were the Oslers, whose crystal fountain astounded all who saw it at the Great Exhibition in 1851; and the Elkingtons who amazed the world with their wonderful process of electro-plating whereby base metals could be coated cheaply, effectively and splendidly.

It was the wide-ranging activities of these and others that gave Birmingham its title of the 'City of a Thousand Trades' and allowed it to catch hold of new opportunities. In this wise, as one trade declined another was discovered and pushed forward. This feature of Birmingham's industrial history was at its most obvious at the end of the nineteenth century. The traditional crafts of gun making, brassware and jewellery were declining slowly, but as they did so a transport revolution gave hope for alternative work. Throughout the land, people were to be seen riding on bicycles. Seeking an alternative use for shell-making machines made idle during a downturn in the gun trade, the Birmingham Small Arms Company shifted into making cycle hubs in 1893. By this date, Joseph Lucas was turning out the 'King of the Road' bicycle lamp and was laying the foundations of a celebrated electrical engineering business, and by the early years of the twentieth century Lucas was moving into supplying goods for the fast-emerging car trade.

Amidst the cluster of those responsible for the British automobile industry were two men with strong connections to Birmingham. The first was Frederick Lanchester. Born and raised in London, he came to Birmingham in 1888. Seven years later, in Taylor Street, Nechells, he created the first four-wheel car which was petrol driven and was all British. First driven on the road early in 1896, this vehicle was the 5bhp Stanhope Phaeton and, like all other early motor cars, it looked like a carriage that could have been drawn by horses. Crucially, this vehicle was the first anywhere designed to run on tyres filled with air. These tyres were hand made by Dunlop, then based in Dublin but soon to move to Aston Cross, Birmingham and thence in 1915 to Fort Dunlop, Erdington, Birmingham.

The second pioneer of the British car industry who was based in Birmingham was Herbert Austin. Born at Little Missenden, Buckinghamshire in 1866, his people farmed land that was overlooked by the Cotswold Hills. When he was four, his father took up the post of farm bailiff for Earl Fitzwilliam in Wentworth, Yorkshire and Austin received his education at Rotherham Grammar School. But as he stressed later, 'strangely enough, even in my very early years it was for things mechanical I had the greatest love'. Fascinated by geometrical drawings, Austin developed a keen eye for size and proportions. At the same time, he was deeply attracted to the music of the great composers and to works of art and for the rest of his life his passion for the mechanical was infused with an urge to make things that were artistic. ['The life story of Sir Herbert Austin K.B.E., reprinted from *The Autocar*, 23 and 30 August and 6 and 13 September 1929, p. 3].

From Rotherham Grammar School, Austin went to Brampton Commercial College, after which he was apprenticed to his father's brother who was an architect. Showing dissatisfaction with this profession, his parents sought for him an engineering apprenticeship with the Great Northern Railway in 1884. As he awaited a vacancy at the company, his mother's brother visited from Australia. Excited by the talk of a land of promise, Austin joined his uncle on his return to Melbourne. Over the next few years, the young Yorkshireman carried on with his drawing whilst he was an apprentice at Longland's Foundry Company. Here he received 'a thorough training as a mechanic' and took out his first patent – for a locking plate for a railway fish-plate bolt.

After his apprenticeship, Austin became the manager of a small engineering business which carried out work for an Australian firm, the Wolseley Sheep Shearing Machine Company. Noticing several weaknesses in the machinery, he pointed them out to the customer and suggested improvements that were acted upon. Impressed by the engineer's knowledge and ability, Frederick Wolseley, the owner of the company, offered Austin the post of manager. The offer was taken up and Austin began to travel Australia, talking to sheep farmers and recognising the vital need for reliable equipment for those in the outback who were distant from suppliers and swift repairs. This awareness led him to make significant changes to sheep shearing machinery, changes which had a major and long-lasting impact.

Notably, Austin's trekking also impressed upon him the importance of good and fast means of movement:

> It was during my work in the Australian bush that my life's greatest ambition found birth. It was then that I discovered the urgency of the transport need, for I was able to observe the difficulties and dangers under which the 'outback' settler was compelled to live and labour. Embedded in my memory, and never likely to be effaced, are journeys through the bush in every kind of conveyance . . . It was in these same isolated places, and greatly affected by such circumstances, that I made a kind of compact with myself that I would one day, by some means or other, build motor cars that could be used by these lonely yet loveable people of the bush . . . ['The life story of Sir Herbert Austin', p.6].

Because of the difficulties with sub-contracted engineering work, the Wolseley relocated to England, but problems continued and thousands of defective machines were sold and then bought back. In an attempt to counter these pronounced aggravations, Austin was made manager of the British company and he and his family returned to England in 1893. Quickly, he turned his attention to the necessity of turning out high-quality goods that were inspected properly before they were despatched. These were tasks that he was able to address more effectively after the Wolseley moved to Birmingham. The transfer was encouraged by the fact that the city was the source for much of the company's machinery. But Austin continued to be unhappy with the standards of some suppliers, and he took the Wolseley to the larger Sydney Works in Alma Street, Aston, where the business could make more of its own parts.

At the Sydney Works, Austin started making other products, such as machine tools, textile machinery and bicycles. Perhaps affected by a visit to Paris, where he had examined the 'very crude internal combustion engines that were in existence at the time', he built a tri-car which had two wheels at the front and one at the back. Finished in 1895 at his home, swiftly he took it out on the Coventry Road. The next year, the budding car maker persuaded the board of the Wolseley to support his automobile venture and in 1896 he produced the Wolseley Autocar Number 1. This had two wheels at the rear and one to the front, and a year later it was followed by another three-wheeler. It was this vehicle that Austin ran to Rhyl and back in 1898. He averaged a speed of 8mph, carried two passengers and had no breakdown on the 250-mile plus trip.

These were exciting years for the nascent automotive industry which effectively had originated in Germany in 1885 when Gottlieb Daimler had fitted one of his engines to a bicycle and given rise to the idea of the motorcycle. The next year Karl Benz had run his first motor vehicle on the road and so began the age of the car. These German pioneers had influenced a number of Britons, although both Lanchester and Austin seem to have developed independently

Herbert Austin (right) pictured with the Wolseley Tricar, around 1895.

their own thoughts and practices, and in 1890 Frederick Simms had acquired the rights for Daimler's engine patents in the United Kingdom and its empire. In turn, these patents were sold on and as a result in December 1896, the Daimler Motor Company was registered. Three years later came the registration of the Lanchester Engine Company of Birmingham – soon to become the Lanchester Motor Company.

Austin himself was a key figure in the fast-moving development of the British car industry. After his work had ended, he laboured on his vehicles late into the night and tested them on the road at weekends. As he recalled, he had to resolve various concerns:

> Apart from the ignition troubles, which were the first and quite the most serious difficulties experienced, probably the engines proved the most satisfactory part of the primitive cars. Only the hot tube type of ignition was available. Tyres constituted the second most serious trouble. No present-day motorists would take to the road if they had to put up with the pneumatic situation as it existed thirty to thirty-five years ago. Third ranked the problem of transmitting the power from the engine to the rear wheels. Why the pioneers fixed on the clash type of gear, the one and only survivor of all the many that have been tried and resurrected ad nauseam,

is a mystery to me to this day. Possibly the comparative feebleness of the
engines of the period compelled attention to an efficient transmission, no
matter how noisy and difficult it was to operate at first. ['The life story of
Sir Herbert Austin', p.9].

Arising from these problems, Austin introduced the gate change principle
for gears, of which he claimed to be the originator and which later was adopted
throughout the car industry. Despite the dilemmas, the long hours and the hard
work, this was a thrilling time. Wherever Austin and other pioneers drove their
cars there was exhilaration amongst the experimenters and an excitement
amongst the onlookers. Invigorated by such happenings, Austin had a vision of
everybody driving cars.

The initial phase of Austin's endeavours ended with his victory in 1900
in the small car class of the One Thousand Miles Trial put on by what became
the R.A.C. Driven by himself, this Voiturette was his first four-wheeler and had
been built the year before. The positive publicity arising from the win led to a
marked increase in orders for Wolseley cars, yet, Austin's employers were slow in
pushing forward his talent in making vehicles. This tardiness led the engineer to
approach the great shipbuilding firm of Vickers Sons and Maxim with a
suggestion that it take over the machine tool and motor side of the Wolseley. The
proposal was taken up and in 1901 the new business of the Wolseley Tool and
Motor Car Company Limited was launched.

Herbert Austin became the general manager, although with hindsight he
felt he had made a mistake with this decision. Indeed, he believed that he should
have started building cars on his own account – even if it had been in a very small
way and in a slow process that would have been somewhat unsafe.
Notwithstanding his later reservations, Austin made a success of the venture and
in the first three years increased the annual turnover of the firm by over 800%.
The greater part of this growth was propelled by cars and not machine tools. As
for the vehicles themselves, some advanced cars were made for racing but the
greater part were products for the general market and which gained a high
reputation for their reliability and good performance.

Increasingly drawn to starting up his own business, Austin struck out for
himself in 1905 after he had a disagreement with the board of Vickers. With a far-
sightedness that few recognised at the time, he bought for £7,750 a property in
Longbridge, which then was deep in the Worcestershire countryside and lay seven
miles outside Birmingham. Friends tried to discourage him, telling him that
mechanics would not travel so far to work, but Austin ignored them. The small
factory had been purpose-built recently by the printers White and Pike and the
newly-independent businessman was attracted by modern facilities which were
close to road and rail links, with room for expansion. There was another pulling
factor. Because Longbridge was in a rural spot, the air was clearer than in smoky
Birmingham. This less polluted atmosphere was important because it helped to

achieve a good paint finish for the slow drying coach enamels that were used then.

Compared to the £100,000 capital on which most motor concessions and agencies were run, Austin had just £15,000 – and even part of that had been put forward by the son of an old friend, Captain Frank Kayser. However, about a year afterwards, Harvey du Cross joined the firm. He was the managing director of the Swift Cycle Company and was the son of the chairman of Dunlop. Amongst the employees taken on by Austin was Mr W. A. Howitt, his private secretary from the Wolseley. Howitt later explained that first and foremost, Austin was a worker who could do all types of work on a motor car and 'was not ashamed to take his coat off and demonstrate to a workman, who might seem a little confused, the right way to go'. [Mr W. A. Howitt, 'The late Lord Austin, K.B.E., LL.D. J.P. Biographical Impressions by his Private Secretary', in, *Austin Magazine*, July Jubilee Issue, 1955, p. 2].

A grafter who was plain in his speech and dress, Austin was a talented engineer and designer whose mind soared to the possibilities of what might be. Like Boulton, Watt, Gillott and all the other heroes of the Birmingham workshop, his practicality was inspired by vision and on the wall of his office at Longbridge was displayed the belief that 'Most everything worthwhile is born of

Austin's Motor Works, Northfield, (now Longbridge), in the early 20th century.

some dreamer's dream'. Austin's dream was to build cars at his own factory and
see those cars driven on the road by a public able to afford motorised transport.
He realised his dream.

From the first, Austin was determind that his cars would 'represent the
embodiment of all the best features in automobile construction'. This meant that
'only the highest class of material will be used' and that the supervision during
manufacture 'will be such as to ensure the very best results'. Importantly,
Longbridge differed from most car factories in that it brought together the
building of the chassis and various car bodies for fitting. By early 1906, the
Austin Endcliffe was in slow production, and it was 'in every way a fully fledged
car – a tremendous advance over the horseless carriage style and the early Austin
design of 1895 and 1900'. A touring model with a four cylinder engine, the
Endcliffe had a horse power of between 25 and 30. [*Austin Through the Years*,
Birmingham: 1959, p. 1 and 3].

By 1907, Longbridge had 400 workers who were able to build by hand
147 cars. Over the next seven years, the number of employees grew to 2,000
whilst annual output of various models extended to 983. Along with Austin
himself, these men – and later women – played a vital role producing munitions
during the First World War. Indeed, 'the total record of deliveries of munitions
and other materials of war by the Austin Motor Company alone since 1914 is
staggering in its immensity'. This output included over eight million shells, 650
guns, 2,000 aeroplanes, half a million night tracers, 682,000 percussion tubes,
167,000 burster containers and almost 50,000 shrapnel heads. Added to this
were 2,000 lorries, 480 armoured cars, 148 ambulances, 750 touring cars and
light vans, 1,603 limber wagons and 2,000 Lewis gun carts. Finally, The Austin
also manufactured large quantities of spare parts for vehicles and aeroplanes,
2,500 aeroplane engines and a variety of other equipment. ['How engineering saved
the Empire. The story of the Austin Motor Company's activity during the Great War', in,
Supplement to The Graphic, 18 January 1919, p. 1].

Women were crucial to the war work of The Austin and they made up a
sizeable proportion of the 20,000 people collaring at Longbridge by 1918. Many
of these employees worked in new parts of the factory. Pushed forward by the
needs of a war economy, the area covered by the works increased from the ten
acres of 1914 to 60 acres by 1919. Austin's vision of a green-field site was
vindicated fully for had he 'bought a factory or site hemmed in by streets in the
confines of Birmingham, development such as that which has taken place at
Longbridge would have been impossible'. [Howitt, 'The late Lord Austin,' p. 1].

In particular, the government was able to buy two farms next to the main
Longbridge works and upon which were built the North and West Works –
factories specifically erected for munitions. Longbridge itself is sited on land
rising towards the Lickey Hills and these slopes did pose problems for
construction. Scores upon scores of thousands of cubic yards of earth had to be
excavated for the new buildings, whilst the top of Cofton Hill was lopped off to

Midland aircraft workers put on a patriotic face on the steps of The Austin Aircraft Works at Longbridge during the First World War.

make a level area of 73 acres which was suitable for the landing of aeroplanes. This lay behind the South Works, which included the original factory and which itself had grown considerably. In recognition of his service to his country, Herbert Austin was made a Knight of the British Empire in 1917, whilst the Belgians honoured him with the Order of Leopold. The accolades were given poignancy because a German sniper had killed his only son, Vernon James, in 1915.

With the coming of peace, Austin appreciated the imperative of switching his spectacular works back to motorcar making. As with other manufacturers which had focused on war work, there was severe dislocation and a loss of jobs. Since 1914 the head of a public and not a private concern, Austin acknowledged that:

> I faced the most difficult period of my life. I found that reorganisation called for greater effort than did original organisation. Four years of idleness – idleness so far as car production was concerned – meant that a great deal of leeway had to be made up. The four cylinder 20bhp car was placed on the market at an unprecedentedly low price. There were years of hard struggling when it seemed at times that I should never win through, but I like to remember that throughout this whole period I did not lose confidence in the possibilities of the industry that had been so near to my heart for very many years. ['The life story of Sir Herbert Austin', p.13].

Still known locally as 'The Orstin', Freddie Henry began his apprenticeship at the factory in 1926 and described the Twenty as a fine car with advanced styling, disappearing hood and enclosed spare wheel. He believed that 'The Old Man' focused on this car because of the success of the Model T of his close friend, Henry Ford. However, the Twenty was large and expensive, with prices beginning at £695, and although it was mass produced its sales collapsed as the short post-war boom turned to depression in 1921. Output that year fell drastically to 2,246 Twenties from 4,319 in 1920. So desperate was the situation that a receiver was appointed, but the Longbridge factory was saved by another dream of Austin himself. [Freddie Henry, '"The Old Man". The story of the first Baron Austin of Longbridge, 1868-1941, for Austin apprentices and ex-apprentices everywhere', Birmingham, December 1983, p. 14].

Aware of the need for a cheaper car, he believed that such a vehicle could save not only the company but also open up driving to a new market. That is why he himself viewed 1922 as the critical year for the future of Longbridge. For it was then that Austin introduced the 'Seven', a car with a four-cylinder engine (of 747cc) and room for two adults and two children. This car helped to democratise car ownership and owed much to two clear characteristics in Austin. According to Roy Church and Chris Mullen, he was 'an engineer who, in addition to expressing a strong social purpose in extending car ownership, possessed an acute visual sense, and regarded the act of drawing and intuitive problem solving as more significant than the act of mathematical calculation or written description'. [Roy Church and Chris Mullen, 'Cars and Corporate Culture: The View from Longbridge 1905-1989', in Barbara Tilson, edited, *Made in Birmingham. Design and Industry 1889-1989*, Studley, Warwickshire: 1989, p. 195].

Herbert Austin at the wheel of his Austin Seven prototype.

Austin was convinced that there was a market for a small-sized car, but he was given little encouragement by his committee of shareholders and banks. Consequently, he reverted to the practice of experimentation used when he had been at the Wolseley: he developed the 'Seven' as an individual. His first design concepts were done at his home of Lickey Grange, after which he instructed Stanley Edge to work on the project. Edge was a draughtsman in the car drawing section of the Longbridge drawing office and for eight months he lived at Lickey Grange so as to help Austin. As Jonathan Wood has made clear, the eighteen-year Black Country lad Edge 'was more than a mere interpreter of his master's thoughts. He was destined to play a crucial role in the Seven's creation, namely the initiation and design of the small four-cylinder engine that lay at the heart of its appeal'. [Jonathan Wood, *The Austin Seven*, Princes Risborough, Buckinghamshire: 199, p. 5].

After this period, the design of the new car was moved secretly to Longbridge where construction began and the board was won over in April 1922. The Seven was shown to the world in July of that year and Austin proclaimed that it was intended as a decent car for a man who now could only afford a motorcycle and sidecar and yet was ambitious to buy a motor car. This, 'the motor for the million', came out at £225, but in March 1923 it was reduced to the keenly priced sum of £165. Advertised extensively as 'Cheaper than Taxis,

Shopping a Pleasure', the Seven was a great success and *The Autocar* pronounced that it 'has made motoring possible for thousands who could not otherwise have enjoyed its advantages'. So popular was the car that the question was posed: 'What was more important to the middle class? A baby or a baby Austin'.

Sir Herbert himself recognised the key factor in the success of the Seven. He was aware keenly that during the First World War, the Americans had taken advantage of the fact that European car producers were geared to war work. This allowed the automobile manufacturers of North America to gain a good advantage in the immediate post-war years, when British car makers had to concentrate on products for which their factories were now best equipped. For example, Longbridge turned out commercial vehicles, agricultural tractors and 20bhp cars. But as Austin made plain:

> Later on, however, Longbridge busied itself with the manufacture of the small-powered car, and it was here that England scored. Despite the undoubted brilliance of our competitors and the unique opportunities that had been theirs, they overlooked the small car need . . . As soon as it was recognised as a practicable proposition, the Austin Seven was hailed with delight by those people who stood in sore need of mechanical transport but could not afford to pay a big price therefore. ['The life story of Sir Herbert Austin,' p.14].

Significantly, the appeal of the Seven was international. From 1927, the Dixi Company of Germany built a left-handed version of the Austin Seven under licence. The next year, this business was taken over by BMW which continued to produce the Dixi until 1931. It was BMW's first car. The Seven also appeared under licence in France from 1928. This French model was produced by Lucien Rosengart in the Peugeot factory. Nor was the United States of America immune to the allure of the 'Seven', and from 1929 an American version called the Bantam was brought out. Interestingly, in 1933 the Japanese firm Jidosha-Seizo began building a car modelled on the 'Seven' and called a Datsun. Austin himself purchased one of these vehicles and found that 'unlike the European and American versions of the Seven it was a badly finished vehicle and the ride was most unstable'. In 1934, the Japanese business changed its name to Nissan, and after the Second World War it sent a team of engineers to Longbridge to learn how to make the Austin A40 under licence. [Henry, 'The Old Man', p. 22].

The cheapness, attractiveness and reliability of the Seven allowed Longbridge to ride out the worst of the Depression of 1929-31. This severe downturn in the economy had its worst effects on the staple industries such as coal mining, textiles and ship building. Compared to the desperate situation of many workers in these sectors, overall the middle class prospered. For those in regular work, real wages were rising as the cost of living declined and with a decreasing birth rate, the middle class had a greater disposable income. Much of this spending money went on Austin Sevens. Indeed, the car's production peaked in 1935, after which there was a decline until its output was ceased four years later. By the outbreak of the Second World War, 291,000 Sevens had been built.

Although this model led the way during the inter-war years, The Austin also brought out other strong selling cars, such as the Ten-Four saloon, the Cambridge Ten and the Austin Taxi. This was front wheel driven and had a rear engine and central steering. By 1934, The Austin was producing 44 models based on nine types of chassis. Amongst them was the Twelve, and as the Second World War beckoned, the Seven itself was replaced by the Eight, which was powered by a larger engine. Production at Longbridge had now reached 90,000 cars a year. Much of this increased output had been achieved because the factory was reorganised to bring in American style flow-line principles and conveyor systems. It had also become a self-contained plant with its own foundry, forge, press shop and paint shops that supplemented the engine, bodyshell and final assembly sections.

As in the First World War, Longbridge proved itself to be a vital source of munitions for the British. As early as 1936, with the prospect of conflict looming, Austin had been appointed chairman of the Government Shadow Factories Scheme for making aircraft and their engines. Now made a baron for his support of Lord Rutherford who split the atom, Austin oversaw the building of a shadow factory at Longbridge itself. This East Works was cunningly hidden from the enemy and from Cofton Park 'you couldn't tell there was a factory. It was like a field and trees, an extension of the park. The camouflage was marvellous'. There were other preparations for war. Deep shelter tunnels were constructed which gave protection for 15,000 workers; 120 acres of glass roof were blacked out; Air Raid Precaution personnel were trained; and a Home Guard Unit was set up. [Letter from D. Harrison of Rednal, in, Carl Chinn, *Brum Undaunted: Birmingham During the Blitz*, Birmingham: 1996].

During the war, The Austin shadow factory made 2,866 planes such as Fairey Battles, Hurricanes, Stirlings and Lancasters; and 56,485 Mercury and Pegasus engines and engines sets. The main works was as busy with making goods essential for the successful prosecution of the war. Each week it sent out almost 500 vehicles – including ambulances, fire engines, troop carriers and gun tractors – and a multitude of other products. These included hydraulic motors for gun turrets; Horsa glider fuselages; balloon cable cutters; oil and fuel tanks for four-engined bombers; components for Rolls Royce engines; exhaust rings for Bristol aero engines; tails for bombs; Vickers and Hispano machine gun magazines; armour piercing ammunition; magazines for tommy guns; ammunition boxes; service helmets – made on presses previously used for making panels for car bodies; steel helmets for fire watchers; and driving gear for Churchill tanks. The Royal Navy also received Longbridge wares, such as marine engines for lifeboats; depth charge pistols; 110,000 magazines for Oerlikon anti-aircraft guns; and hemisphere pressings and mechanism plates for mines. [*How*

Longbridge Spanned the Years of the War. Austin War Production in Pictures, Birmingham: 1946].

Fortunately, The Austin was attacked only once and the *Luftwaffe* did not hinder its output. Still, that daytime raid did leave its tragic mark. A number of workers were killed, and through attending their funeral, Lord Austin caught double pneumonia. He did not recover and died on 23 May 1941 following a heart attack. His wife died a year and a day later. Both are buried in churchyard of Holy Trinity, Lickey, close to their home at Lickey Grange and overlooking Longbridge. Survived by his daughters, he was the first and last Baron Austin of Longbridge.

'The Old Man' was succeeded as chairman of the Austin Motor Company by Ernest Peyton. His technical director was Leonard Lord. He had been managing director of the Morris, Wolseley and MG Companies and had been responsible for the dramatic upturn in the fortunes of the Morris – then Britain's leading car manufacturer ahead of Austin. Praised by Richard Williamson as 'one of the giants of the British car industry', Lord was born in Coventry in 1896 and was a powerful and important personality. He had come to Longbridge in 1938 as works director and had introduced a range of Austin Lorries. Regarded as Austin's heir, Lord became chairman in November 1945. [*I Remember Longbridge. Sunday Mercury Special Publication*, 10 August 1998, p. 7].

Earlier that year, on 10 June, an Austin Ten had become the first British car to be exported to the USA since VE Day on 8 May and it was Lord who was

The 250,000th Austin car for export rolls off the production line at Longbridge in a huge post war effort, as Austin chairman Leonard Lord is congratulated by Norman Mighell, acting High Commissioner for Australia. (circa 1946)

to lead the significant post-war export drive by The Austin. On 25 June 1946, Longbridge produced its millionth car, and the next year the company announced the first British light car that had been designed completely since the war. This was the A40 Devon saloon. It had an unprecedented success on the world market. In total, Longbridge produced 344,025 Devons – of which 77% were exported. At a time when the United Kingdom was struggling to recover from the massive costs of the war and was desperate for income from abroad, the Devon earned the country the great sum of £85 million from overseas markets.

Under Lord's strong and targeted leadership that took advantage of the post-war seller's market, other vibrant models were brought out – such as the luxury A135 saloon and a new Metropolitan taxi – and production records were broken weekly. Indeed, in 1948 the output from Longbridge attained the figure of 136,000 vehicles – more than the total for the whole of the British car industry in 1946. This was a remarkable achievement and in 1949 Austin became the leading car producer in the United Kingdom when it overtook the Nuffield Corporation – the former Morris Motors group. The next year annual production at Longbridge grew to 157,628 units and in 1951 the company introduced the new A series engine with the A30. It was a small car engine that became acknowledged as one of the best in the world and would later power the acclaimed Mini.

The huge rises in output led to major reorganisations of the layout of Longbridge and an ambitious programme of expansion. In particular, in 1951 the company opened Car Assembly Building number one, better known as CAB 1. Encompassing 60,000 square feet of glass in its walls and roof, it was 250 yards long and boasted three moving production lines and underground tunnels along which components could be carried so as to keep the track working full out. CAB 1 was also one of the first car plants to use electronic controls for selection, sequencing and supply of parts to the assembly tracks.

Despite the success of Austin, the world car market was increasingly dominated by the great American car makers such as Ford and Vauxhall, and it was becoming obvious that the two leading British car companies needed to merge if they were to be able to compete successfully. This union came about in April 1952 with the formation of the British Motor Corporation (BMC). Amongst the names that were brought into the corporation was one that had a deep resonance for Austin: it was that of Wolseley Motors, which Morris had bought in 1927. Lord Nuffield became chairman of the new company, with Lord as his deputy, 'but there was no doubt that Austin was the senior partner of the so-called merger. BMC's headquarters were based at Longbridge, Lord was also joint managing director and shared the job with George Harriman, his long time protegé.' [The Society of Motor Manufacturers and Traders Limited, *The Motor Industry of Britain Centenary Book 1896-1996*, London: 1996, p. 12].

Formed to combat American competition, BMC soon had to react to the problems posed by the mass importation of small cars. Following the 1956 Suez

Crisis, petrol rationing was introduced in the United Kingdom and this led to motorists buying more economical models, many of them made in Germany. In response to this threat to BMC, Lord exploded, 'God damn these bloody awful bubble cars. We must drive them off the street by designing a proper mini car.' To achieve his objective, Lord turned to Alex Issigonis who had designed the popular Morris Minor, which had come out in 1948 and was the first British car of which one million were made. Unusually in the modern car industry, Issigonis had been responsible for every aspect of the plan, including the door handles and the small knob on the lid of the glove compartment. [The Society of Motor Manufacturers, p. 140].

The son a Greek father and a mother from Bavaria in Germany, Issigonis had come to England as a young man. After his time at Morris, he left in 1952 to work on designs for the Alvis company in Coventry and four years later accepted Lord's invitation to join BMC at Longbridge. Issigonis was left largely to his own devices in designing the new small car – although Lord had stipulated that it must be powered by the A series engine. Backed by a small team of helpers, Issigonis 'was responsible for creating the entire car. It bristled with ingenuity and was a triumph of front wheel package driving, from its transversely mounted 848cc BMC A Series engine incorporating the gearbox in its sump, to the all independent rubber based suspension. The Mini is, without qualification, the most technically significant car in the history of the British car industry. And it sold for under £500.' [The Society of Motor Manufacturers, p. 141]. Issigonis himself recognised his individuality when he proclaimed that he was 'the last of the Bugattis, a man who designed whole cars. Now committees do the work.' [A. Hope, 'The Genius Today', in, *The Autocar*, 25 August 1979, p. 34].

With an Austin Mini produced at Longbridge and a Morris Mini coming from Cowley, Oxford, the new car was launched in 1959. Fearful, that its radical look would not appeal to the mass market, the Mini was priced at £496 – which was about £30 less than it cost to build the car. Conspicuous value for money as it was, the underpriced Mini captured the imagination of a new age. Along with the Beatles and Carnaby Street, it symbolised the Swinging Sixties and the creative forces that were making Britain the focus of attention for young and trendy people across the world. So great was the impact of the Mini that today it is clearly one of the icons of the later twentieth century. Yet the Mini did not really make money, although it was an outstanding concept and was spectacularly popular. As a result, cash problems began to mount for BMC. Other difficulties were also becoming evident. The Morris side of the business was aimed overwhelmingly at the domestic market and as a result it was starved of investment. This lack of investment would become a recurring theme in the decline of the British car industry.

By 1962, BMC was turning out 200,000 Minis a year. That year, the company brought out another highly successful model from Longbridge – the Austin 1100. Quickly this became the most popular car in Britain, but it was also

Alex Issigonis with one of the first of his new Mini Morris cars in 1959.

priced too low. The lack of full appreciation for the importance of marketing and pricing was a long-standing one in the British car industry. Although a designer as well as an engineer, Lord Austin himself had seen the look of a car as a secondary aim. His main interest was in the chassis and not in the body, and 'the design of a car was governed by practical considerations, such as its ability to turn corners quickly'. [Church and Mullen, Cars and Corporate Culture, p. 197]. Similarly, Lord was an engineer first and foremost and he believed fervently that the primary objective of a car manufacturer was to build 'bloody good cars and they sell themselves'. [The Society of Motor Manufacturers, p. 141].

Lord himself had retired in 1961 and was replaced as chairman of BMC by his deputy, George Harriman. By this time, Longbridge covered 165 acres and had 21,000 workers who could make up to 193,810 vehicles a year. Significantly, about 3,250 employees had worked at the factory for between 25 and 50 years. For many of them, Longbridge was their life and that of their families. This is emphasised by the experience of the Berringtons. Leonard Berrington's grandfather was a coachmaker at The Austin before 1914, when wood – especially ash – was used in making the bodies of cars. Leonard's father then served an indentured apprenticeship as a coach trimmer under Herbert Austin and went on to work in the Body Experimental Department for more than 25 years. Leonard himself began his own apprenticeship in Number 2 machine shop at Longbridge in 1942, and apart from his army service, remained with The Austin for 45 years. His eldest daughter, Elizabeth, became the fourth generation of Berringtons to work at Longbridge. [*I Remember Longbridge*, p. 7].

Longbridge was (and is) like a small town. Indeed, more of the complete process of car manufacture took place there than at any other plant in Britain. This embracing of car making in its entirety ensured the uniqueness of Longbridge. Amongst its facilities it boasted a 60,000 square foot Design Office; various office blocks; a foundry which made 270 tons of castings weekly; a drop forge shop where 400 tons of finished parts were produced and which was famed for its hammers pounding into the night; tool making rooms; engineering blocks; a car assembly plant; a body finishing line; an upholstery section; testing, cleaning and inspection sections; and a Sales Block and Exhibition Hall. [Austin Through the Years].

In 1964, BMC built 730,682, a record number of cars, and took 35% of the British market. But the underpricing of the Mini and Austin 1100, and the dependence on these small cars that were front-wheel drive, led to cash problems. A recognition of this situation in 1966 led to a merger with Jaguar, a manufacturer of medium and large saloons. The new venture was called British Motor Holdings, but two years later it was joined with the Leyland Corporation, which recently had taken over Rover, to form the British Leyland Motor Corporation.

This union had been encouraged by Harold Wilson's Labour Government, which was beset by severe economic problems and feared a collapse of BMC under the pressure of falling profits. The new chairman of the car company was Sir Donald Stokes, the chairman of Leyland and a key figure on the Industrial Reorganisation Committee. This had been set up by the government in 1966 with the aim of increasing the competitiveness of British industry. Stokes had an unenviable job. British Leyland encompassed the Austin, Morris, MG, Wolseley, Jaguar, Daimler, Rover and the Triumph car marques as well as eight commercial vehicle names. This was a cumbersome collection of businesses, each of which had its own distinct history, approach and models. These structural complexities were compounded in the workplace by restrictive practices, over manning and disputes between employees and managers. But perhaps these factors have been exaggerated in explaining why British Leyland struggled and thus have overshadowed another major difficulty faced by the corporation.

Crucially, British Leyland's factories were filled with ageing plant. This was a predicament evident throughout British manufacturing. No government then or since has grasped the need to encourage the long-term investment which would have allowed British manufacturers to update their machinery and compete effectively in a global market. The lack of funding inevitably led to the bringing out of new models which ignored the strong traditions of first-rate engineering, attractive design, and keen price which had marked out both Austin and Morris. In the case of Longbridge, the highly-popular Austin 1100 was replaced by the Austin Allegro 'which, sadly, was manifestly inferior, both visually and mechanically, to its predecessor . . . On a broader canvas, the failure of the Allegro marks the beginnings of the indigenous motor industry's decline as a volume car producer.' [The Society of Motor Manufacturers, pp. 159-60].

Attempting to compete in both the specialised and volume car markets, commentators argued that British Leyland was in need of rationalisation and a clearer focus. This realisation led to a power struggle between two leading figures, finance director John Barber and George Turnbull of Austin Morris. Unsurprisingly, Turnbull stressed the importance of volume sales, whilst Barber pushed for a move upmarket through Rover and Jaguar models, which would have led to less sales. Barber's view prevailed and in 1973 he became deputy chairman. However, before he could press ahead with his aims, the British economy was overwhelmed by the recession of 1974, largely induced by the raising of oil prices. Running out of money, British Leyland collapsed. Confronting a dire situation, the newly-elected Labour Government guaranteed the corporation's capital and instructed its industrial adviser, Sir Don Ryder, to investigate the corporation's future. He recommended that British Leyland should be split into four divisions. One of them was to be cars and this sector of the company should continue to have a presence in both the volume and specialist car sectors. Accordingly, in 1975, the British Leyland Motor Corporation became defunct and was renamed British Leyland. Effectively, the company was nationalised for the government held 99.8% of its shares.

British Leyland's hardships were founded upon the country's economic ineptitude and reflected the deeply-entrenched difficulties of the British car industry in general. In 1972, Britain had produced 1,921,311 cars, but by 1975 this figure had dropped substantially to 1,267,695. British Leyland limped along, desperate for reinvigoration through sustained investment, the bringing out of new models and strong leadership that energised the workforce. Recognising the ongoing precariousness of the business, in 1977 the board appointed Michael Edwardes as chairman and managing director. A year later, the magnitude of his task was made clear when figures showed that BL was now the eleventh biggest car manufacturer in the world. Yet, it brought out 743,000 vehicles, well below the 1,769,000 of Renault in ninth place and massively less than Ford, the second biggest car producer in the world with 6,462,000 vehicles, and General Motors, the market leader, with 9,482,000 cars.

Almost immediately, Edwardes announced that 12,500 jobs would have to be cutback if the company were to survive. The majority of these losses would not have been compulsory but would have arisen from the non-replacement of men and women who retired or left their employment. Still, they affected many lives and represented a loss of future jobs – and also they led to plant closures. Even as these plans were drawn up, BL was swept along in the wave of another global recession. Triggered by rocketing oil prices in 1979, the serious economic downturn caused an almost catastrophic fall in British car production to 923,744 units in 1980. The recession was exacerbated by the rising value of the pound. This had been caused by the growing national income from North Sea oil and a positive stock market reaction to the election of a Conservative government under Margaret Thatcher in 1979.

In response to a rapidly deteriorating situation, the newly knighted Edwardes announced a Recovery Plan. It indicated the need for another 25,000 job losses over a two-year period and the full and partial closure of thirteen factories. Published in September 1979, the plan was acclaimed by those national newspapers that believed that the British car industry was over manned, under productive, led by weak management and dominated by militant trade unions. It cannot be denied that there were problems between management and unions and that there was a need to embark on a programme of rationalisation, but contrary to popular mythology, Longbridge in particular was not strike prone. Indeed, most walkouts were wildcat, short term and unofficial, and although they had 'real' causes they were influenced by an underlying dissatisfaction with 'the rigors of the production line' – such as isolation, repetitive tasks and monotony. [Jon Murden, "Life on the Line": Strikes and the nature of work in the Post-War British Motor Industry', in, *Retrospect. Journal of the Birmingham Historical Association*, no 1, summer 2000, p. 4].

The Edwardes Plan, as it became known, was opposed staunchly by the Leyland Combine Trade Union Committee. This was chaired by Derek Robinson, the senior convenor at Longbridge and a man who was vilified by much of the press as 'Red Robbo'. Disdaining to take account of decades of lack of investment and of decline and revelling in a negative image of lazy, strike-prone car workers, media pundits focused on Derek Robinson as the sole cause of the adversities of the British car industry. The fact that he was a Communist enabled them to portray him as an outdated militant. As a result they were able to disregard not only the historical problems of British car making but also what many people regarded as the increasingly anti-manufacturing stance of the Conservative Government.

The Longbridge works committee facing the press during a Longbridge dispute in September 1976. Pictured from the left are: Vic Plouten, Derek 'Red Robbo' Robinson, Ron Dredge, Jack Jones, Dave Haddon, Dennis Hurst and Alan Moore. *Picture by Paul Delmar*

Fearing that BL might collapse if they opposed the Edwardes Plan, and also feeling that the days of Robinson and his type of union activist were past, the workers of BL overwhelmingly backed Edwardes when he put his proposals to them directly instead of to the unions. Emboldened by this result, the BL management asked Robinson to withdraw the trade union response to the Edwardes Plan. He refused to do so and was dismissed in November 1979. His sacking was not because of a strike but because he had exercised his democratic right in opposing a certain move. Still, there was little popular support for Robinson. Deeply-affected by the winter of discontent in 1978, when strikes had seemed to dominate the life of the country, the mood of the public had swung towards curtailing the power of trade unions. This feeling was as obvious at Longbridge. The unions brought out the workers on strike, but at the subsequent mass meeting the majority of those present rejected the reinstatement of Robinson.

One of those who strongly supported Robinson was Dick Howell. Later a significant figure in the Battle for Longbridge, Dick had started work at the factory in 1969. Within a couple of months, the men in the engine plant (now Powertrain) had asked him to become a shop steward. He remembered that in the early 1970s, 'we had 35,000 working at Longbridge and the comradeship was out of this world. If anyone was in trouble there was always someone to jump in to help'. Dick feels still that the sacking of Derek Robinson was 'political and unfair'. The convenor wanted expansion not contraction of the car industry and 'some of us tried to get him reinstated. But it was not the wish of the majority of the workforce or his union, unfortunately. This was a black day – a man who had done his utmost for the workforce did not get the backing he deserved. This upset me to the point of tears and at this stage I did not want to remain a shop steward, but carried on at the request of Derek himself.' [Letter from Dick Howell to Carl Chinn, June 2000].

Freed from conflict with the workforce, Edwardes turned his attention to one of the major problems of BL: its products. He was of the opinion that great names like Rover, Austin, Morris, Jaguar and Land Rover had become subordinated to a Leyland uniformity that stifled enthusiasm and local pride. In order to reassert respected marques, Edwardes renamed the company BL Ltd and created two new divisions: Austin Morris, for the volume car market; and Jaguar Rover Triumph, for the specialist sector. At the same time, he understood that it was essential for the whole company to ally itself with a major international car company. In 1979, he achieved his objective by signing a memorandum of understanding with the Japanese company Honda to develop a joint model. Until this agreement came to fruition, it was vital that BL bring out its own new models and end its dependence on the Austin Allegro (1973), Morris Marina (1971) and Mini (1959).

Using computer-aided design, attention at Longbridge was turned to developing a 'supermini'. Launched as the Austin Metro in 1980, it was a family hatchback car that was attractively styled and comfortable and was economical to drive at a time of increasing petrol prices. Designed for a specific market, examples of the Metro had been shown to the public at special clinics at which the responses were noted. Brought out from the new West Works, the Metro was produced using high technology facilities that were at the cutting edge in the British car industry. Indeed, the number of welding robots in Britain doubled with the fitting out of the new works. Although it was popular, the sales of the Metro adversely affected those of the Mini and thus did not increase the total of small car sales. Nor was it a source of large profits.

Despite improvements and cut backs, BL continued to struggle and in 1981, Edwardes initiated a Corporate Plan which envisaged drawing back the company's output to 600,000 vehicles a year. He resigned as chairman in 1982. By then, BL was operating only two car manufacturing factories at Longbridge and Cowley, and its total workforce had been slashed to 87,000, about half of its figure in 1977. Market share had also fallen noticeably to 17.8%, but productivity had risen sharply – especially on the Metro line at Longbridge. Days lost through labour disputes had also declined and there was the hope of profitability in the near future.

Models initiated by Edwardes continued to appear after his departure and during the tenure of Harold Musgrove. A Brummie born and bred, Musgrove was committed fully to Longbridge, and to this day still owns three

The 500,000th Austin Metro rolls off the line at Longbridge on 15 September 1983. The then chief executive Harold Musgrove is pictured sitting on the bonnet.

Rover cars. In 1984, the Austin Maestro hatchback was brought out from Longbridge, followed in 1984 by the Austin Montego. That year, the Rover 200 four door saloon went into production at CAB 2. Unlike the Maestro and Montego, this was the first car to be built at Longbridge jointly with Honda. Significantly, it was not badged as an Austin. The end of the proud Austin name was nigh. In 1986, Graham Day was appointed chairman of BL and soon after he renamed the company Rover Group. Originally a bicycle company that had pioneered the modern safety bicycle in 1884, Rover had begun to make motorcycles in 1903. This move was followed two years later by the production of Rover's first cars. In 1919, the company bought the design of what would become the Rover Eight. This small car had been made by the Ariel motorcycle company of Birmingham and Rover manufactured it at a new factory in Tyseley, in the city. After some years of hard trading with various models, it was decided in 1933 to make Rover 'One of Britain's Finest Cars' with 'a discreet and understated image of typically British quality'. The move was successful, and from the later 1930s the company also had shadow factories at Acocks Green, Birmingham and at Solihull. In 1947, this latter plant was the site for the development of the Land Rover – a four-wheel drive utility vehicle that gained rapid popularity across the world. [Rover. A Brief History, Rover Group, 1997, p. 6].

Rover continued to have a cachet in the motoring world after the Second World War and, like Jaguar, it maintained its prestige under the ownership of the British Motor Corporation and British Leyland. It was for this reason that Day decided that all new saloon models should be called Rover, whilst the MG badge would be reserved for sports cars and the Land Rover brand would be developed in the four-wheel drive sector. This change of name emphasised a move into niche sectors of the car market, itself brought about by a realisation that BL had the output of a specialist producer even though most of its cars were focused at the mass market. Aiming at lower-volume but hopefully more profitable marques, Day saw Rover Group's future as a competitor to Mercedes-Benz and BMW. The Rover 800 exemplified this shift in strategy. Unlike the 200, which was seen as a rebadged Honda Ballade, the 800 was an executive saloon developed in full co-operation between the two businesses.

In 1987, the Austin name was dropped. To hundreds of thousands of Brummies and West Midlanders it was a bad and upsetting move. The fact that the Rover Group was heading for higher status models should not have precluded the keeping of a name which was associated with origins of British motor manufacturing, the democratisation of car ownership and engineering of the highest quality. The dismissal of the name Austin seemed to negate all the achievements of Longbridge, its founder and its workers over the previous 81 years.

The same year as Austin disappeared, BL achieved a small profit before tax and interest, but Day knew that £1 billion worth of investment was needed over the next five years if the Rover Group was to fulfil its potential. This presented a worry in that the company was state owned and the present Conservative Government was set vehemently against nationalised industries and instead strongly favoured the free market. A number of BL subsidiaries, including Jaguar, had been privatised already, but the main company itself seemed to garner little interest amongst potential buyers. Fortunately, one interested party did emerge and so the decision whether or not to support Rover Group with public funds did not have to be taken. In August 1988, British Aerospace paid the government £150 million for Rover – on condition that the company was not sold within five years. The acquisition appealed to BA because it sought a regular cash flow to balance its large but irregular payments from the sale of planes.

Whatever the arguments for or against the loss of the Austin marque, under Day, the Rover Group carefully and determinedly rebuilt the image of its products. In this campaign, it was greatly helped by the introduction of the celebrated K series engines, which appeared first in 1989 with the new five door Rover 200. This engine 'marked Rover's return to the self-sustaining world of car manufacture, with a novel form of engine construction nobody had used before'. Tellingly, as with the Mini, the Metro had been powered by an A series engine, the design of which went back to 1951. Britain's most prolific and long-lived engine, it was so highly successful because of the vision of its original conception that allowed it to meet emission regulations into the 1990s. Still, neither BMC nor British Leyland had been able to fund replacements and it was an indictment on the lack of investment in the British car industry that the K series was the first new engine to come from Longbridge in almost forty years. [Eric Dymock, Rover. The First Ninety Years. One of Britain's Finest Cars, Sutton Veney, Wiltshire, 1993, p. 173].

Rover spent £200 million on developing the K series engine and won the Dewar Trophy for its outstanding qualities. The engines were conceived in 1984 by a team which worked under Roland Bertoldo and was taken ahead under the direction of Sivert Hiljemark, Rover's head of Powertrain engineering. An outstanding feature of the K series engines is that each one is made of aluminium. Attractive because of its light weight, aluminium is expensive – but the designers of the K series ensured that the engines were sufficiently strong without becoming too heavy and too dear.

The new Rover 200 models were acclaimed by the press and as Eric Dymock has shown, 'smooth-running and quiet, they were furnished the way a Rover was expected to be. The decor was unselfconsciously arranged for the British market'. Other models derived from the basic design of the 200 soon followed. These included the booted four door 400 of 1990, whilst in the same year the K series engine was fitted to the Metro, now called a Rover 100. Two years later, the return to more traditional brand values was flagged up when the new 800 featured a version of the classic Rover radiator. This was the first time this grille had been used for almost twenty years. A luxurious coupé was added to the 800 range and in 1993 the gap between it and the 400 was filled by the

600, a two-litre saloon. Both the 800 and 600 were made at Cowley, whilst the smaller Rover models, including the Mini, continued to be produced at Longbridge. [Dymock, Rover, p. 176].

It seemed that Rover had turned the corner and once again was becoming a well-respected and successful maker of good-quality cars. One of the most important figures in this transformation was John Towers. Born in Durham in 1948, he became a student apprentice with Perkins Engines in 1966. An engineer and a manager, Towers spent time both with the Varity Corporation and Massey Ferguson before becoming manufacturing director of Land Rover in 1988. He had a major and long-lasting impact upon the company as a whole, as was emphasised by Jon Griffin, business editor of the Birmingham *Evening Mail*. For Towers:

> then held a variety of posts across the Rover Group, including project development director, and a meteoric rise to fame within the group saw him rocket to chief executive. In that role workers still recall the down to earth engineer who preferred casual shirts and jackets to suits, and liked to ignore his private parking space. He was said by many to have played a major role in the development of Rover's best-selling models of the late 1980s and early 1990s, notably the Land Rover Discovery. He also became skilled at handling problems with the unions. He arrived at Rover in 1988 in the middle of industrial action, a baptism of fire which quickly gave him experience. Just three years later, many union leaders praised him for his work on Rover's New Deal programme that promised jobs for life in exchange for the adopting of new Japanese-style flexible work practices and flexibility. [*Evening Mail*, 18 April 2000].

Towers oversaw a sharp and positive change in the fortunes of Rover. New models had been introduced, imaginative advertising was attracting attention to those models, and 'the stunning' Viking badge had been adopted. With a company that was growing in confidence, Towers attempted a buy-out from British Aerospace which would have seen a joint takeover by Rover's management and Honda. But in a move that was regarded as 'one of the biggest industrial surprises of the decade', Rover Group was sold to BMW in 1994. As was sharply observed by Phil Williams of the *The Birmingham Post* in March 1998, 'no-one had noticed parent company British Aerospace playing commercial footsie under the boardroom table in Munich'.

The purchase by BMW 'devastated' senior staff who were involved in the plan for the management buyout. Their intentions were revealed by Professor Garel Rhys, then and now a leading analyst of the car industry. He had been contacted by two Rover managers shortly before the announcement of the purchase by BMW. As told to co-author Stephen Dyson, then reporting on the *Sunday Mercury*:

BMW buy Rover from British Aerospace in January 1994. BMW's chairman Bernd
Pischetsrieder shakes on the deal with BA chief executive Dick Evans.
Picture by Paul Webb

They explained that the decision to sell to the Germans had been made
above their heads and expressed feelings of betrayal. News of the £800
million sale shocked the industry. No one was more surprised than
executives at Honda which still holds a 20% stake in Rover . . . Professor
Rhys, of Cardiff Business School, said, 'Senior managers at Rover were
committed to a management buy-out. They were happy for Honda to
own 30% or even 40% of the company, but wanted to retain the rest to
keep Rover British. Now they are feeling just as betrayed by British
Aerospace as Honda. Their morale and commitment is low.' [*Sunday
Mercury*, 6 February 1994].

Professor Rhys issued a warning that was full of foresight. He cautioned
that 'everything will depend on how BMW treats Rover management. If Rover's
long-term strategy is changed, the effect will be felt throughout the company'.
Richard Burden, Labour MP for Northfield was dismayed at the news. He
denounced the sale, explaining that 'it should never have come to this.
Management and workers at Rover should have been involved in discussions at
a much earlier stage.' Many people agreed wholeheartedly with these comments,
as they did with Richard Burden's attack on the appalling way in which the affair
had been handled by British Aerospace and the government. In particular,
questions were raised by workers, managers and informed observers about the
role of Michael Heseltine, the Secretary of State for Trade and Industry in the
Conservative Government. It was felt that the government should have backed a
management buyout that would have been supported by Honda. There was no

doubt that the relationship with the Japanese company had been productive and had helped to turn around the image and fortunes of Rover. It was obvious that Honda was as taken aback by the decision as were the workers at Longbridge, but it was stated that the Japanese had not wanted to increase their stake in Rover to more than 47.5%.

There were several reasons that may have affected the desire of BMW to buy Rover. It was believed by some observers that BMW wanted to purchase a volume car producer to secure its own future and to prevent a take-over by a larger company. And even though Rover was moving towards the specialist car market, it still had the capacity and ability to produce large numbers of cars both at Longbridge and Cowley. Secondly, it was clear that BMW was drawn in by the Land Rover factory at Solihull. This was a strongly performing element within the Rover Group and was distinguished by superbly designed and engineered products such as the Range Rover, Defender and Discovery. Finally, in Birmingham and the West Midlands it was felt that the revitalised Rover was beginning to bite into the market dominated previously by BMW and Mercedes-Benz and thus BMW wanted to control a competitor.

In 1995, a year after BMW's purchase, Longbridge began to turn out saloon and five door versions of the new 400 series, as well as a new three and five door hatchback 200 which was aimed at the younger driver. Both products were part of the 'Portfolio' range which also boasted the two-seater *MGF* sports car. The widely respected MGB name had been dropped in 1980, and the MG marque had been applied, perhaps ill-advisedly, to sporty versions of the Metro, Montego and Maestro. In 1992, Rover had reintroduced the idea of the MG sports car with a car that was MGB based. However, the new *MGF* had no forerunner on the production line and was a completely fresh car. Significantly, it did not result from the partnership with Honda. It was Rover's first all-British car since the Austin Montego of 1984 and was widely praised for its performance, road holding and quality. Like the other two Portfolio models, the *MGF* was developed by a specialist project team and was part of a distinct range that was manufactured at Longbridge. This achievement of bringing out three new models from the same factory in the same year was justifiably seen as a 'remarkable feat'. [Longbridge. Still making History After 90 Years, Rover Group, 1996, p. 1].

These Portfolio cars were powered by K series engines. Apart from the *MGF*, their body shells were made at Longbridge and all were painted in the state of the art Number 3 Paint Shop. This covers an area of two and half football pitches, incorporates 1,350 tons of steelwork and has a conveyor system, which is six and a half miles long. Built at a cost of £42 million, Number 3 Paint Shop was matched by Number 2 Paint Shop which had been upgraded with a £38 million investment in the late 1980s and now required only a sum of £3 million to be spent on it. The assembly of the high volume cars took place in CAB 1, whilst the niche models were assembled in CAB 2 – which had been mothballed since 1989. Crucially, through Powertrain, Longbridge also supplied the engines for all Rovers and for many customers outside the company. In addition, Powertrain was responsible for producing the suspension and braking components for the Portfolio and other models.

Feeling that 'Munich was cutting him out of the loop', Towers resigned from Rover in 1996 during the filming of the BBC series 'When BMW Met Rover'. By now he had been awarded the CBE for his services to industry. Despite the departure of Towers and the misgivings of those who felt that Rover should have been sold to Honda, it seemed that BMW was keen to invest in a company that had been starved of funds. Plans were drawn up to improve Rover's plants and allow the development of new models. Cowley benefited from new design and manufacturing technology and was chosen to produce the Rover 75 – a car which gained great plaudits from the press and motor industry analysts for its excellent design and superb engineering. The decision was also taken to build a new engine plant at Hams Hall in North Warwickshire, whilst Longbridge was marked out as the factory that would produce the new Mini. This was an exciting project that galvanised the workforce. By the late 1990s, the preparation for the construction of buildings for the manufacture of the new car were evident and hopes were high that soon money would be spent on the rest of the works.

However, there were some unnerving signs. In 1998, Rover lost £642 million. Of course, these figures were of grave concern to BMW, but matters were not helped by what some people saw as the company 'shooting itself in the foot'. Firstly, the manufacture of the Metro was stopped early in 1998. Now known as the Rover 100, it was still a popular model and was withdrawn without a new car ready to take its place. Obviously, the lack of a high selling vehicle in the volume car market had serious implications for the profits of Rover. Then, in October of that year, the launch of the acclaimed Rover 75 was overshadowed by the threat of closing Longbridge.

With no sensitivity for time and place, the announcement was made at the Motor Show at the NEC – Birmingham's National Exhibition Centre in Solihull. Patrick Fuller, the editor of *Autocar*, was there that day.

> We were in a hall when the car was unveiled with a brass band and we all felt very good about it – it looked terrific – and minutes later the then chairman of BMW stood up and started telling us why British workers weren't producing the car quickly enough and there was a lot of work to be done. It was exactly the wrong message at the wrong time to give about the new car and frankly the introduction of the car never recovered from those negative headlines at the time. [Carl Chinn Afternoon Show, BBC WM and BBC Coventry and Warwickshire, 16 March 2000].

Under questioning, Bernd Pischetsrieder, chairman and chief executive of BMW, announced that production at Longbridge was up to a third less than at BMW's German factories and that closure was a possibility if matters did not improve. It was noticeable that no mention was made of facts which could explain the disparity in production. The Birmingham factory was adversely affected by ageing machinery, whilst it was a place which made cars and did not merely assemble them. Naturally, less cars were produced at a car making plant than at a works aimed at assembly.

The British trade unions were deeply concerned at the threat to close Longbridge and entered into protracted negotiations over the issue of productivity. BMW was keen to introduce the type of flexible working agreement which prevailed in their German factories. By this, workers banked up their hours. When there were lulls in demand, then they would have time off but these hours would be held in hand for when output was stepped up. This meant that in times of high demand there would be less overtime pay. Close to Christmas 1998, the trade unions came to an agreement with BMW over flexible working, but worries continued to arise. Technical problems bedevilled the Rover 75 and overall, without a major presence in the volume car market, sales slumped in 1998 by over 25%. This led to Rover's losses worsening to £750 million.

A growing preoccupation with the future of Longbridge seemed to be offset in June 1999 when BMW signed an agreement with Stephen Byers, the Trade and Industry Secretary of the British Government, to invest £1.7 billion at Longbridge. This deal was subject to an input by the government of £152 million. It appeared that there was now a real basis for Rover to move forward and for Longbridge to have a secure future as a crucial element in the Rover Group. Indeed, Professor Joachim Milberg – the new chairman of BMW – stated unequivocally that the investment would mean that Longbridge would become a world class factory for the twenty-first century.

Yet even this moment of hope was soon darkened by difficulties. Because it may have contravened complicated rules about competition and state assistance to private companies, the proposed grant quickly became the subject of a lengthy investigation by Mario Monti, the European Competition Commissioner. As concern mounted over whether the government help would be allowed, informed commentators began to realise that the closure of Longbridge was still an option. Rover was continuing to make redundancies and was, according to BMW, losing £2 million a day. BMW was blaming much of its losses on the strong pound. Despite what were, in hindsight, warnings, no-one was prepared for the shocking news on 14 March that BMW was intent upon breaking up Rover Group. This rocked British industry and led to arguably the most determined and successful fightback by British workers since the Second World War.

CHAPTER TWO

Stabbed In The Back

By Stephen Dyson

T he darkest chapter in Rover's history began very quietly on Tuesday 14 March. *Suddeutsche Zeitung*, a regional German newspaper, carried a story suggesting that BMW was about to break up its British subsidiary. To start with, nobody took it very seriously. There had been numerous similar reports in the past few months, and the German car giant had strenuously denied them all. After all, hadn't BMW pledged a £3 billion investment in Rover only months before? Hadn't contractors already commenced work on the £1.7 billion rebuild of the company's Longbridge plant in Birmingham to start making the new Mini? Surely this was just more wild press speculation, despite BMW worries about the strong pound, and the protracted delays to the £152 million Government grant aid sought to underwrite its huge outlay.

In the early evening of that first day, however, it became apparent that there was something very different about the latest rumours. BMW refused to deny them. And then, as the night wore on, they released a statement that sent a shiver down the spines of the whole British nation. 'The Board of Management of BMW AG has been working on different scenarios to restructure Rover Group Ltd,' a company spokesman said. He went on: 'The scenario referred to in the article of the *Suddeutsche Zeitung* as a plan is just one of the conceivable variants. The decision preferred by the Board of Management will be presented during the regular Supervisory Board meeting on Thursday 16 March and published afterwards.' [Unless otherwise indicated, quotes used in this book are either from the *Evening Mail* or from the authors' own notes of the dates in question].

This short, carefully worded statement triggered media frenzy. Every news bulletin ran the breaking story as their main item, and, on the morning of Wednesday 15 March, it filled the front end of every national newspaper. Not that anyone had the real facts. BMW kept its shock plans under cover for the next day's board meeting, leaving the world's media to a day of conjecture and guesswork from car industry experts. Many said that BMW would keep Land Rover, dispose of Longbridge and take production of the new Mini back to Germany. Some indicated that US car giant Ford was the favourite to ride to the rescue of Rover. Others mentioned that Volkswagen and Vauxhall were interested in the ailing British car firm. Basically, nobody knew what would happen.

Union leaders and politicians were enraged. Labour MP Richard Burden, whose Northfield constituency contains much of Longbridge, said BMW was 'playing with workers' lives'. He added: 'It would be a gross breach of faith if BMW deviates from its stated plans for Longbridge. This has been a bolt out of the blue. This is playing with the lives of the 50,000 people whose jobs depend on Longbridge. BMW has made a commitment to the British people and

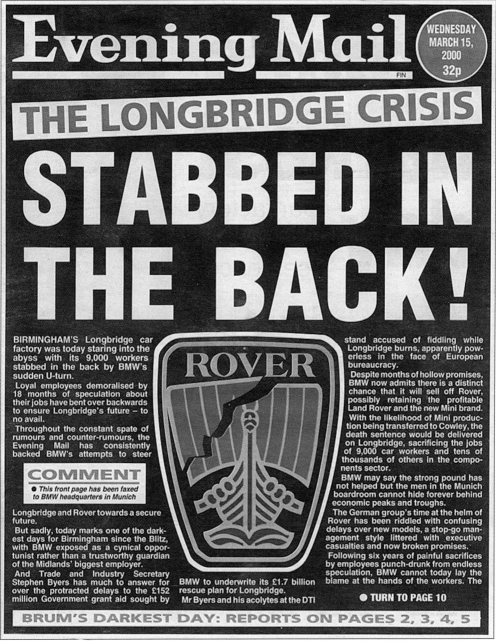

The memorable front page of the *Evening Mail* announcing the Longbridge crisis on 15 March 2000.

the British people have made a commitment to them. It is up to both sides to keep those commitments.'

Tony Woodley, the chief car industry negotiator for the Transport and General Workers Union (TGWU), was even more direct when BMW refused to discuss its plans with unions. 'The situation is bloody outrageous,' he stormed. 'It is not something we are going to accept. If this company thinks we are going to go quietly, it is sadly mistaken.' Woodley was speaking after a 30-minute meeting with Professor Werner Samann, the current Rover chief for BMW, who told him he was not in a position to reveal anything until after the supervisory board had met.

Woodley hastily packed his bags to fly to Munich himself, intending to demand an audience with BMW chairman Professor Milberg. He travelled on what must have been an angry flight with Terry Pye, national organiser of the Manufacturing, Science and Finance union (MSF), Duncan Simpson, of the Amalgamated Engineering and Electricians Union (AEEU), Tom Glennon, Longbridge works convenor, Bert Hill, a senior Midlands organiser for the GMB general union, the MSF's Brian Barnes and the TGWU's Dave Osborne. As the party arrived at Birmingham International Airport, they were all waving copies of that day's *Evening Mail*, the front page headline of which summed up the mood of the whole of the West Midlands: 'Stabbed In The Back!'

Tony Woodley, the senior Rover trade union organiser, arms himself with a copy of the *Evening Mail* as he prepares to leave Birmingham International Airport on 15 March for a flight to Munich for crunch talks with BMW bosses. He was flanked by (from left): Duncan Simpson, of the AEEU; Tom Glennon, then Longbridge works convenor; Bert Hill, senior GMB organiser; Brian Barnes, of the MSF union; and Dave Osborne, of the TGWU. *Picture by Alan Williams*

Headline news outside Rover's
Longbridge plant on 15 March 2000.
Picture by Richard Lea-Hair, Newsteam

That's exactly how Rover workers said that they felt after six years of changing shifts, losing bonuses and increasing productivity. 'This is like a punch in the face', said Kevin Pearce, aged 32, a Longbridge worker for ten years. When he heard the news he could not sleep. Phil Harris, aged 51, who had worked at the plant for 27 years, said: 'There is just a feeling of despair at the moment, and it is very hard on people who have young families. We have been working so hard trying to push these programmes forward that BMW have brought in and we seem to be back to the same situation as we were in before.' Fellow worker Michael Brown, aged 52, from Selly Park, said: 'You get the impression they are just looking for an excuse to get rid of Longbridge.'

By the evening of that black Wednesday, the news got worse. There was to be no rescue by Ford, Volkswagen or Vauxhall, according to new leaks. Instead, the parts of Rover that BMW did not want were to be sold to a little known London-based venture capitalist firm called Alchemy Partners. This latest conjecture was confirmed at an incredible press conference in Munich the next day, along with more stunning news, best described by Jon Griffin, the *Evening Mail*'s Business Editor, who flew out to Munich to record the crisis.

> The shock in the massed ranks of the world's media was palpable. Not only was Rover Cars being hived off to an obscure venture capitalist with no track record of car production, but Land Rover was up for sale too. [17 March 2000].

Land Rover, the jewel in the crown of the Rover empire, was to be bought by Ford, it emerged within 24-hours. This was a bolt from the blue, as BMW had been expected to keep the lucrative Solihull-based firm, but at least most observers felt its future, and that of its 10,000 workers, stood a good chance under Ford. A good chance, however, was *not* what many people felt the left-over bits of Rover faced with Alchemy, previously known to many only for a £5 million deal to take over the Fatty Arbuckle's restaurant chain.

BMW confirmed that it intended to keep the new Mini for itself, transferring its proposed production from Longbridge to Rover's Cowley plant near Oxford, where the Rover 75 would continue to be built. Cowley's 3,500 workers and another 2,000 at Rover's body pressings plant in Swindon would, for now, remain with BMW. Alchemy, meanwhile, would 'purchase' the remainder of Rover at Longbridge, although this was planned to be a golden sale, with BMW pumping hundreds of millions of pounds into the deal in terms of assets, debt write-offs and redundancy payments. Alchemy planned to massively reduce capacity at Longbridge, building the remaining old Mini and the ageing Rover 25 and 45s under the MG badge only whilst parts remained in stock. Ultimately, the plant would only produce MG sports cars, leading to the direct loss of 5,000 or more jobs. Then there was the knock-on effect to jobs in the supply chain that depended on Longbridge – which some industry analysts estimated to be more than 50,000.

Despite the enormity of these moves, BMW's Professor Milberg curtly brushed aside the wave of criticism he faced at the Munich press conference held after his board meeting on Thursday 16 March. 'Given the situation,' he declared, 'given the high value of the pound, we were concerned that we would continue to run up very substantial losses with Rover. We have done a hell of a lot, a hell of a lot. It is with the staff and the workforce in mind that we were looking for a solution that would allow Rover to continue, and not to be dismantled. We have found a solution. The decision was not easy for us but there was no alternative.'

When questioned further, Milberg pointed the finger of blame firmly at the high value of sterling, which he said had increasingly caused mounting losses for Rover.

When BMW took over Rover in March 1994, one pound was equal to 2.53 Deutschmark. By the end of 1998, the exchange rate was one pound to 2.79 Deutschmarks, deteriorating further to 3.12 Deutschmarks by the end of 1999, and today the exchange rate is 3.18 Deutschmarks to the pound. The British government has made the situation at Rover, which as such was already very difficult, even more of a problem due to the ongoing debate on the exchange rate and the possibility of Britain joining, or not joining, the Euro. Then there was the squabble within the EU commission regarding the structural assistance and grants for our

Longbridge plant. And last year, sales of Rover cars dropped worldwide by more than 80,000 units in comparison with the year before, a decrease by 25%. [Evening Mail, 16 March 2000].

It was almost as if Milberg was saying to the world: 'What else could we do?' But if he thought his explanation was the end of the matter, he was so, so wrong. For a start, there was TGWU union leader Tony Woodley, a man whom the world had already seen very angry on Wednesday after the crisis emerged. Immediately after the 16 March press conference, he was apoplectic. Warning that Rover workers could mount an all-out strike, Woodley announced: 'There is one thing for sure: we have made it clear that any thoughts of breaking up Rover and any thoughts of doing business with a venture capitalist, who are clearly only there to make a quick buck and run, is not on our agenda. We have made it extremely clear that if the supervisory board takes a decision that is a *fait accompli* we will be in dispute with this company.' They were strong words. But they came from a man who had done more than anybody in recent years to ensure Rover's future. And he was ready to do so again.

In the days that followed, Jon Moulton, the managing partner of Alchemy, was at least honest about his stark intentions. On Friday 17 March, he said: 'We are not going to be a mass producer of cars...We will be a medium volume producer for the specialised market.' Asked about job losses, he replied: 'We cannot say at this stage that it will be X or Y number. It is possible a very substantial portion of the workforce will be gone.' He added: 'Regrettably, production at the moment exceeds sales. We have not got vastly optimistic ideas of unit sales.'

Anger at this carve up was not just confined to union leaders. Sue Smith, of the *Evening Mail's* Bromsgrove office, interviewed former Rover boss Harold Musgrove, now chairman of Worcestershire Acute Hospitals Trust. On 18 March, he described what was happening to Rover as 'rape' and added:

I am appalled at the Department of Trade and Industry and the Treasury who have allowed themselves to be put in this position. I am ashamed that we have allowed the people of Longbridge to be let down. They have worked their cotton socks off. I have the greatest respect for the workers of Longbridge. They are excellent car makers. The only thing is they haven't got any cars to make. BMW has made a mess of their product planning. It is amateurish.

Even German citizens themselves were somewhat ashamed of BMW's actions. Griffin of the *Evening Mail* had been in Munich for two days covering the story, and before he came home on 18 March he ventured into the streets of the city to ask the German public what they thought.

Security guard Marcel Hutil, aged 32, said: '…They do not really like the workers, they only like money. English workers are the best in the world and the English unions are much stronger than the German unions. But BMW do not care.' Medical student Michaela Griesbeck, aged 24, said: '…I have great sympathy for the British workers. They have kept their part of the agreement, and I think that BMW have acted very badly indeed.' Art student Gunnar Becker, aged 28, said: 'BMW's actions are not actions to be proud of. If you have a company, you have some responsibility for the workers and they have thrown away that responsibility…'

These were just a few of the reactions to BMW's actions. There were hundreds more – many far harsher. It was such a jolt to the British unions, government, media and general public that Rover's fortunes had been transformed in less than nine months. On 23 June 1999, Trade and Industry Secretary Stephen Byers had been pictured shaking hands with BMW's Milberg in London, after completing discussions which appeared to have secured the future of Rover. Now that same Byers, somewhat beleaguered, was being blamed by much of the media and opposition politicians for his ignorance of BMW's change in plans. Yet he was determined to concentrate his mind on the bleak scenario faced by thousands of workers in Birmingham and the Midlands. Visiting the second city on the Friday of that first week, he announced that a new

Trade and Industry secretary Stephen Byers (left) and Professor Joachim Milberg smile for the cameras after a deal was announced that pledged to save Rover on 23 June 1999 – nine months before the latest crisis. *Picture by John James*

Trade and Industry secretary Stephen Byers is questioned by the *Evening Mail*'s political correspondent Shaun Connolly on his way to Birmingham on 17 March 2000. *Picture by Kirsty Wigglesworth*

The Rover task force discusses the crisis at one of its regular Saturday meetings on 25 March 2000. Pictured fourth from the right, with a beard, is chairman Alex Stephenson, faced by Birmingham city council leader Albert Bore, fifth from the left. *Picture by Trevor Roberts*

taskforce was to be set up, headed by Alex Stephenson, chairman of the regional development agency, Advantage West Midlands. The group was to be given a £152 million aid package to spend on workers made redundant by the Rover crisis. The money was planned to help retrain Longbridge workers, assist other businesses create more jobs and soften the blow on the community.

On that taskforce, and among other Midland experts, sat Labour MP Richard Burden, whose constituents would be badly affected by the BMW-Alchemy plan, and former Rover managing director John Towers, now representing the Birmingham and Solihull Training and Enterprise Council. Byers met them during his visit, ostensibly to discuss the taskforce. But at the same time, the very beginnings of an alternative idea were broached between the three of them. Basically, both Burden and Byers wanted a clued-up opinion on whether the latest development for Rover was avoidable. Who better for that was there than John Towers? It was not much of a plan that was hatched at this stage, only a careful and polite question and answer session, yet it is worth recording. Speaking two months later after the crisis, on 15 May, Towers told me:

> We had a discussion round the main headings, with the fundamental one being: was there another way? Were BMW persuadable, and could that other way lead to a far less harmful outcome for BMW, Rover and the region? We decided there was sufficient concept material for the others to say to me: 'Let us get these ideas written up in more detail'. We agreed that I, Richard and Stephen would review that and see whether there was something we could do.

So the seeds were sown, but more of that later. For now, Burden and Towers sat down with the rest of the taskforce to think the unthinkable: how to react if Longbridge virtually closed. Because, however attractive an alternative bid might have been, at this stage there was the serious need to consider the reality for those who would be affected if the Alchemy purchase went ahead.

The McHughs exemplified those families that were at peril, and their story, which appeared in many papers at the time, portrayed how it would have been the end of the line for a tradition spanning more than 50 years. Danny McHugh, aged 40, had worked at the plant for 20 years – ever since his father Daniel, who was a foundry man there, got him a job. Mr McHugh senior, now aged 81, had started work at the plant in 1956 and left in 1983 after spending all of his 27 years' service at the North Works. Danny's 46-year-old wife, Marjorie, spent three years there as a punch card operator, and her late father Sidney Jeffries was a Longbridge toolmaker for nine years, spanning the Second World War. The family's house even looks out on to the factory. Two days after BMW's break-up was announced, Danny said: 'We've got Longbridge running through our family like words through a stick of rock. If it were to close, dad would find it so upsetting. It's like a family tradition.'

Joe and Dawn Clarke of Linden Avenue, Great Barr, with daughter Amy, taken on 10 May after the Phoenix buy-out. *Picture by Paul Pester*

The McHughs were not alone. Joe Clarke, aged 32 with a wife and daughter, had been an engine assembler at Longbridge for 12 years. He told the Evening Mail:

> 'This closure could affect our whole family. In our family there is me who works at Longbridge, then there is Dawn's father, my brother-in-law and my mother, who all work for companies who do about 30% of their work for Rover. All those jobs could be at risk. But I would say that is fairly typical. The incomes for whole families will be wiped out. In south Birmingham it will close shops and other services that depend on the Rover workers. A whole community will be decimated. It is incomprehensible to see how all these people will manage. My skills are not transferable and there will be thousands of other people also looking for work.'

The job losses would have also cascaded through the region's car industry. 'You cannot underestimate the economic importance Rover has for Birmingham, the Midlands and Britain,' stressed Russell Luckock, chairman of Birmingham car parts manufacturer A E Harris. 'For every job lost at Rover, there will be five lost at a supplier,' he continued in his interview with the *The Birmingham Post* on 16 March. And his estimate was deemed to be conservative. Shopkeepers in the Longbridge area also braced themselves to watch the heart being ripped out of their community. Sara Hussain, from the Spar near the plant, said: 'If Rover shuts, then it would absolutely kill our trade.' Karen Richards, owner of the local Rednal Café, explained that: 'It would become a ghost town around here if Longbridge went. Without Rover, I don't think we could survive.'

Russell Luckock, of A.E. Harris, a car components supplier which would have been badly hit by BMW's original plans for Rover. *Picture by Andrew Fox*

Sara Hussain pictured on March 15 at the Spar in Longbridge, which she said would be badly hit if Longbridge closed. *Picture by Neil Pugh*

These examples were just a snapshot of how BMW's sell-off of Rover to Alchemy, a management team who, to start with, intended to turn it into a niche sports car company, could have created abject misery. It was an immense prospect for anyone to face, and one that the new taskforce busied itself to comprehend. As Byers said at the launch of the taskforce: 'This is a very important group, one that has a real responsibility to face the challenges now upon us and offer some real hope, not just to the workers of Longbridge, but to the wider community. We must not underestimate the effect BMW's decision has had. By working together, we can achieve far more than if we did things as individual groups or organisations.'

As well as Stephenson, Burden and Towers, the following politicians and experts were drafted onto the think-tank: Prof Kumar Bhattacharyya, of Warwick University Business School; Councillor Albert Bore, leader of Birmingham City Council; Councillor Gerard Coyne, chairman of the urban and economic regeneration committee on Birmingham City Council and a representative for the ward of Longbridge; Nick Paul, regional chairman of the Confederation of British Industry; Councillor Colin Beardwood, of Worcestershire County Council; Professor Mike Wright, vice chancellor of Aston University; David Ritchie, regional director of the Government Office of the West Midlands; Rosemary Thew, regional director of the Employment Service; Sue Battle, chief executive of the Birmingham Chamber of Commerce and Industry; and Graham Broome, chief executive of the Automotive Industry Forum. A lot of people, with a lot of expertise in business, industry, jobs and retraining. None of them promised an easy solution, but all of them pledged to pull together in an attempt to lessen the impact of the Rover crisis. And while the experts talked and planned for the worst, the story continued to unfold.

CHAPTER THREE

Rallying For Rover

By Carl Chinn

Longbridge is a symbol of Birmingham's manufacturing prowess. The largest car factory in Britain, its products have affected profoundly the lives of British people. We Brummies and West Midlanders are proud of that, just as we are proud of our other industrial achievements. Through Longbridge and other factories, we have shouted out to the world that we are a folk talented in the taking of metal and the forging and fashioning of it into things of beauty and usefulness. The history of Longbridge itself has spanned almost the whole of the twentieth century and its growth has matched that of our city. To the great majority of us, the two are intertwined. Longbridge is an essential element within Brum and we could not imagine a city without it.

Throughout the south west of Brum and in Bromsgrove, tens of thousands of lives are affected directly by the success of the plant, whilst most local traders and small businesses need the spending power of car workers.

An aerial shot of the Rover plant at Longbridge. *Picture by Adam Fradgley*

Elsewhere in our city and in the Black Country, scores of thousands of more people are reliant upon Longbridge for their well being because of the work it gives suppliers to the car industry. Even those of us like myself who have no connection with Longbridge understand its significance without having to be told it. We, too, are proud of the achievements of its workers and recognise that Longbridge is a beacon of Brummagem manufacturing.

An old fashioned Mini and a new style *MGF* roll off the assembly line at Longbridge.
Picture by Alan Williams

That pride in Longbridge was enhanced by our experiences during the 1980s, when we lost 40% of our manufacturing jobs and went through the worst recession in our history. We came out of that dark period and into the 1990s as a city moving swiftly and assuredly towards the leisure, professional and other service industries – but as we did so, we did not turn away from our affinity to the making of things. We believe passionately that we still have a role to play in manufacturing endeavour and, despite job losses, the size and impact of Longbridge proclaim that we are yet a manufacturing city of significance. Brummies have clung hard and fast to our belief that not everyone can serve, that somebody has to make something. And we are good at making things in Brum. But since at least the 1970s, we have been buffeted not only by unfavourable economic conditions but also by governments that have seemed to set their face against the interests of manufacturers.

Throughout that time we have watched as long-established and important firms have disappeared and we have lived under the shadow of the threat of the end of Longbridge. In the late 1970s, the clear implication was made that if the workers did not back the Edwardes Plan then the factory was in danger of closure. And that threat was much more obvious in the dispute between the management and the unions over the sacking of Derek Robinson. The concerns over the future of Longbridge were as apparent in the 1990s, but it seemed that whatever was said and whatever the crisis somehow Longbridge survived.

Perhaps that is why the *Suddeutsche Zeitung* story of 14 March did not immediately cause great worry. Of course, the article perturbed folk, but after all we had been living with major stories about Longbridge since the launch of the Rover 75. It was not that we were complacent about the future of the factory, it was just that we had been there before. Rapidly though, a wearied acceptance of yet another anxiety over Longbridge's future turned into deep disquiet as BMW confirmed that its board was soon to issue a statement about its intentions towards Rover. That growing uneasiness was exacerbated by the extensive media coverage of the affair.

On the Thursday 16 March of the fateful announcement, I left my teaching at The University of Birmingham and went to BBC WM to present my afternoon show. When I arrived, my producer, Fran Daly, told me that the BMW press statement was expected at any time and that the management had decided that we would have to focus on Rover if the story broke whilst I was on air. Just before 2pm, I met with Liz Cave, the acting managing editor, and Tony Wadsworth, the programme editor. We discussed the probability of my show having to change and, if it did, the need to move fast to get reactions not only from trade unionists, politicians and commentators, but also from the general listeners and, most importantly, Rover workers at Longbridge and elsewhere.

Taking my seat in the studio, I had a quick chat with my first guests and as we came out of the news and travel at 2.06, I began to introduce them. As I did so, Jaspal Bilkhu, who drives my show, told me in my earphone that we had to go immediately to Munich for the BMW press statement. The interviewees were ushered out and I was joined by Tony Wadsworth, who was able to provide me with commentary if I needed it, whilst Howard Bennett came in to work with Fran. Howard is the producer of Ed Doolan's consumer and current affairs show on BBC WM and BBC Coventry and Warwickshire and is well used to handling stories that are breaking.

The next two hours flew by as information and reaction sped in. I spoke to BBC WM's news journalists in Munich, discussed the implications with correspondents from BBC Midlands Today, interviewed politicians and talked with outraged trade union officials. One of the first people to come on the show was Richard Burden. Not only was he angered by the news but also he was offended personally. As Labour MP for Northfield, in which constituency most of Longbridge falls, he had been given repeated assurances by BMW about their long-term commitment to the factory and its workforce. Contending that BMW had 'ratted' on Longbridge, Richard's sense of betrayal was intensified by his assurance that BMW had been supported fully by the workers, the government with 'an unprecedented grant', by the city council, the local chamber of commerce, the training and enterprise council and Advantage West Midlands.

Roger King, representing the Society of Motor Manufacturers and Traders, also had a personal involvement. A former apprentice at Longbridge and Conservative MP for Northfield, his feelings were 'strained'. He accounted for the long-term decline of the factory 'on a failure to identify the true path of progress' on which the company should have embarked. Successive managements had never really identified the market at which Longbridge cars should have been aimed. This problem had been exacerbated by the dropping off in the Rover-buying public. A view from a serving Conservative MP was provided by Julie Kirkbride, Conservative MP for Bromsgrove, into which constituency Longbridge spilled over. She believed that the government 'had a lot to answer for' because of the high value of the pound and the European Commission investigation into the grant of £152 million.

Terry Pye, national secretary of the MSF, gave an immediate trade union response to BMW's plans. A Brummie himself and a man who is able, committed and determined, Terry became a leading figure in the battle to save Longbridge. He expressed vividly the mood of so many people:

> It's a devastating afternoon. It's devastating for the people of Britain and it's devastating for the people in the West Midlands . . . It was a complete bombshell. We have been holding discussions with the company over months and months about the future and despite the difficulties which the company has experienced with the strength of the pound, with the grant aid and with the competitiveness of the market, there's always been an optimism that together we can pull through. And there's been a commitment by BMW towards introducing the medium car into Longbridge. And now we find it's all crumbled into dust. It's a complete bombshell.

Terry told me that he and the other union leaders in Munich had been 'taken by complete surprise' about the news that Land Rover was to be sold to another major manufacturer, whilst the proposed move of the Mini to Cowley was 'another blow for Longbridge. It's bad enough knowing that the R30 (a proposed new car) isn't coming in there, that obviously puts everybody's future in doubt, and now we have this situation about the Mini . . .' Yet for all his upset and indignation, Terry held up the possibility of firm resistance to BMW's plans. He pronounced that 'we've made it perfectly clear to this company that we have no intention of going along with their plans, of seeing this great British company

. . . broken up and sold off to people who are later, in our opinion, going to asset strip and throw thousands of our members on the dole'. ('Asset stripping' was a phrase constantly rejected by the Alchemy, as we see on page 96).

Throughout the programme, interviews were interspersed with comments from the listeners. They poured in, expressing fury, dismay, dejection, disgust and shock. Then we received a couple of calls from workers at Longbridge. Unsurprisingly, neither man wanted to be named, fearful that if they spoke out and were identified that they would be amongst the first to lose their jobs in any take-over. The first of them, Steve, explained that things at Rover 'had gone backwards since they stopped making the Metro. We were still selling it and then as soon as we stopped selling the Metro, Peugeot sales went through the roof. It was not a good move by BMW at all.' Expressively, he told us that in Longbridge itself everyone was 'absolutely devastated. And it's not just us, it's the companies that actually work directly for Rover.' Nobody had walked out, but 'people had downed tools for about two hours to listen to your radio station'. Steve understood that industrial action would not 'get us anywhere'. It was a perceptive comment, which was shared by the great majority of workers at Longbridge. When the time came to fight, they knew that they would have to adopt new, imaginative and radical means to challenge the adverse decision of a major international company.

Steve shared all of the emotions of the general public but he also shouted out one other feeling – a deep sense of treachery. He said the workers had done everything that had been asked of them by BMW. They had given up their annual pay rise and special deals 'to try and get the company forward and they've stabbed us in the back totally . . . We couldn't have done more as a workforce. If this company hasn't gone forward it's down to bad management not down to the workers. We don't have strikes here, we don't have problems here at all. So they can't blame the workers.' Steve also put forward the view that most of the workers believed that they had been let down by the government.

Soon after, I took a call from Stuart who worked at Gaydon and wanted to stress that this research centre should not be forgotten. In his mind there was no doubt that Rover produced a first-class product: 'We've been slated time and time again by the motoring press. I can't answer for them, but they are partially to blame for what has happened and certainly the government should have handed over the money that we were promised and argued with the European Commission about the legalities of what was going on. Certainly it's been happening within Germany.' These were themes picked up by many other West Midlanders: the culpability of certain motoring correspondents and the fact that British governments needed to support manufacturing more decisively. Another caller, Tom from Coventry, worked for a supplier of Rover and brought to the fore the potential job losses for firms in the component industry. One of his other observations was shared by many people, the belief that Rover should have continued with its relationship with Honda and should not have been sold to BMW.

Just when it seemed that Longbridge was to be modernised, the workers had been told they had no future with the German company. This sense of disloyalty was more pronounced because the workers had not got a clue as to what was happening. Nobody had bothered to inform those whose livelihoods were in jeopardy. One of the last people with whom I spoke was John, who was at work in Longbridge. He and his workmates were 'gutted' and he had felt strongly enough to walk out. By now, news was coming in that the London *Evening Standard* was calling on the government not to become involved in saving Rover, as we shall see in Chapter Nine. John was appalled at this: 'for anyone to say that about anybody that's making a living anywhere in the world is just disgusting'.

Prior to my show ending at 4pm, I summed up what had taken place over the previous two hours. Throughout the afternoon, I had sought to act objectively and in the manner of a BBC presenter, reporting the facts and asking questions which teased out effects and possibilities. But as the news approached, I knew I had to say something about how I felt. I told the listeners that this had been one of the hardest shows I had ever presented 'because you know where my heart is'.

Straight after my programme I drove to Longbridge because I wanted to show my solidarity with the workers. There were few people around, for the employees were still on their shift, but those folk who were about plainly were in a state of depression. That night, it was as if a pall was hanging over Brum and the West Midlands. Like everyone else, I listened to the news and read avidly the *Evening Mail*. Swiftly, the full implication of the statements by both BMW and those of Alchemy sank in. It looked as if Longbridge was to end up as a small factory making sports cars for the niche market. The manufacturing symbol of Brum would be felled and with it would be chopped our confidence in ourselves.

That Friday 17 March was Paddy's Day of course, and on the morning I had spoken about the history of the Irish in Birmingham at the Saint Patrick's Day Breakfast at Birmingham's Council House. Longbridge dominated the conversation and in the grace before we ate, Monsignor Tom Fallon asked us to pray for the factory and its workers. Thence, I went to open a new Irish business in Bournville, not far from Longbridge. Unsurprisingly, the happy occasion was darkened by the unhappy prospects for Birmingham and its car workers. That evening, I gave a talk to the local conference of the Federation of Master Builders. Again, everyone was fretting about the news. The builders all knew that heavy job losses at Longbridge and elsewhere would have serious implications for their own companies. Before and after my talk, various members of the press had contacted me, but what could I say that was different to the thoughts of anyone else? However, when I came home, something occurred which gave me the opportunity both to say something different and to act.

It was about 10pm when I got back, and my wife, Kay, told me that Our Dad, Buck, had phoned to talk to me about Longbridge. I called the old man and he and Our Kid, Darryl, came over to see us. They'd been talking with Our Mom, Sylvia, about the Rover crisis and about what could be done. All of them believed that I had to stand up and be counted. As a public figure who had consistently defended Birmingham, Our Dad and Our Kid told me that I had a duty not to hiver and hover on the sidelines. Kay agreed. Similar thoughts had been sweeping through my mind all day, but the words of my family convinced me to try to think of a way in which I could help to galvanise public opinion.

I was also influenced by the determination of Tony Woodley, the national secretary of the TGWU. It was obvious that he did not think that it was all over. He had proclaimed fervently that BMW's arrangement with Alchemy was not a done deal. Similarly, Duncan Simpson had proclaimed that BMW's plans could be stopped. Although less fiery than Tony, as national negotiator of the AEEU, Duncan's contribution to the battle for Longbridge was profound. So too was that of Terry Pye. His words on my show had impressed themselves upon me. If men like these were going to fight, then the rest of us needed to jump into the fray by their side.

My immediate reaction was to call for a march that would rival the great rally led by Thomas Attwood in 1832, when a quarter of million folk had met in Brum to clamour for democracy. But as Our Kid said, whilst a march was a cracking idea to show everyone's support for Longbridge, we also needed to think of how the factory could be saved. His idea was to push for some kind of municipal ownership. This pulled me in because I am a great supporter of municipal activity. Knocking ideas around, I came to the opinion that the councils of Birmingham, Bromsgrove and the Black Country should have a role to play, but so too should the workers. It was their livelihoods that were at stake and they should have a major say in the running of Longbridge. I also realised that the workers and councils would need the expertise and finance of leading businessmen.

Early on the morning of Saturday 18 March, I rang Ian Dowell, the editor of the *Evening Mail*, at his home and left a message with my thoughts. Within a few hours, Ian rang back and we had a long chat. He was excited by the idea of a march and pledged the total support of what is popularly known as The Mail, but Ian also encouraged me to think more deeply about the economic considerations of any plan to save Longbridge. As our conversation wound up, Ian arranged for me to be phoned on the Sunday afternoon by Jon Griffin, his business editor. My mind was now buzzing and I rang Tony Woodley on his mobile to leave a message alerting him to my intentions and asking him to telephone me so that I would do nothing that would step across trade union plans.

Next, I spoke Liz Cave of BBC WM to appraise her of what I was planning as I knew that my actions would have implications for the BBC. Liz assured me that she would talk with her senior managers to find out their views. However, she felt that so long as I acted in my position as community historian and did not associate the campaign with my work for the BBC, then there should be no problems. Given the BBC's remit of impartiality, it was essential that I adhered to Liz's instructions. Of course and quite properly, I would be precluded from talking about Rover and Longbridge on my own show. As it turned out, Liz's thoughts were verified by her bosses. Finally, I rang Ed Doolan – for whilst I could not comment on the march on my own programme, because both it and the Rover crisis were such big stories, I was able to talk about them on other shows, so long as I was introduced as Carl Chinn, community historian and made no attempt to capitalise on my own role in the BBC.

As planned, Jon Griffin spoke with me on the Sunday afternoon and I made another call to Tony Woodley to tell him what I had done. I did not expect a quick response because I recognised that he must have been overwhelmed with calls and that his overriding priority had to be the immediate interests of his members. Still, at 7am on Monday 20 March I was heartened to receive a message from Tony. He said that it was really good to hear that someone else felt that the game was not up and that we could battle against BMW's plans. I rang Tony back and as we discussed possible sites for a rally after the march, I stated that I would be suggesting Cofton Park because it was next to Longbridge. Tony was not sure about this venue as local union officials were keen on something happening in the city centre. Nevertheless, he told me to go ahead with my plans but to be ready for calls from his people – for later that day the unions would be meeting and the issue of a march already was on their agenda.

From its first editions on 20 March, The Mail covered its front page with the exhortation, 'March for Longbridge!' and declared that it:

> backed plans for the biggest public rally ever held in Birmingham to try and save Longbridge from 'death by a thousand cuts'. The rally at Cofton Park, directly opposite Longbridge is being called in an attempt to stop the sale of the giant UK car factory to venture capitalists Alchemy Partners in advance of the six-week deadline for the deal. Evening Mail historian, Dr Carl Chinn, a contender as the city's first directly-elected mayor, is urging more than 250,000 people to flock to Longbridge to launch a campaign to hand the factory over to Midland ownership. He wants private entrepreneurs with first-hand knowledge of the car industry to come to Longbridge's rescue and for the 366 acre site to be sold off to a new "people's co-operative" comprising councils throughout the West Midlands, Longbridge worker representatives and car industry bosses . . . Dr Chinn told the Evening Mail: 'I feel passionately that the people of the West Midlands have got to start to fight against what is happening at Longbridge. If we do not fight this, the Midlands will be finished as an industrial region. This is about the future of Birmingham as a centre of manufacturing. If we do not make any stand, irrespective of our colour, creed or politics, we are going to end up in four or five years' time with mass unemployment and nothing else.'

In that first edition of The Mail, Ian Dowell rallied Brummies with his assertion that 'the double-dealing management of BMW have broken our hearts but not our spirit. We are not going to allow Birmingham to be wiped off the car making map without a fight.' Crucially, the idea of the march was also supported fully by Sir Ken Jackson, leader of the powerful AEEU. An intense defender of manufacturing industry, he announced that: 'People are disgusted with BMW and I am sure that any way of highlighting that would get massive public support and sympathy'. Soon after the first Mails hit the streets, I went on to Ed Doolan's show to discuss my plans. In the ensuing fortnight, Ed's programme played a vital role in giving the unions and me the opportunity to talk about the march. Although local independent radio and television stations gave the march general publicity, none of them talked with me about it – probably because I was a presenter on the BBC. Without their coverage and unable, quite correctly, to mention the march on my own programme, we would have had a major problem of publicity for the rally if we had not had the support of The Mail and the chance to talk with Ed Doolan on BBC WM. Ed questioned me as to why I was acting. I answered that in ten or twenty years time when my grandchildren asked me what had I done when Longbridge died, I didn't want to reply shamefaced that I had done nothing. Many people rang in to Ed's programme giving their firm backing for the march and I declared that now was the time when we said, 'No More'. Now was the time when we started to fight back.

As soon as I was off the air, I drove to Q Gate at Longbridge. That gate came to have a great effect on the consciousness both of the region and the nation. It is the main entrance into Longbridge and for weeks it seemed as if the eyes of Britain and Europe were fastened upon it, upon those who went through it and upon those who gathered outside to support the workers. Cofton Park lies across from Q Gate and TV stations parked their cars on the footpath adjoining the park and set up their cameras and equipment on the grass. Outside the factory, I talked with several workers. Amongst them was Anil Chandra, a quality engineer. Anil aroused for me the way in which BMW's announcement had shattered both him and his fellow workers. As he later wrote, when the news broke on 16 March:

> My heart sank deep and a feeling of loss overcame me. This could be seen and felt all around Longbridge this day. When I arrived at home I cried in despair. After thinking and reviewing why, I concluded that a major part of my family's life and mine was based around the plant at Longbridge. Adding to this was the consistent confirmation before 14 March that the BMW Group stood firm behind us. We were shown the scaled model for the new Longbridge plant, our future security with BMW, and our families were also invited to view this future plan. This demonstrated to all the commitments to us, so yes, I then realised why I was shaken to the ground with the events that occurred. [Letter to Carl Chinn, June 2000].

Outraged Rover worker Anil Chandra
at Q Gate, Longbridge.
Picture by John Reavenall

Anil proved himself to be an articulate champion of Longbridge and regularly spoke to the press. On the morning of 20 March, he told the local media that he was surprised that the task force had been set up so quickly and he wondered why it had been given £152 million. Surely, that cash would have been utilised better in investing in existing jobs at Longbridge? Anil also questioned why the workforce had not got an option to join with the management in a buyout. One of Anil's colleagues, Ken Bullers, soon put together a business plan for saving Longbridge and with Neil McLean, they discussed it with John Hemming, the Liberal Democrat leader on Birmingham city council, who would become vital in the Battle for Longbridge. After their meeting, the three workers backed the efforts of John Hemming and ensured that the press knew how successful the factory had been under the leadership of John Towers. During that time in the mid-1990s, a profit had been shown and the workforce had been motivated because they had been led by a car man who knew about engineering and good quality products.

For much of the rest of the 20 March I was on the phone. I spoke with Edward Crew, Chief Constable of the West Midlands, who assured me that the police would not object to the march. He was pleased with the suggestion of Cofton Park for the rally because it was on the outskirts of the city and this meant there would be less interference with the normal activities of the citizens of Birmingham. Edward gave me the names of senior officers whom I should contact to discuss the details of the day of action. I also chatted with officers from the City Council about using the park and Tom Glennon, then the Longbridge Works Convenor.

A man of integrity and thoughtfulness, Tom is imbued with the highest principles of the trade union movement. Convenor since 1997, he held his post through his election by the shop stewards at the plant. Longbridge is a prime example of a federated system of trade unionism that operates via the Joint Shop Stewards Committee, which is chaired by the convenor. Members of all unions accept combined decisions. Belonging to the TGWU, Tom was also part of Rover's joint involvement committee, which was comprised of senior managers, personnel and trade unionists and which oversaw the future strategy of the company, investment and models.

Tom brought home to me how much of a terrific jolt the BMW decision had been. Throughout 1999, he had other senior trade unionists had been told by BMW's senior management that Rover was in great financial difficulties, but that there was no likelihood of the company going under. Indeed, it was made plain that BMW and Rover were in it together and they would sink or swim as one. Tom was shocked on the evening of 14 March when he received a call at home from a Rover manager who warned him that things were serious and that there had been a story in a German newspaper. The next day, Tom joined Tony Woodley and other leading trade union officials to meet with Professor Werner Samann, Rover's boss, at the company's headquarters at Warwick. They were informed that there were three options for Rover: to shut the business; find a buyer for it as a going concern – and that had proven impossible; or to sell to Alchemy. Straight from that harrowing encounter, Tom and his fellows went to Germany to meet Manfred Schock, the trade union representative on the advisory board of BMW, and Professor Joachim Milberg, the head of BMW. Even then, the German company kept things from the trade unionists, telling them at first that no decision had been taken about Land Rover and then stating that this part of the company was to be sold.

Although he was about to retire on 31 March, Tom was of great help to me. I explained that I did not want to do anything against the wishes of the trade unionists at Longbridge, and Tom assured me that my involvement was welcome. He fully supported a march and advised me to make contact with local officials from the TGWU, AEEU, GMB and MSF. I contacted as many of them as I could. Amongst them was Ray Griffiths, regional secretary of the AEEU, who typified the resolve of senior trade unionists to fight for British manufacturing. Later, I also got to know Ray's colleague, Tony Murphy, regional officer of the AEEU, who was also very helpful and dedicated to the workers. Then, on the evening of 20 March, I was phoned at home by Dave Osborne, the Birmingham-based organiser of the TGWU. Dave informed me that the unions had decided that they were going to have a march from the city centre and that they hoped to follow it with a rally nearby. We bounced thoughts around and agreed to combine our efforts. I appreciated that the trade unions themselves were the bodies representing the men and women of Rover whose futures were at risk. It was right and proper that they took the lead. I saw my role as supporting them and helping to reach out to people who were not connected to the car industry and who may not have been trade unionists.

Over the next week I did become aware that there were mumblings amongst a few politicians and senior trade unionists that I was becoming involved only to get publicity for myself. Those rumours were hurtful and malicious. More upsetting were the murmurings that were put about that my call for a march was an attempt merely to gain attention for what some people suggested was my proposed campaign to be the elected mayor of Birmingham. Indeed, as the battle for Longbridge was carried on, it became obvious that someone was feeding this rumour to the national press. On 29 April, following the pull-out of Alchemy from its negotiations with BMW, Patience Wheatcroft wrote a piece in the business news of *The Times*. She was dismissive of John Towers and stated that his proposal was 'currently little more than a touchy-feely nice idea that happens to coincide with one of its proponents' plans to become mayor of Birmingham'.

Although I was not named, it would seem that I was the person who had 'plans to become mayor of Birmingham'. My response to that intimation is two fold. I was never a proponent of the Phoenix Bid. I had no money to put into such a project nor did I have any expertise in big business, engineering, marketing or design. Throughout the campaign I was a vociferous supporter of Phoenix, but that is all. Secondly, whilst my name has been bandied about as a possible candidate to be mayor of Birmingham, it is a frivolous assumption that I fought for Longbridge because I may have wanted to hold such a position. I did what I did because I am a Brummie who is proud of my city. I had no hidden agenda. Passion for my city courses through my being and, apart from my family, the thing I care most about in my life is Birmingham. Significantly, no decision had been taken then about whether or not Birmingham should even have an elected mayor. The Democracy Commission only reported in July 2000 about the possibility of such an office and has recommended that in March 2001 there should be a referendum in which the voters of Birmingham determine the issue. Finally, an election would have to be held. It is fanciful and wrong to think that I acted because perhaps some time in the future I may have stood as a candidate for a post that did not yet exist. It should be reiterated that I am a historian, writer and broadcaster. I am not a politician. A politician may have been capable of such machinations. I am not.

Thankfully, the shop floor workers and shop stewards with whom I campaigned knew that I did what I did because I believed in the cause. They would have quickly sussed me out if my intentions had been self-serving and they would have dropped me. I came to know and become mates with men like Carl Lanchester and Ian Robinson and since the victory in the Battle for Longbridge our families have clicked and we have continued to meet. I am grateful to them and men like Terry Reilly, a shop steward of Number 2 Paint Shop, and Paul Parsons, a shop steward in the West Works, who have made it plain to me that they were pleased at my involvement and knew that I acted as a Brummie for the best interests of Brum. If anyone is to judge me then let it be the people to whom I belong. I shall stand by their judgment.

Despite certain undercurrents from elsewhere, Dave Osborne and I worked well with each other. Full credit must be given to him for his diligence and ability to organise what proved to be the biggest march and rally in Birmingham for more than a century. I was in regular contact with him on the phone (and we met for the first time on Wednesday 22 March) and I gave him my contacts, advice and support. But it was Dave Osborne, the Longbridge Joint Shop Stewards Committee, Alan Weaver, the TUC's regional organizer, and other trade unionists both from Longbridge and Land Rover at Solihull who were on the march committee who pulled everything together so effectively. Dave himself stated in The Mail on 21 March that 'the aim of the march is to ask for public support in our campaign to reverse the plans of BMW and for the company to talk to us about other action they could take'.

After a long discussion and taking account of the views of Tony Woodley and other leading union officials, Dave and myself concurred that the march and rally should be on Saturday 1 April. I was booked to give a keynote address to a national oral history conference that was to be held in Birmingham over that weekend, but the organisers understood my reasons for having to cancel. We aimed for a Saturday so as to allow as many members of the public to join us as was possible, and we specifically avoided all mention of a 'demonstration'. For both of us, that was a negative word and we wanted to put out a positive aspect to our plans. Rightly, Dave and his team were adamant that it was important that the rally should be from Birmingham city centre to Cannon Hill Park. This was for two reasons. Firstly, there was the issue of the symbolism of gathering in the middle of Birmingham and then walking to a spot not too far away. Secondly, the trade unions wanted to emphasise that the march and rally was not only for the workers of Longbridge but also for those in the Rover Group as a whole. A mass meeting in Cofton Park would not have met this latter objective.

Following our initial talks, on Tuesday 21 March, The Mail led with the call, 'Will You March for Longbridge' and gave the date of the great rally. It also published my cry to owners of Minis and Austin Sevens to attend. Later, we had to drop this appeal because of logistical problems such as car parking and because Birmingham could have been gridlocked by an influx of Austin vehicles. In an imaginative piece of editorship, Ian Dowell gave a hotline number for people to state publicly that they would be marching. On both 23 and 24 March, whole pages of The Mail were given over to these promises and thousands of names were printed.

In the 21 March edition of The Mail, Richard Burden gave his wholehearted backing for the day of action. His contribution to the saving of Longbridge cannot be underestimated. Although Richard and myself were not in regular contact, we did speak several times over the ensuing weeks and I was aware always of his deep commitment to the cause. His secretary, Polly Rance, stressed the number of hours he put into the campaign to save Longbridge. Throughout those 56 days, many of the workers were aggrieved at what they saw

The *Evening Mail*'s campaigning front page of 21 March 2000 asking for people to attend the great march for Longbridge.

as the lack of support from the Labour Government. Seeking an accessible target for their anger and dismay, some of them focused their ire upon Richard because he was the local Labour MP. I defended Richard and sought to stress both his personal and political dedication to The Austin. Richard did sterling work both behind the scenes and in public through his comments to the press and his questions in Parliament.

After The Mail hit the streets, I was again interviewed by Ed Doolan and urged the people of Birmingham and the West Midlands not to abandon the men and women of Longbridge and to come out in their tens of thousands – if only to line the streets and applaud the marchers. By now we had begun to make an impact upon the national media and the *Financial Times* printed a photo of me outside Q Gate at Longbridge and in the caption mentioned my call for action. Throughout that day I continued to speak with leading figures locally. In particular, I believed that it was essential that the rally was non-political and had all-party support. As a result, I rang Albert Bore, leader of the Labour Group and of Birmingham City Council; David Roy, leader of the Conservatives; and John Hemming, leader of the Liberal Democrats.

On the evening of 21 March, David Roy rang me to assure us of the full backing of the Conservative group and told me that representatives of the party would march and rally with us. The next day, John Hemming gave me the same pledge on behalf of the Liberal Democrats. John also discussed with me his belief that Longbridge could be saved and detailed his interview in the *The Birmingham Post* of the previous day, which will be assessed in Chapter Five. Soon it became obvious that John was to become a pivotal figure in the battle for Longbridge. A millionaire and highly successful entrepreneur in e-commerce, he stood up publicly and proclaimed to the West Midlands that there could be an alternative to the Alchemy deal and so heartened the workers and the public; he brought together many of the figures who were crucial in supporting John Towers and the Phoenix Bid; he acted as a spokesperson for the group until asked to stand down; and he was an intelligent and vital conduit of information for all of us. At no time did John ever suggest there was a connection between his actions and his politics. He strenuously avoided all links to the Liberal Democrats when discussing Rover and proved himself to be a man of honour.

Albert Bore contacted me on the Wednesday 22 March. Obviously, he was behind the march, but as the leader of the council he was actively involved in a multitude of other matters to do with Longbridge. That day he had attended a variety of meetings and told me that it seemed apparent that no white knight on a charger was going to come to Longbridge's rescue. In such circumstances, Albert Bore's duty was to seek solutions that were the best possible for Birmingham and to focus his mind on what could be done by himself and the council. At the same time, he ensured that the resources of the city were put behind both the rally and the march. Consequently, council officers were crucial in the smooth running of the day of action. They were headed by Derek Stanford and Lee Tomkinson of the events section of Leisure Services, and Steve Hall of Transportation. Collectively, their expertise, advice and wholehearted assistance should not be overlooked. Albert Bore also authorised the placing of posters about the march in pavement advertising sites across Birmingham.

On that Wednesday evening, I went to the Yardley Ex-Servicemens' Club to give a talk to several hundred people attending the Hay Mills and Yardley Aged Dinner Fund. It was an emotional night. When I walked in, the elderly Brummies cheered and called out to me to keep fighting for Longbridge. In my talk, I declared that we would never surrender and that we would fight and fight and fight to keep the factory open as a volume car producer and to keep Rover together. Everything I said was received with acclaim, for many of the people there had worked at, or had relations working at, the Land Rover works in Solihull. When I came home, the enormity of what could happen to Brum if we failed sank in, and I felt my confidence dropping. I rang Tony Woodley and his conviction that we could win reinvigorated me.

Each day more information was coming out which hardened the belief held by so many in the West Midlands that BMW had acted unfaithfully towards the workers of Longbridge. On 21 March, The Mail's industrial correspondent, Chris Morley, had written a piece in which Rover workers spoke of BMW's 'cruel deception' by inviting families to a preview of the £1.7 billion plans to transform Longbridge. Just weeks before, 'employees, their partners and their children had been given special tickets to see the expensive display at the giant site's conference centre – while BMW bosses were secretly talking to Alchemy Partners about carving up Rover'.

> One man, who declined to be named, said . . . 'There was a large scale model, photographs and plans and the bosses kept telling us not to believe what we read in the press but instead to listen to them. That is why the anger is so deep. It was truly and utterly a complete deception.'

In Brum and the West Midlands, the mood was intensifying against BMW and in favour of the workers. Roger Perks, headteacher of Baverstock School in Druids Heath, Birmingham, brought to the fore the way in which lives would be wrecked by the 'downsizing' of Longbridge. A show of hands during assembly 'revealed that over two-thirds of our pupils have parents or relatives working in some capacity with Rover and it is obviously going to be a hard and testing time for them'. He could not express too strongly his disgust and anger at the way the employees had been treated after doing everything which BMW had asked of them. An admired headteacher, Roger hoped 'that this will be a lesson in life to the pupils that they must develop skills and qualities which are transferable and obviously they will have to consider more mobility in the future where and for whom they work'. [*Baverstock Telegram*, 20 March 2000, p. 1].

I was now in almost hourly contact with Dave Osborne and the momentum for the rally was growing. On Thursday 23 March, it was announced that the marchers would assemble at 10am at Jennens Road, just off Masshouse Circus. Dave and his fellow trade unionists were working tirelessly to arrange a huge rally in little time. They were attending to a multitude of important matters such as gathering points, the need for drop off locations for coach parties, and marshalling. We had no idea as to how many people would be attending, but Dave was receiving scores of calls indicating the presence of trade unionists from across Britain. They would swell the numbers of those from Longbridge, Solihull and also Gaydon – which we were also fighting to save. In this light, we thought that the march might involve up to 50,000 people.

Obviously, such a mass gathering meant that the trade union rally committee needed the assistance and co-operation of many different bodies. Amongst them was the West Midlands Police. Their involvement was coordinated by Superintendant David Shaw, who ensured that the handling of the whole event was outstanding and exemplified community policing at its best. Similar praise should also go to West Midlands Fire Service, West Midlands Ambulance Service and the St John's Ambulance. Many men and women from these organisations gave invaluable advice and help and neither the march nor the rally could have taken place without them.

Throughout that week and the next, the letters page of The Mail was filled with views about the Rover crisis. Many were from Longbridge workers such as P. Smith who urged 'the Birmingham community and businesses to join us on April 1. The more of us there the more TV coverage it will bring. All we ask is a few hours of your time . . . Let's not see Longbridge bulldozed like so many other industrial factories.' Other letters were from those who saw Longbridge's plight as a worrying symbol of the decline of British manufacturing. I. Mansbridge of Manchester stressed that 'what is being visited on the Midlands has been the experience of one industrial region after another. Westminster has crushed Britain's manufacturing like an insect under foot.' [24 March 2000].

One of the most informed and persuasive letters was from Steve Shaw, a Labour councillor for Longbridge Ward. It was in the form of an open letter to the Prime Minister, Tony Blair, and it explained how Longbridge's workers had virtually 'jumped through hoops' in accepting changes to shift patterns, working practices and conditions of pay. In return BMW had promised them job security. However, Steve believed that there was a chance to save jobs by exploring the possibility of finding an alternative buyer for Rover; clarifying the new strategy of Alchemy for MG cars; taking whatever steps were necessary to support the regional economy by ensuring that Longbridge remained a volume car producer; and demonstrating a commitment to the locality by allowing to go ahead a PFI bid for the regeneration of Northfield centre and by providing resources for the Northfield relief road. [23 March 2000].

Soon after my decision to call for a march, I had spoken with a pal of mine, Brian Travers of the world-famous UB40. He pledged the band's support and told me that they would all turn up to show their solidarity with the workers of Rover and the people of Birmingham. This was wonderful news, but only what I had expected from men who are as passionate about Brum as myself. As explained by Carol Beirne, UB40's assistant manager, many members of the band were unemployed in the late 1970s and 1980s 'and they know the sort of difficulties that Rover families are going through at the moment'. UB40's support was reported in The Mail on Friday 24 March and it proved important for publicity and morale. I did leave messages with a number of other leading entertainers from Birmingham asking them for their backing, but none of them responded. UB40 not only got in touch but even though they were locked away in the recording studios, they made themselves available for interview on BBC WM and BBC Coventry and Warwickshire and on independent radio. This latter medium was important because it gave us added coverage, especially towards a younger audience.

I also contacted the two main football clubs in Birmingham. Alan Jones, secretary of Birmingham City, responded immediately and gave the full backing of the club. He told me that no officials would be able to attend the rally because on that day Blues would be at home to Wolves, a big local derby. However, the kick-off time would be put back so to allow fans to attend the march and rally and still get to the ground in time. On the morning of the march, the first edition of The Mail carried two pages that highlighted the support of ten well-known people. Three of them were connected with Birmingham City. They were David Sullivan, president and co-owner of the club; David Gold, chairman and another co-owner; and Martin O'Connor, captain of the first team.

The march route had also been published in The Mail on Friday 31 March and had been discussed on Ed Doolan's show, whilst Brendan Joyce of the Garryowen night-club in Small Heath had promised that the proceeds of a special night should go towards the cost of the rally. In the end, he handed over £5,000. That Friday evening, 200,000 leaflets and 5,000 posters about the march and rally came off the printing presses. This was another of Dave Osborne's initiatives. The posters supplemented those of The Mail which were prominent in the front windows of homes and shops across the city. In red and blue lettering on a white background, they proclaimed the message 'Don't Let Rover Die' – beneath which were the words Evening Mail. The poster also featured the Rover symbol with a crack running through it – a clever and eye-catching visual image that appeared regularly in the paper itself.

Early on the morning of Saturday 25 March, I went up to Transport House on Broad Street to pick up leaflets and posters. Everywhere men and women were collaring. Some were pasting posters on to placards, others were bundling leaflets and yet more were discussing where they would go that day to hand out leaflets to the public. I chatted with Dave Osborne and shook hands with most of the trade unionists that were present. Taking several thousand leaflets and scores of posters, I went to leave, but just before I did so, I was stopped by a shop steward. His name was Carl Lanchester, of Number 3 Paint Shop at Longbridge. He recalls what pushed him to approach me in the build up to the rally:

> The Paint Shop was saying, 'Who's going to speak for us? Who's going to tell em what we're goin' through here, the hardships, the financial hardships.' People were hocked up to their eyeballs. 'What we going to do? How we going to get out of it?' They said, Big Phil Sidhu who it was, he said, 'You've got to get up there, you've got to tell em.' And I thought, 'Well, I've got no chance of getting up there.' Which proved right when I phoned Tommy Glennon and he says, 'Carl I can't even get up there myself.' He says, 'You can try but you're wasting your time.' So how could we get our voice heard at Cannon Hill? It was only when I went down to Broad Street on the Saturday before the rally to pick up leaflets to distribute over Birmingham I had me first stroke of luck and that was when I came down the stairs from the canteen I bumped into you, Carl. And I thought, 'That's the man. That's the man that can get our message over.' And I had that conversation with you, I told you what we were thinking, what people were desperate for at Longbridge and you said, 'Phone me up tonight.' And I did and that was really the turning point. When I got back to work on the Monday I told all the blokes what had happened, I told em I'd seen you. I said that you were going to put our point over on April the 1st and 'Yeh, we would have a voice.'
> [Tape recording by Carl Lanchester, 17 July 2000].

Over the next few weeks, both Carl and myself came to believe that fate had stepped in to push us together.

On the Saturday afternoon 25 March, I went with some of my family to the Villa as we always did when the team was at home. We went down the match early because we wanted to hand out leaflets. I stood outside the old Holte pub; Our Dad went up to the North Stand; and Our Kid stood with Our Mom and his father-in-law, Billy Hughes, outside the Doug Ellis Stand. A Dubliner, Billy himself had worked for years at the Rover in Tyseley and was keen to help in whatever way he could. Billy was helped by his best mate, Harry Gillan – a Protestant from East Belfast who is now in his 80s. This was just one small example of how we all came together and how differing beliefs did not affect our over-riding devotion to the cause. That day, we gave out thousands of leaflets. Only a handful of people wouldn't take one and there was just a single bad incident. This bloke took a leaflet from Our Dad and as he went past he screwed it up, chucked it on the floor and shouted: 'I hope they all lose their jobs'. He never knew how lucky he was. Our Old Man comes from a tough working-class street and was ready to put one on the bloke. Luckily, Our Dad held himself back, because we all knew that the national media was ready for just one slip from anyone associated with the rally and march.

The involvement of my family meant a lot to me and highlighted at a personal level the way in which Brummies and West Midlanders were bonding together for a common cause. My own convictions, and my support for Longbridge, are deeply informed by my background. For almost the last 20 years I have steered clear of party politics because I believe that my historical and community work should not be associated with a particular political standpoint. That does not mean that I do not have strong and often radical opinions. I do. I am noted for my research into the lives of the poor, women and ethnic minorities and as someone who believes in the rights of those people and of the working class. For me, the battle of Longbridge was not only about fighting for Brum but also it was about fighting for the British working class.

I am fortunate that I am well off and that I grew up in a prosperous family. Our Dad was a bookie and we lived a big house, but both he and Our Mom come from the working class and have remained loyal to their roots. Our Mom grew up in a back house in Whitehouse Street, Aston and both Our Nan and Granddad Perry were raised in poverty in the back streets of Brum. Our Dad's mom and dad had also lived through very hard times in Sparkbrook before we became bookmakers. Just a generation away from back-to-back Birmingham and two generations away from deprivation and having to rough it, both me and Our Kid were brought up to be working class and not to turn our back on our own. I hope that we have never done so. We know where we come from and to whom we owe our loyalty.

As the week of the march beckoned, it now became a matter of tightening up the details. Dave Osborne and his committee continued to do the bulk of the work, whilst I focused on the issue of entertainment at the rally. We knew that many people might go straight to Cannon Hill Park and we realised that if there were as many marchers as we anticipated, then it would take at least an hour for them all to get into the arena. I was convinced that we needed to have music to entertain people until we were ready for the speeches. Thankfully, the responsibility for all the arrangements was taken over by a team of chaps who gave their services for free and who brought various skills to the operation.

First of all there was Jimmy Franks, a local radio personality who has wide expertise in the management of big events. Jimmy had phoned me as soon as he had seen my call for the march in The Mail and offered me his help. As it turned out, he did a wonderful job in compering the events at Cannon Hill Park until the speeches. Secondly, there was Phil Smith. Like Jimmy, I had known Phil for several years and he is a man whom I admire for his abilities. Well versed in theatre management and promotions, Phil had been the events manager for Birmingham City Council before he had taken up a post at the The Birmingham Post & Mail. Recently made redundant and trying to set up his own business, Phil empathised with the workers. He stage-managed the event at Cannon Hill

Park and liased with the companies that Leisure Services had brought in for the staging.

Finally, there were Andy Bucknall and his mate, Mark Guest. I came to know and respect Andy whilst he was a mature student at The University of Birmingham. A lad from Kingstanding, he is now working as a tutor specialising in music at City College. Andy plays regularly in a band and is involved in the promotion of young local groups. Mark Guest works in the voluntary sector and is in the band Fantastics. Together with Andy, he co-ordinated the running order of the performers and arranged for passes with Special Events Security, the company hired by the city council. On the day of the rally, Fantastics were joined by Dub Angels, an amalgam of two bands associated with Andy Bucknall; Will French; Andy Wickett, the original singer with Duran Duran; the Icknield Male Voice Choir; Laurie Hornsby; and Saiboo, a duo which included Brian Bannister, a folk singer from Kings Heath in Birmingham who had written a song about Longbridge called 'Rover's Clock'. It included the appeal 'just have one more crack, working on the track, One more chance to make those engines roar'. He spoke about his words and the sentiments behind them on BBC Midlands Today around the time of the march, explaining that 'as a musician I can't really help, but if the song helps a little bit to keep this place open then it will have been worthwhile, and that's what I'm trying to do'.

It was astonishing how many people and organisations were offering help – although not always were we able to take it up. Amongst them were Ian Darby of the Rover Owners' Club and Dave Hollis of the Mini Club. They could have brought hundreds of cars to Brum, but as stated previously, for safety reasons we had to decline their offer. Then there was Andrew S. Baker from Midland Radio Links who offered us the use of his company's Motorola two-way radio hire fleet for the day of the march; and the MAC, Warwickshire Cricket Club and The University of Birmingham, which freely opened their car parks for coaches and other vehicles. Finally, we had the services of Bryan Sheppard, chief executive of BID, who came along freely to interpret the speeches for those who were deaf. He had replied to my request for someone to carry out this role after I had been approached by Roger Sutton, public relations officer for BID – the charity that provides services for the deaf in the West Midlands. An ex-British Leyland employee himself and someone who is profoundly deaf, Roger had urged me 'not to forget the deaf community and please book a qualified BSL interpreter for the speeches you intend'. [Fax to Carl Chinn, 24 March 2000].

I was also receiving scores upon scores of letters of support from individuals and organisations such as the Austin Village Preservation Society, the Birmingham Irish Business Group, the Birmingham Irish Community Forum, and the Human City Institute. Many of the letters detailed ways in which Rover could be saved and kept together. With years of experience in trying to improve the conditions of working people, Bill Banning of Hall Green, Birmingham, suggested a workers' co-operative; Chris Morton of Tamworth advocated that

Gordon Brown should use the government's reserves to buy Rover and allow the workers and blue collar management to form a syndicate; Maureen Verney of Kenilworth argued that 'there must be many like us who would willingly put shares into Rover'; John K. Lyon of Harborne, Birmingham, called for nationalisation; Susan Lewis of Sutton Coldfield wanted the government to lower the tax on British cars; and Alan Heath of Solihull promoted the idea of changing production at Longbridge from petrol engines to a new fuel power, such as hydrogen, electric or solar. [Letters, 14 March, 20 March, 21 March and 22 March].

Others emphasised the resolve of people to act. Anne M. A. was one of them:

> We cannot continue to lie down and see our industrial heritage eroded in this fashion. It is about time we stood up and be counted. My heart goes out to all the Rover workers. BMW have acted in a despicable manner . . . and I do not think that the government has done very much. I think they have been very lax. I think it is up to every citizen to attend your rally . . . I should love to be there. Unfortunately, due to being in very poor health I cannot attend (I am awaiting two operations). However I shall be there in spirit, I thought that in writing to you with my support I can do the next best thing . . . I hope the rally goes well with a good turnout. Show the world that we are proud of our industrial heritage and are not prepared to tolerate these catastrophic effects on our region, indeed country. [Letter 20 March 2000].

Another of those who could not attend was Bill Jordan, former head of the AEEU and now General Secretary of the international trade union movement, the ICFTU. He had to be in South Africa for that organisation's conference and sent the heartfelt wishes of himself and his wife, Jean, 'for a successful rally and its consequent positive impact on the efforts to save Longbridge and the wider Rover manufacturing complex'. A Brummie born and bred, Bill declared that Birmingham's future would be determined by 'the legacy of invention and innovation bequeathed by the other BMW, Boulton, Murdock and Watt, that still courses strongly through the arteries of the city and its people'. [Letter 24 March 2000].

Aston born and bred, John Houghton drew to the fore the spirit of defiance in Birmingham through a poem.

> Rise up you Brummie might,
> Let's not go down without a fight.
> The time has come to be counted,
> Save our jobs the call must be chanted.
> From Birmingham's past industrious life,
> in its long past it has known strife.

So I give you a call from the heart,
Join our ranks and take your part.
In this we must succeed,
To counter this deadly deed.
Come on Birmingham let's unite,
We can make them put it right!
[E-mail 20 March 2000].

But it was not only Brummies who were moved and motivated. Robert 'Rupe the Fish' Stevenson sent the full support of the Coventry Retail Market, stating that 'we firmly believe that we need a great British industry and a working future for our children. We must stand together or divide we shall fall. I was at the House of Commons last week and even the security guards there were in support of your cause. We urge everyone to show solidarity for one of the last remaining Great British institutions lest we become an island for tourists and holidaymakers. We've lost our coal, farmers and fish industry, don't lose our car industry.' Brian Griffiths of Bilston captured the sense of solidarity in the Black Country when he wrote that 'at my local pub, a mixed bar, a few weeks ago we were united in one thought – that we felt we must go out and do something, voice our opinion and show the government how strongly we felt. (This has never happened before on any other issue as people usually have so many different views.)' [E-mail 29 March and Letter 30 March 2000].

Dave Osborne and other local trade unionists received similar letters and heartened by such mass backing, we addressed the logistical issues of the march and rally. Transport was one of our major preoccupations and early in the campaign, I phoned Phil Bateman, corporate affairs manager of Travel West Midlands. It was late at night and Phil seemed to be a little bleary-eyed when he answered his mobile. It turned out that he was on holiday in Australia and that I had woken him and his wife in the middle of the night! Laughing at my discomfort, Phil gave me the names of people to contact at his company. Before I could do so, I was rung by Peter Snape, Labour MP for West Bromwich East and chairman of Travel West Midlands, the biggest bus operator in the region. He assured me of his personal support for the cause and told me that his company would provide free travel to and from Cannon Hill Park. It was a magnificent gesture, enhanced by the fact that many of the company's buses were emblazoned with posters giving details of the rally. Thanks to Chris Roberts, area manager Birmingham, Travel West Midlands also arranged to pick up the members of the Birmingham Irish Pipe and Drums Band from the vicinity of Cannon Hill Park and take them to Masshouse Circus to head the march.

On Wednesday 29 March, it was revealed that Derek Robinson was to march with us and so make his first high-profile public appearance for years. The next day it was confirmed that the leaders of the 'big four' manufacturing trade unions of Britain would all walk and speak at the rally. Indeed, Bill Morris, head of the TGWU, was emphasising the importance of the event by cancelling a visit to the world trade union congress in South Africa. Then, on the eve of the march, I received a phone call from Adrian Fitzpatrick, a Brummie through and through who had gained a high profile nationally through his large and often successful accumulator bets on various sporting events. Adrian has become wealthy through his flower-selling business and he let me know on the day of the rally that he and his people would be standing outside his warehouse at the bottom of Hurst Street in order to hand out tens of thousands of carnations to the marchers. The story was publicised by The Mail and on the radio.

That Friday morning 31 March, I made an emotional appeal on Ed Doolan's show for the people of Birmingham and the West Midlands to stand tall and proud and to walk with the men and women of Longbridge and Rover. I also gave details of road closures and where disabled and infirm people could park so as to join us at the rally. Then I went off to Cannon Hill Park for an interview on the lunchtime edition of Midlands Today. After my own radio show, I attended a secret meeting called by John Hemming to pull together everyone concerned in saving Rover and Longbridge in particular – but more of that in Chapter Five.

On that day, The Mail led with the headline 'Save Us!', and on the evening I spoke to Carl Lanchester again. Once more, he urged me to speak from the heart, to tell people what it was like to be unemployed and to let them know how the lives of tens of thousands of people would be affected by the closure of Longbridge. He added that the workers in his Number 3 Paint Shop were no longer dismayed and dejected, they were angry and ready to battle and they wanted me to give them and the world a clarion call of defiance. That night, I couldn't sleep and I paced the floor until Kay told me lie down. In fact, I hadn't slept properly for several nights because my speech was going round and round in my mind. I couldn't get Carl's words out of my head and they convinced me of the approach I should take. I would speak from the heart and shout out our defiance. And although I had never been poor, I did know the bitterness of joblessness. I had been on the dole for almost two years in the mid-1980s, after which for another three years, I had been in irregular and insecure work. In fact, the last time I had signed on was in the summer of 1989. I was then in hourly-paid employment at an adult education college and, of course, there was no work during the summer vacation. I hated signing on and I loathed the thought that I had no purpose in my life. Like so many others, I knew what the workers of Rover and Longbridge were facing and what effect joblessness would have upon their lives and upon our city and region. We would not let this happen. We would fight for Longbridge. We would fight for Birmingham and the West Midlands. We would fight for British manufacturing.

CHAPTER FOUR

The March For Rover

By Carl Chinn

Saturday 1 April was the most stirring day of my life. I think that tens of thousands of Brummies and West Midlanders feel the same. All of us were touched by the solidarity that was so evident and were inspired by our collective action. For over two weeks, events had overtaken us and we had been powerless. Now we had an opportunity to act and to control something. We were intent upon proclaiming to the world that we had not packed it all in. We believed fervently that the march and rally would make a difference. It did.

At 7am, the BBC sent a Rover 800 to fetch me to Masshouse Circus for an interview by BBC News 24 and by Bob Platt of Radio 5 Live. There was extensive media coverage of the preparations and I was just one amongst many people whom the press wished to talk to. In particular, journalists were questioning the TGWU's Tony Woodley. Throughout the Rover crisis, Tony shone as a beacon of trade union resistance to the plans of BMW. From the first, he was resolved not to give in and to save Longbridge and try to keep the Rover Group united. A strong and forceful character, only he will ever really know how much effort he put into the campaign. From my own perspective, I was aware of Tony's strenuous negotiations with BMW, his firm lobbying of the government for support for his aims, and his talks with John Hemming about putting together an alternative bid to Alchemy. Tony's efforts and doggedness were always matched and enhanced by Duncan Simpson of the AEEU. The two of them made a formidable force on behalf of the workers.

As early as it was, people were beginning to gather and by 10am, the marshals were directing folk down from Jennens Road to the car park beneath Masshouse Circus itself. Sometimes the marchers came in small groups and then, every ten minutes or so, as various buses offloaded their passengers, there was a surge of folk arriving. I remember looking across Masshouse Circus to the Lower Priory and seeing bunches of people with their Mail placards moving towards us and feeling my spirits soar as they came closer. Then I turned behind me and Jennens Road was filled with thousands upon thousands of people. Rising proudly above them were scores of beautifully coloured and evocatively illustrated trade unions banners proclaiming support from across the nation.

There were those from the car workers at Dagenham, the Ipswich Branch of the TGWU, the Oxford and District Trades Council, the National Union of Mineworkers Yorkshire Area, the Liverpool University MSF, Keighley Trades Council and many more. Then there were the banners from Birmingham and the Midlands, including those of the Land Rover Joint Shop Stewards and the Fire Brigades Union number 7 region. And everywhere, there seemed to be banners

The intricate banners of many union branches were displayed during the march.
Picture by Sam Bagnall

from Unison branches, such as those in Gloucester City, King's College, London, Southwark and elsewhere. In fact, the Birmingham branch of Unison provided one of the biggest single contingents in the march and uplifted the walk with the blowing of whistles. Melodic sounds were played by Travis Walters and other members of the Rover Tomcats jazz band, and further liveliness was provided by a group of schoolchildren from Birmingham's George Dixon School and Sixth Form. Led by their head teacher, they carried a banner extolling their support for Rover and were accompanied by young South Asian Brummies playing Bhangra drums.

Significantly, we were joined by Hans Koebrick, a BMW worker from Berlin and an active trade unionist with IG Metal. He had arrived because he felt so strongly about what BMW was doing to Rover. He told The Mail: 'They don't care about destroying thousands of jobs and although I am not directly affected I want to show my support for Longbridge and also I could be involved in the next crisis.' Many people who worked for suppliers of Rover joined such trade unionists. Amongst them was Tony Finnerey. He and his fiancée, Rebecca were to be married soon and their wedding preparations were overshadowed by a nightmare of uncertainty about Tony's future. There were also over 100 employees, almost half the workforce, of Stadco. This Shrewsbury firm makes panels and depends upon Longbridge for 90% of its business. But large numbers of those present were neither trade unionists nor connected to the car industry. They were like Janice G. Bissell of Perry Barr, Birmingham. She had 'nothing whatsoever to do with Rover. I am a middle aged woman but I felt that I had to be along side' the marchers. [Letter to Carl Chinn, 2 April 2000]. Similarly, Mary Weaver of West Heath, close to Longbridge, had come along to show her concern for the safe future of the economy in the Midlands and told The Mail: 'This is not just going to affect manufacturing. It will have an impact on retailing and everything else if thousands of people lose their jobs. I live in a road of 30 houses – and nine of those depend on Rover for their incomes'. Tellingly, there were also disabled people such as Pamela Williamson in her wheelchair, which was pushed by her pals. Her dad had worked at Longbridge, as did her two brothers, and she declared in the paper that 'nothing could keep me from marching today'.

This massive gathering heartened the thousands of car workers and their families who were there. They carried scores upon scores of banners and flags, one of which declared that members of the Smith family of Northfield had 600 years of service at Longbridge. Body shop worker Gary Crowe summed up the views of the workers when he told The Mail that 'it is a great show of support for us at a time when morale is very low. The worst thing is, not knowing what's going to happen'. Other Rover workers stressed how their lives had been badly affected already. Dave Jordan of Longbridge was accompanied by his son, Daniel. He had bought a new house last September 'on the strength that I would have job security. Now I fear that I could lose it. I've been a seat builder at Rover for 14 years and I don't know how I would get another job. I worked for 10 months at the Oxford plant and I signed a contract saying that I would get a job working on the new Mini, but that's all gone through the window.' Tracey Morrell was another person facing bleak prospects. A 32-year-old single mother with two daughters, Tracey of Bromsgrove said in The Mail that she had been 'devastated to hear that Rover was going to be sold. If I lost my job, it would make day-to-day living difficult. We were looking forward to going away this summer, but I don't know whether to book anything now. We just wanted to be here to give our support and show how angry we are at what they are trying to do'. Julie Cartwright was one of the many relatives of car workers who was unable to join the rally. From Brierley Hill in the Black Country, she was eight months pregnant and her husband, Andrew, who had worked at Longbridge for twenty years, would not let her march. Still, 'I was with you in spirit. When our baby is born and old enough to understand, I will tell him how both you and their Daddy marched to try and save his job and those of thousands of others'. [Letter to Carl Chinn, 4 April 2000].

The mood of the marchers was neither excited nor sombre. Overwhelmingly, it was a dignified gathering, distinguished by feelings of

The Birmingham Irish Pipe and Drum band heading the march on 1 April. From left to right: piper Frank Brennan; drum major Basil Howe; piper Marion Doyle; piper John Miller; piper Bill Grigg; and drummer Brendan Mulvey. (Not visible were piper Gerard Weir; Maurice Long on the bass drum; drummer Bob Barcas; and seven-year-old drummer Joel Grigg.)
Picture by John Palmer.

John, from Kingstanding, stood near to Moor Street station for this shot. He worked for Land Rover (Axle Division) from 1958 to 1985, which was on the corner of Aldridge Road and Wellhead Lane, Perry Barr. It is now gone and its site is part of the campus of the University of Central England. John was forced to retire from work because of multiple sclerosis. Although he was unable to take part in the march, he came to Moor Street to give his support as the walkers went by.

determination and defiance and by an assurance that we were in the right, that we were marching for a just cause. Just before 11am, the Birmingham Irish Pipe and Drums Band was in place at the head of the march. I knew all of their members well and, with Dave Osborne's agreement, I had asked them if they would lead us. They were honoured to do so, for nothing of course. Close to them was Ray Egan of Harborne dressed as John Bull and holding a sign which roared out 'No Surrender. Save the Rover. Save British Jobs', (Ray and his patriotic image are described fully in Chapter Ten). Before them was a Mini, a Rover 75 and the Land Rover Discovery of John Hemming. As a councillor in Acocks Green, John drives such a car because it is a good vehicle and so many of his electorate work at the Land Rover plant in Solihull.

Behind the pipes and drums, Terry Pye and other trade unionists held a sign calling out, 'Keep Rover Running'. Then came Tony Woodley, Duncan Simpson and the leaders of the four main unions represented at Rover: Bill Morris of the TGWU; Sir Ken Jackson of the AEEU; John Edmonds of the GMB; and Roger Lyons of the MSF. Accompanying them were local Labour MPs such as Richard Burden and Dennis Turner of Wolverhampton South-East. Peter Snape, who is also the chairman of the West Midlands Labour MP Group, voiced their collective anger when he stated that: 'BMW has betrayed the trust of its employees. We are here to show we won't stand by.' Amongst the other leading personalities were Baroness Christine Crawley, a former Labour member of the European Parliament, Councillor Albert Bore, John Hemming and Derek Robinson.

Just to the rear of these people, and rightly taking the prime position, were the Joint Shop Stewards of Longbridge. They carried their banner which gave the names of each of the unions and featured a Mini. Clearly visible near to the front was one of the largest banners in the march. It was that of The Mail emblazoned with the defiant message, 'Don't let Rover Die'. Amongst those holding the banner were editor Ian Dowell, his head of news and co-author of this book Stephen Dyson (in bed with tonsillitis for four days before the march) and Malcolm Stent, a well-known local personality, playwright and folk singer cum comedian. Like all of us, Ian was:

> overwhelmed at the response from members of the public. We are here to show the world that we are refusing to let the major car manufacturing industry die in Birmingham. We want a major firm to step in at the eleventh hour and we want the Mini back. The Mini is Birmingham's car and after all the development costs have been borne in Birmingham. It would be terrible if it went to another part of the country or worse overseas. [*Evening Mail,* 1 April 2000].

It seemed that each and every person was carrying a placard with a poster upon it. Many of them were supplied by the unions, others by The Mail, but

The very front of a march that involved some 80,000 people on 1 April. Walking behind the
front row, among others, are Terry Pye, Tony Woodley, Bill Morris and John Edmonds.
Picture by Roy Peters

great numbers were handed out by the *Socialist Worker*. After the march, many people wondered how such a small party was able to produce so many placards. There was some concern that the Socialist Workers, or Swappies as they were called by the workers at Longbridge, would try and rush to the head of the march from New Street Station and so hijack the event. It would have been impossible for them to have done so for three reasons. First of all, the huge numbers of people involved precluded anyone taking the march over. Secondly, Dave Osborne and his committee had authorised hundreds of stewards from amongst Longbridge's workforce. They were not prepared to let anyone take the march away from the Rover workers and the people of Birmingham and the West Midlands. Thirdly, the police were liaising effectively with both the trade union marshals and with Special Events Security.

Joe Clarke headed the Longbridge stewards. Holding a megaphone, he actually led the whole march. A key figure on the Joint Shop Stewards Committee, Joe and his wife, Dawn, were featured in many newspaper articles and television programmes. He ably put forward the case for Longbridge and through so doing, he showed the general public that Longbridge workers were not militants to be feared. Amongst the other marshals at the head of the march were two other shop stewards, Pete Logan and Noel Moloney. I would get to know both of them better in the coming weeks.

At 11am, Dave Osborne gave the signal to move off. It was a misly, mardy day but the damp and gloomy weather had not kept people indoors. By the time the last of the marchers left Masshouse Circus, over 45,000 of us were walking towards Cannon Hill Park. Our numbers were to be swelled by people who joined us along the way and by those who awaited us in the park. At the rally itself, there were at least 50,000 folk who had come together. In addition to them, it was estimated that at least 30,000 people had lined the streets to applaud the marchers. These figures are important. There have been attempts to downplay the hugeness of the march and rally. They are wrong and uninformed. Those of us involved in the planning of the event know with certainty that at least 80,000 people walked, rallied or lined the streets for Rover.

On a day when he 'wouldn't have wanted to be anywhere else in the world', Richard Williamson of the *Sunday Mercury* captured the impressive variety of folk who were intent upon crying out against BMW's plans.

They came from London, Merseyside, Plymouth, Sheffield, Oxford and Bristol to show solidarity with Longbridge. Middle-class ladies in lipstick rubbed shoulders with the revolutionaries of the Socialist Workers Party, teachers and college lecturers walked with car workers and bank clerks. There were 80,000 of us and it was impossible not to be moved by the sight of so many good and decent people willing to stand up and be counted. For all the anger seething away in the city it was a good-natured crowd that tramped through the Bull Ring to a barrage of whistles and

Thousands of protesters approach the
Masshouse Circus area in Birmingham
city centre during the march on 1 April.
Picture by Steve Murphy

The marchers pass under the old Bull Ring Shop
Centre bridge. An aerial view of the mammoth m
Picture by Adam Fradgely

hooters and beating drums. We roundly booed the man who dared to drive past at the wheel of a BMW but even that was done with a laugh. You'll Never Walk Alone blasted out of a shop in Sherlock Street as staff urged on the marchers who trooped by with flowers in their hands and smiles on their faces. This was not a funeral march and we were not on our way to a wake. 'It isn't over for Rover,' said the banners and we all desperately wanted to believe that.

We did not walk as a beaten people with our heads bowed. We marched with our heads held high to show the world what our region had achieved in the past and what we could achieve in the future. Our pride was swelled by the cheers and applause from onlookers all the way of the march. Moor Street Queensway had been closed to traffic and the road was filled with supporters, and as we passed the historic heart of Brum at the Bull Ring, shoppers and traders called out their encouragement. Just ahead of us, the walkway linking the Bull Ring Centre with the Pallasades was packed with the faces of folk who waved, clapped and gave us the thumbs up. All along Smallbrook Queensway, passers-by urged us on, and as we marched down Hurst Street we were strongly backed by shopworkers and others. Near to the bottom of that street, Adrian Fitzpatrick and his people thrust carnations into our hands and as we came along Sherlock Street our confidence was waxing.

The people of Highgate, Balsall Heath and Edgbaston turned out in great numbers to raise our spirits as we marched through their neighbourhoods and onto the Pershore Road. Many waved Union Jacks and crosses of Saint George, and every other house had 'Save Rover' posters in their windows. Shouts of 'Keep fighting!', 'Never surrender!', 'That's the way!', and 'Go on, show em!' rang out and looking back along the march it was a wondrous sight. The line of people wound back further than the eye could see. It was as if the whole of Brum had stood up to be counted. We were all there, English and Irish, Afro-Caribbean and South Asian, Scots and Welsh, Jewish and Gentile – all of the people of Brummagem bonded in our common purpose and in our belonging to each other. We were showing the world who we were. A people proud of our manufacturing and proud of our multi-cultural identity. We should not be overcome.

As we went along the Pershore Road, I rang Phil Smith to tell him how far away we were so that he could ensure the performers were ready. I updated Phil as we turned into Edgbaston Road and approached the gates of the park. Just inside them stood George Purcell, a security guard from The University of Birmingham, who had brought along his Austin Seven. There could have been no better greeting for us and no finer symbol of why we were marching. Austin's dream had made Longbridge the biggest car factory in Britain. We were not going to allow that dream to be chucked into the miskin of history.

The edge of the arena of Cannon Hill Park was dotted with knots of

Laura Grigg, pushing three-month-old Oran, and Anthony Duffy on the march for Rover.
Laura and Anthony are two of the organisers of the St Patrick's Day Parade in Birmingham,
now the third biggest in the world, and their attendance emphasised the support of the
Brummie Irish for Longbridge. *Picture by Roy Peters*

people who had been unable to make the march, and just by the bandstand I
heard people calling my name. The cry had come from a woman and her
husband who were standing by an old and frail lady in a wheelchair. She was
wrapped up warm against the cold and drizzle and as I got by her, she drew me
to her and hugged me. She had insisted to her daughter that she be there with
us. After a short chat I went to move away and she called after me 'God Bless
you, ma lad. God Bless all of you and God Bless Brummagem.'

I was deeply moved by the old lady's steadfastness, and tears welled up
into my eyes. As I left her, I could feel the spirit of my own people who were
dead. There was Our Nan, Lil Perry, who herself had been a shop steward, her
husband, Our Grandad Perry, and her sister, Our Aunt Win Martin. The three of
them had grafted in factories all of their lives and I knew that they were with me,
strengthening me and pushing me on. Then I heard the music, which was blaring
out from the speakers by the stage at the far end of the arena. The sound of the
instruments was accompanied by a noise like the pounding of a great press. It
was Laurie Hornsby's anthem for Birmingham. As we poured into the park,
Laurie's words struck deep into our souls:

Okay our streets didn't look so pretty but we made things here in this city
that carried our name and proved our worth
and sold in every corner of the earth.
cars and lamps and nibs and the like
and pots and pans and buttons and bikes,
Nuts and bolts and sauce and beer,
Where were they made? Right here!

In Birmingham, city of a thousand trades
Forward in mind, forward in heart
Every tomorrow is a brand new start
In Birmingham, never pulling down the shades
We roll up our sleeves and do what we can
Forward goes Birmingham!
[Laurie Hornsby, 'Birmingham', from *Wallop Mrs Cox* album, 2000].

Laurie grew up in Handsworth, on the borders with Smethwick, and throughout his childhood the thumping of a press from Evered's brass foundry had disturbed the sleep of his family. Seeking to escape the noise, Laurie's dad moved the family to West Heath – where now they were kept awake by the hammering from Longbridge! Tellingly, Laurie's song came to him whilst he was walking in Cofton Park.

The head of the march swept into the arena and the great host began to fill the park. To my right, close to a tower for TV crews and technical equipment, stood my family. Our Mom is badly affected by rheumatoid arthritis and can't walk far. Nor can Our Mom's sister, Lynne Baker, because of her osteo-arthritis. I'd insisted that Our Dad and Our Kid stayed with them in the park. With them were Darryl's wife, Sandra; their daughter, Natalie and sons, Séan and Daniel; and Darryl's father-in-law, Billy Hughes. Our Kid was blarting with the emotion. In fact, I think that we all had tears in our eyes for much of that day. He grabbed hold of me and then I kissed Our Mom. They were urging me to 'Do it! Show em!' Next to them was an old friend, Joe Mattiello. Joe is the head of a leading Italian Brummie family and was a mate of my Great-Uncle George Wood. A former shop steward himself at Fisher and Ludlow's and now in his late 70s, Joe's appearance also meant much to me. So too did that of Tommy Nolan. I'd drunk with Tommy years ago in the 'Royal Oak', Sparkbrook and then, as now, Tommy was a shop steward with the TGWU.

I moved away from my family and was immediately interviewed by Liz Copper of Midlands Today. I was struggling to keep a hold of my feelings. Emotion was surging through me and I was barely able to express myself. I told Liz that it was a wonderful day: 'the feelings, the emotion, the crowds lining the streets to applaud everyone. We're not going to give in. We're going to keep fighting and fighting until we mek sure that Longbridge has a future. Rally for

Rover!' Shaking hands and clasping hold of people, I was approached by Barrie Roberts. A prominent local Conservative, he wanted to let me know that he and other Birmingham Tories were present and that they were with us. His words once again indicated the breadth of our local support and the lack of connection with national politicians. I made my way backstage. Just as I did so, I spotted my wife, Kay, and our three daughters, Tara, Catríona and Rochelle. Our lad, Richard, was studying in London and couldn't be with us but he had rung up the night before to give us his best. Kay hugged me and wished me luck and went off to find Our Mom and Dad.

The various performers were entertaining the crowd as it gathered and Jimmy Franks and Phil Smith were doing a cracking job of making sure that everything went smoothly. Finally, it seemed as if everyone was in the park and UB40 were introduced. They were greeted with prolonged cheers. Brian Travers captured the thoughts of all the band when he explained that 'we're just here to support any of the initiatives that can alleviate the hardships the Rover workers are going to be going through. And let's see if we can change this.' Lead singer Robin Campbell then spoke. He had been an apprentice toolmaker at Longbridge in the 1970s and he pronounced that 'We are the same as all of you people. We are disgusted at the way Rover workers have been treated.' Robin was followed by Ed Doolan, speaking in his private capacity. Like all of us on the stage, he was honoured to be there and he roared: 'Don't let this emotion die!' Then he urged people to ring him the next morning to speak to Bill Morris and Richard Burden and to let the world know about the rally.

She was only aged seven, but Sarah Jay, of Wordsley, let her feelings be known on the march. *Picture by John Reavenall*

The lady with the bushy hair and glasses is Paulette Bagley. Behind her is Tony Moore, of West Heath, Birmingham. He wrote in when the Evening Mail published this picture to explain that he had been at Longbridge for 13 years, following his father, Colin, who had been there for 41 years until 1999. On Tony's shoulders is his friend's son, Teal Howard; to the left is Lynda Howard; Tony's wife, Jane, is on the left of the picture next to Ken Brock, in the cap; to the right of her is colleague, Richard Howard; and on Richard's shoulders is daughter, Shaye. Also pictured behind the little girl is Gerry Boland, turning; behind him is Chris Walford; on the right of the picture, in darkened glasses, is Ken Bagley; and the two chaps smiling behind him are Bob Dillon and Richard Nunn (in glasses). Mr Nunn also wrote in to explain that he, the Bagleys, Mr Dillon, Mr Walford, Mr Boland and Mr Brock were part of the test driving team at Gaydon. The majority were made redundant, although Mr Nunn and Mr Bagley were transferred to Land Rover.

Local celebrities on the stage before the speeches join in the singing of *You'll Never Walk Alone.*
Left to right: Jimmy Franks; UB40 members Robin and Ali Campbell, Astro, Norman Hassan,
and Brian Travers; Carl Chinn; UB40's Earl Falconer; Ed Doolan; UB40's Michael Virtue; Steve
Roche, conductor of the Icknield Male Voice Choir. Behind are members of the choir. (Jimmy
Brown of UB40 was also on stage, but is out of shot.) *Picture by Roy Peters*

As UB40 and Ed Doolan went off the stage, the Icknield Male Voice
Choir moved forward. They had already sung 'When the Saint's Go Marching
In!' and the powerful 'You Can hear the People Sing'. This last song could not
have been better chosen. Its first words are 'Can you here the people sing, singing
the song of angry men, it is the music of a people who will not be slaves again'.
I introduced the choir for the second time and called upon the crowd to sing with
them for Brummagem, Longbridge and the West Midlands. Then the chords of
'You'll Never Walk Alone' were heard. I beckoned UB40 and Ed Doolan back on
stage and holding hands we sang. The choir was fervent and was joined by
50,000 voices. It was an awesome sight. As far as the eye could see, banners and
placards were held aloft and people were raising their arms in the air or clasping
each other's hands as they sang to let the Rover workers know that never would
they be deserted.

As we finished, Tony Woodley took the microphone and brought on the
speakers. Tony addressed the crowd first. He was forceful, pertinent and showed
his mettle in handling hecklers from far left groups. These had clustered near to
the stage, but their chants and catcalls soon quietened as the Rover workers
made it clear that they wanted to hear what Tony had to say. He recounted the
details of BMW's actions and connected the anxiety over Rover's future with
worries elsewhere in the country.

The number of people here shows the emotion and the anger that people feel in the West Midlands and the country as a whole. We are dealing with a tale of deceit, lies and betrayal – the break-up of one of the greatest companies in the world. It is industrial sabotage of our manufacturing industry, creating the worst industrial crisis for two decades. This is not just about Longbridge. Every part of the country will be affected by the disastrous decision by BMW to cut and run. They have behaved dishonestly and dishonourably. We are not prepared to be treated like cannon fodder or the second-class citizens of Europe. [*The Birmingham Post*, 3 April 2000].

Tony called upon the Prime Minster for his personal intervention: 'We need his help and we need the financial assistance of this Government. They have a responsibility to Rover, to Britain, and to British manufacturing industry. Without their help it will be a disaster.' Jon Griffin of The Mail proclaimed that Tony's speech was 'a devastating tirade against BMW and a chilling analysis of the implications of a proposed Rover carve up'. It was.

Bill Morris spoke next and stressed a personal bond with Birmingham. He told the rally that he had arrived in the city over 40 years ago as a sixteen-year old: 'Birmingham gave me my home, my education and my first real job. It was in Birmingham that I joined my union and first fought for workers' rights. I am proud to say that, like you, I am a Brummie and more than that I am proud

The crowd is in a defiant mood. The 'Blair dummy' of No 3 paint shop is prominent.
Picture by Edward Moss.

The rally in Cannon Hill Park. Longbridge union convenor Adrian Ross is leaning against the rails (front left) and his predecessor from the 1970s, Derek 'Red Robbo' Robinson, is on the second line behind him, slightly to the right. To the right of Derek is former Powertrain shop steward Barry Hardeman, now retired. On the right of the picture, the white man with the moustache (next to the Asian man holding the Socialist Workers banner) is Howard D Jones. In the centre, wearing a fluorescent jacket with a shaven head, is lorry driver Neville Lacey. His fiancée June White, who completed the entire march despite severe back problems, can be seen next to him with curly hair, partly hidden by a flag post. *Picture by Roy Peters*

Roy Peters is a professional photographer who took scores of evocative shots both of the march and the rally, *writes Carl Chinn*. For him, as a Brummie, and as someone committed to the rights of workers, 'The Rover Rally was a memorable day and one that I shan't forget. I have taken pictures for the Labour Movement since 1980/81 – the T & G is just about my oldest client – but I have never witnessed, nay been a part of, anything like that day.' At the rally, Roy stood in the small, cordoned-off press area right at the foot of the stage. I spotted him early on and he could see the way in which the emotions of the occasion were sweeping over me. Throughout the speeches of the others on the rostrum, Roy gained eye contact with me and through his facial expressions of encouragement he helped me to compose myself.

to join you in our fight for jobs and our community.' Bill went on to affirm that he would take the fight both to government and BMW, which should be made to account for the devastation it had caused at Longbridge. And he reiterated the points made about the future of manufacturing when he pronounced that: 'There is no point in having a strong pound if it is ripping the guts out of British manufacturing'. Finally, he made it plain that 'before BMW goes it owes a debt to this community, to this city. But more than that, it owes a debt to the workers.' [*Sunday Mercury* 2 April 2000].

Each of the speakers made meaningful points and asserted the importance of the march and rally. Sir Ken Jackson told everyone that 'today's support gives a clear message to Munich that they cannot get away with treating UK workers as second-class workers. You are delivering a powerful message to the Government and to BMW. You are saying that you are not prepared to accept what BMW has done.' Hecklers continued to shout at the speakers, although not as strongly as they had before Tony Woodley had almost overwhelmed them. However, Northfield Labour MP Richard Burden had to cope with more jeering than most.

Many of those in the park were antagonistic towards the government. There were banners emblazoned with messages such as 'Blair Doesn't Care!' and the lads from Number 3 Paint Shop at Longbridge held up a dummy that had the face of Tony Blair. It wore BMW overalls and a placard next to it announced: '50,000 jobs to go & still Blair won't put on his British overalls!' Richard bore the brunt of the anger and alienation of many marchers, but held to his task and finished his speech with the words 'we are not going away'. It should also be highlighted that many of those present were appalled at the lack of support for Longbridge and Rover by the Conservative party at a national level. There was no Tory of national stature at the march nor had the Conservatives in London made any attempt to contact the march organisers.

It was later reported that Clare Short, Labour MP for Birmingham Ladywood and International Development Secretary for the government, should have been one of the speakers. Her absence and that of other cabinet members was taken by some people as a snub. Fiona Gordon, regional director of the West Midlands Labour Party, told the *Sunday Mercury*'s Bob Haywood that Clare did not speak 'because of a cock up' and added that 'there is no question of a snub by anyone. The government has been wholly supportive of Rover all the way through and Stephen Byers has been to Birmingham six times in the past two weeks' [2 April 2000]. There was no cock up. Clare was not down on the list of speakers drawn up by Dave Osborne and his committee. Nor was she mentioned as a speaker on the posters and leaflets about the rally. From my own perspective, I know how much Clare feels for Birmingham. She is a politician whom I admire greatly and I am certain that she would never have snubbed the rally. Indeed she was there amongst the crowd.

Gisela Stuart, the German-born Labour MP for Birmingham Edgbaston, did join us on the platform. In the newspapers the next day, mention was made that the crowd had hectored her and at the rally itself, Tony Woodley felt that this was the case. He informed the crowd that Gisela had 'worked tirelessly to try to deliver the goods over Longbridge'. My own view, and that of many other people present on that occasion, was that Gisela herself was not booed. There was jeering when she came on to the stage but it was aimed at one of the speakers. Gisela did do much work for Longbridge. She is a fine MP and an upright person who is fully committed to Birmingham.

Roger Lyons came after Richard Burden. He proclaimed that the march was a 'phenomenal success'. It was not a 'funeral for Rover, it is a demand for action. BMW has ripped off the skills and know-how of Rover, It is theft.' Moreover, the issue of Rover's future was linked inextricably to the future of manufacturing in Britain. [*Sunday Mercury*, 2 April 2000]. Throughout these speeches I sat next to John Edmonds. He listened attentively to the early speakers and to the reaction from the crowd. I heard him say to himself, 'so they want to boo. They want to cheer'. John then changed his approach entirely and manifested his effectiveness as a public speaker. It was an impressive performance. He asked the crowd what they thought of BMW's actions and there were prolonged boos and hisses. He also gave everyone the chance to cheer. He stated that the rally was not about speeches, it was about messages, 'so let's have some messages. BMW have behaved badly. Alchemy is not an acceptable buyer for Rover. From the government we'll want support.'

Albert Bore, leader of Birmingham City Council, was prominent on the platform and with hard-hitting words and a strong delivery he pronounced that 'what we have seen is the rape of Rover. BMW have taken Rover's 4x4 technology and transferred it to a manufacturing plant in North America where the vehicles built will be BMW-badged.' He asserted that the Rover workforce had done everything that had been asked of them and indicated that if the company was broken up then unemployment in Birmingham would rocket from around 8% to over 12%. [*Sunday Mercury*, 2 April 2000].

Carl Chinn is in fighting mood on the stage at the rally. *Picture by John Reavenall*

I was the last speaker and I had asked for that position. Jon Griffin reported that:

The People's Doctor became the People's Preacher when Dr Carl Chinn received cheers to match the Wembley roar for Villa . . . And under leaden skies, tens of thousands saw Chinn leap to the microphone to rock-style applause from the masses. 'They thought we would surrender, they thought that we would lie down. They do not know us,' he roared. 'I ask you, the people of Birmingham, the people of the West Midlands, the manufacturing people of Britain: Do we surrender?' The response was inevitable, a huge throaty cry of 'No' ringing out immediately across the park. 'If we do not surrender do we stand and do we fight?' A bellow of 'Yes' even louder than the 'No', amid clenched fists and whirling

banners. This was fire and brimstone stuff, with Chinny the preacher ...
He ended on a near apocalyptic note. 'We are fighting not only for British
manufacturing, we are fighting for the working class', he boomed to
further approval. It was stirring stuff, turning the clock back more than
20 years to an era when workers protests were commonplace and unions
held the upper hand across the industrial landscape of Great Britain.
[*Evening Mail*, 3 April 2000].

Before and during my speech, I had to struggle to get a grip of my
emotions as the energy and passion of the crowd surged upon the stage. But as
the assembly before me cried out its approval of what I was saying, I felt the force
of the West Midlanders who had called out for democracy in 1832, of the
Chartists who had striven for the rights of working men and women against the
might of a class-biased state, and of all those trade unionists who had never
submitted to the oppressor. All of them had sought to pass on a life that was
better and more free than their own to their children and their children's
children. As one part of my mind was speaking, I saw those folk from our past
who had never abandoned the fight for justice and I knew that of the same mould
were the people in that great crowd before me.

I called out that for too long we had watched as our mines had become
derelict, as our shipyards had been broken down, as our mills had emptied and
as our factories had been destroyed. And now to Westminster and BMW we said
'No more!' We asked for no handouts from anyone. What we asked for was
investment. Investment in manufacturing. Investment in 'our babbies' futures.
And if they do not think that we would fight for that then never will they know
us'. I stressed that we would stand with the car workers of Dagenham and the
textile workers of Bairds and Courtualds as they had stood by us and declared
that our message was 'clear, simple and unequivocal. We support British
manufacturing.'

With Carl Lanchester's compelling words large in my thoughts, I cried
that: 'They think that Longbridge has no future. Longbridge has got a future.
Let's knock this lie on the head once and for all. Longbridge will have a future
because they will not take the Mini from Longbridge. If they try to take it then
we will stand at the gates of Longbridge to stop them.' I stressed that we were a
people bonded by a common purpose, irrespective of class, colour, creed,
religion or politics and 'we tell BMW – we will fight'. And we had to be clear
what we were fighting for. We were fighting to stave off unemployment, and only
those of us who had stood in the dole queue knew what it was like: it strips you
of your pride, takes from you your dignity and 'chucks our children's futures into
the mud'. We would not let this happen to the workers of Longbridge, to the
workers of Gaydon nor to the other workers. I looked at the crowd and held out
one hand and I pledged to the men and women of Rover that as a Brummie and
West Midlander and as someone who believed in British manufacturing, 'we

hold out our hands. Here's our hands. Here's hearts. We will not desert you. You have been betrayed but we the manufacturing people of Britain will never betray you.'

To both the government and BMW we swore that 'Rover will not die'. As I proclaimed this assurance, the crowd began chanting, 'Rover – will not die! Rover – will not die!' With the shouts quietening, I affirmed that 'we serve warning, if they do not hark to our voice then we will march through the streets of London and take our fight to the doors of Westminster'. The crowd thundered its approval and I finished my speech by announcing that 'when God med me I'm glad and I'm proud that he med me one of you'. Tony Woodley then came back to the rostrum and closed the rally by bringing 'the speeches to a climax. With natural authority he added: "There has been a clear message to BMW today. We are not going quietly." Then to add emphasis once more, "We are not going quietly".' [*Evening Mail*, 3 April 2000].

The march and rally received national coverage on the television from BBC, ITV, Channel 5 and Sky News and it also gained some attention from German TV companies and newspapers. Through our numbers and our pride, we let Britain and Germany know that we threw down our gauntlet of defiance. This had been no gesture of anger and frustration, it had been a clear clarion call for action. Locally, the big event struck a powerful chord with those who had attended. Miss J. Ball of Birmingham wrote to me that on the great day many people were close to tears. There were folk in wheelchairs, infants sitting high on their parents' shoulders and many who were too young to understand the importance of the day. They did not know that 'they were taking part in a historical event, a part of our city's history that would and could affect their lives'. Miss Ball walked behind 'a wonderful elderly lady. She told me her husband had worked in the car industry but sadly had passed away. She was marching as a tribute to her husband and the trade that he had once loved.' The old lady found it hard to walk and pain was evident on her face:

> but she was determined to finish what she had started and marched to the very end. When we reached Cannon Hill Park the look of achievement and satisfaction on her face was a joy to see. This sweet lady to me personified the spirit of Birmingham people. For me the most touching part of that day was when thousands at the rally joined hands and sang 'You'll Never Walk Alone'. Tears streamed down many faces, even the biggest of men could not hide their emotions. We hope and pray our government and the world listen to our cries and realise we are a force to be reckoned with. This was the day the Birmingham spirit shone bright like a beacon. A spirit, a people who will stand and fight when its industry and values are under threat. A people who are hard working and proud. A people of lion hearts and hearts of gold. My people, my city, my beloved Birmingham. [Letter 4 April 2000].

Sheila Coates watched the march in town, supporting the walkers in memory of her husband, a man who had been a car worker at Drews Lane, Birmingham for many years. At first hand she had witnessed factory closures and short-time working 'and the stresses and strains this puts on all the family'. Sheila brought her grandson with her 'and he had his first lesson in Social History. He is only 8 yrs old and didn't quite understand what I was telling him until I asked him how he would feel if his daddy came home and told them there wasn't going to be holidays, nice clothes, pocket money and that mummy's car would have to go, etc – because Daddy didn't have a job anymore and the factory was closing. The look of shock on his face had to be seen to be believed, but I don't think he will forget that march and the thousands of people from all over the country with their banners who demanded the right to work.' [Letter, 11 April, 2000].

Lindsay Sadler was able to make it all the way to Cannon Hill Park. She stood by two teenagers who 'were alternately crying and trying their best to smile. People with bunches of carnations gave flowers to those who had none. Strangers held each others' hands during the singing of "Walk On . . ." I tried not to cry, but the atmosphere was so emotional and the Icknield Male Voice Choir so wonderfully sang "the song for the working man" that I must say that did it for me and I was blarting along with many others.' [Letter, 3 April 2000]. Tom Bradshaw walked for much of the march with his two-year old son, Michael. They couldn't get to the park but listened to the speeches that were broadcast live on BBC WM and BBC Coventry and Warwickshire. Tom was inspired to write a poem about the day called 'Rally for Rover'.

> On Jennens Road we joined as one,
> At Masshouse Circus we massed,
> Down Moor Street we were joined by more,
> As St Martin's we passed.
> At Smallbrook Queensway we would not be swayed,
> No, we'd walk to London and back
> And we may yet have to 'cos, don't forget,
> We want our factories back.
>
> Helicopters hovered high
> As into Hurst Street we turned,
> Photographers and camera crews
> Gave publicity we had earned.
>
> In Sherlock Street the mystery remained:
> How can they treat us this way?
> We thought of homes, but not the detective,

We shall not forget this day.
On Pershore Road our persistence showed,
Then Edgbaston Road to the park
Where speeches were made and tears were shed
And the people made their mark.

So governments and multi-nationals,
Lend us your ear,
We will not lie down and die –
It does not end here.

[Letter, 1 April 2000].

Michelle Mills was also deeply affected. Although now living in Hampshire, she comes from Bromsgrove and her dad, Henry Mills, has worked for Rover for 30 years, whilst many of her friends depend upon Longbridge for their livelihoods. When she heard what BMW was planning she was outraged 'and I was determined I was going to be heard, and if no-one came with me, then I would shout on my own!' She explained that Rover had changed hands some five times since she was a child 'and our family have worked through it. I'm sure that many other families wondered whether Daddy would have a job next week, as we sometimes did. My Dad worked harder than anyone I know, he has learnt every job he can, stretching himself and doing homework at 50 years old to ensure he would keep his job and provide for his family. I am so proud of him.' Michelle rang The Mail and asked about me 'as my dad had talked about what you were doing and I found out about the Rover rally. We drove up the night before to make sure that we would be there for the march and we shouted . . . and chanted . . . and marched . . . and threw our fists into the air throughout your speech.' [Letter, 18 May 2000].

A people welded by our common cause, we marched for jobs now and in the future, but we did not forget the dream of Herbert Austin in the past. Norma Rogers evoked the spirit of 'The Old Man'. Typing a letter in Bromsgrove on 2 April, she was weeping because she was so emotional about all that is happening down the road at Longbridge'. She recalled that often Austin himself could be found in the locality looking into engines and pondering over drawing boards. His cars were tested up Rose Hill, the Lickey, and he had made his home just down the road 'from where I am writing this to you. His body lies in our Churchyard at the top of the aforesaid hill at Holy Trinity. He purchased his groceries from Mr Matthews at Northfield . . . His home was bequeathed to the Institute for the Blind . . . So much history – all soon to be forgotten if we do not stand up to be counted.' Each year in May, the Austin Vintage Car Club drive their cars up Rose Hill and visit 'the great man's grave to pay their respects. The gravestone is cleaned and flowers lay thereon. <u>Let us never forget nor let us forego our heritage</u>'. Norma brought to mind the armaments that were produced in both world wars at Longbridge 'to keep us free and we cannot lie down and let this happen to us . . . We were bombed and survived and we <u>MUST</u> not go under now.' [Letter 2 April 2000].

In the weeks following the march, I was informed that it appeared that certain people at Millbank, Labour's headquarters in London, had branded me 'an out of control Trot'. This was because I had stated in my speech that the battle for Rover, Longbridge and British manufacturing was also a battle for the British working class. It was. It galls many people that none of the major British political parties today seem to even like the mention of the working class. It is as if the workers have been expunged from existence. They have not. At Cannon Hill Park on 1 April 2000, the British working class roared that it has not gone away and that it will not disappear, no matter how much many politicians wish it to. The battle for Longbridge and the working class had not ended. We fought on. [The Millennibrum Project has made videos both of reactions to the march and rally and of all the speeches. These will be available in Birmingham Central Library].

CHAPTER FIVE

Phoenix

By Stephen Dyson

The march for Longbridge was critical in the fight to save Rover. Yet it had not been the only stubborn response to emerge from some angry contemplation in those first few days following the confirmation of BMW's plans. First came a 'Buy British' backlash from local politicians, union leaders and businesses on Sunday 19 March and Monday 20 March, as they queued up to urge consumers to stage a nationwide boycott of BMW cars. Robin Corbett, the Labour MP for Erdington, Birmingham, said: 'The more that people can drive the flag the better. I always drive Rovers personally, so if BMW are waiting for me to go into a showroom they will be waiting a long, long time.' Fellow city Labour MP Lynne Jones, representing Selly Oak, was even more direct: 'BMW have behaved very badly, they have betrayed people,' she said. 'I won't buy a BMW and I would certainly support people not buying BMWs.' Bill Morris, the general secretary of the TGWU, stated: 'People don't have to buy BMWs, they can buy Rovers and that will be supporting British jobs.' Sir Ken Jackson, leader of the AEEU union, said: 'Our members want to hit BMW where it hurts – in the profits.' And Nigel Hastilow, regional director for the Institute of Directors, a former editor of the *The Birmingham Post* and now the prospective Parliamentary candidate for Edgbaston, said: 'I cannot believe that anyone with a BMW would drive around Birmingham after the events of last week.' (Although angered by BMW's plans, Hastilow, speaking in his IoD role, expressed concern before the march of 1 April, fearing that 'on the whole it will be negative publicity'. [IoD Press Release, 30 March 2000].)

This boycott call seemed to have an immediate effect on the car purchasing intentions of British car buyers, angry at what was increasingly seen as BMW's appalling treatment of Rover workers. Just five days later, on Saturday 25 March, an ICM survey commissioned by the AEEU union revealed that 64% of Midland car buyers in the market to buy a BMW were now more likely to look elsewhere. There was an even stronger reaction among established BMW owners, with 77% of those in the region saying they were now less likely to return to the group's showrooms. Sir Ken Jackson said: 'It's the first clear evidence of a public backlash against BMW and their treatment of the Rover workforce. BMW's reputation has been dented by the damage they've caused in the Midlands. It will take some time to recover.'

Meanwhile, other unions also refused to throw the towel in, and began demanding that BMW allow alternative bids to be made to buy Rover, rather than just negotiating with Alchemy. On Wednesday 22 March, various union bosses flew out to Munich again for crunch talks with BMW's Professor Milberg to insist that they wanted to keep jobs, not negotiate payouts. The action followed a mass meeting of Rover's 500 plant shop stewards that unanimously backed the call to oppose the break up of their company.

Up until now, there had been no public airing of any potential alternative bids, with Stephen Byers and Richard Burden keeping any plans that John Towers was developing strictly under cover. But secrecy was not everyone's policy following that first weekend of reflection. John Hemming, a successful businessman, councillor and leader of Birmingham's Liberal Democrats, said that at the time he was increasingly frustrated at the 'media perspective that it was a done deal'. Hemming began talking about the feasibility of an alternative bid to various people, including Richard Burden on Sunday 19 March and Alex Stephenson the next day.

John Hemming pictured at the Rover rally. *Picture by Craig Holmes*

In a concise diary he kept, Hemming recorded on 19 March: 'With my experience of business matters, I concluded that an alternative could be put forward if a good business plan was prepared, but that someone would need to act to do this.' On 20 March, he wrote: 'I needed to find everyone who might be interested in solving the problem …I concluded that public pressure would be important in ensuring that BMW looked at an alternative … I concluded that we might as well have an alternative launched as there was nothing to lose.' With this in mind, Hemming gave an interview to the *The Birmingham Post*'s Business Editor John Duckers, and his plan for an alternative was revealed on the morning of Tuesday 21 March:

> Millionaire Birmingham businessman and councillor, Mr John Hemming, is trying to put together an alternative consortium to bid for Rover. Coun Hemming said last night he was in the early stages of trying to rival Alchemy Partners. But he admitted it would be a very hard job to get a credible offer package off the ground given the venture capital company's lead and the very short timeframe …he said he was nevertheless serious about testing the water. But much would depend on the attitude of BMW… He said: 'We are going through what figures we can and I am very interested in creating an alternative bid. But we recognise that Alchemy has such a lead that it will be extremely difficult to get anything together. I don't want to raise expectations…' He said finance would not be a problem because BMW had already agreed to pay Alchemy a fortune to take Rover Cars off its hands. The West Midlands had the managerial and technical expertise to put together a very experienced consortium team, and, allied with entrepreneurial input, something he could offer, a bid could be feasible … He said he would be contacting BMW in the next few days to register his interest … Coun Hemming said: 'At the very least we need a nucleus of people in touch with each other able to move fast should the Alchemy thing fall to pieces … Moves are afoot – it is about trying to get an alternative.'

That same day, many people contacted Hemming. Among them was John Edwards, who runs the huge Edwards of Stratford Rover car dealership and was to become a prominent member of the final Phoenix consortium. Following a meeting with Edwards, who shared a lot of information about Rover products, things began to move fast. Hemming spoke to the TGWU's Tony Woodley the next day, Thursday 23 March, and his diary entry reads: 'I explain to Tony that I don't mind being a doorman who opens the door for someone else to go through.' Hemming then spoke directly to John Towers, who, according to the diary, said that he had been 'working behind the scenes' and that, although a 'long shot', there was 'no other credible attempt' to put together an alternative. Later that day, Hemming faxed his 'initial expression of interest' to BMW's Prof Milberg. It read:

I represent a consortium of British investors interested in tendering for all or part of the Rover Cars business based in the UK. I would request an opportunity to meet with you in Munich on behalf of my consortium to identify what the next steps would be. I understand that you cannot finalise any arrangements with any other tenderers at the moment, but would request that you give consideration to alternatives, ours included. [John Hemming's diary, March 2000].

Hemming continued serious attempts to gather an experienced management team from within the car industry. Days later, Dr Hagen Luderitz, BMW's chief negotiator for the sale of Rover, contacted Hemming, who then formally submitted an outline bid on Monday 27 March. At that stage, it was called Rover Future. Key players in the Rover drama welcomed the bold move. The TGWU's Woodley said: 'I am delighted with any effort that could lead to a bid to maintain Rover as a genuine, sizeable car making manufacturer in the future.' On 29 March, Rover chief Professor Samann said that Hemming's proposals could be considered. He added: 'He has to come up with a complete proposal. If he is able to do that then yes, we will talk to him.' In his diary, Hemming then recorded:

I am aware that John Edwards has been trying without success to put a deal together supported by the dealers and that John Towers is now interested in trying to do something. Decide to bring all sides together trying to ensure only one consortium rather than three and get AE Sharp to arrange a meeting for Friday. John Towers talks to me and I agree that we should only have one team working on the project. [John Hemming's diary, March 2000].

The historical meeting between Hemming, Towers, fellow Phoenix consortium members John Edwards and Brian Parker, a financial expert, and various other people, including this book's co-author Carl Chinn, took place on 31 March – the eve of the march for Longbridge. It was then decided that only Towers and actual stakeholders in what was to be known as Phoenix would know any details of the alternative bid and negotiations, to ensure that rivals Alchemy were unaware of the strength of the consortium. Although Hemming was one of those excluded from this inner core of knowledge from then on, his role had been – and continued to be – valuable to the group.

It is important to record this 'Hemming factor', because there have since been mutterings among some people over who mattered and who did not in the origins of the alternative bid for Rover. There is no need to go into every tiny detail of any such debates, but history requires the facts to be recorded. Already, in Chapter One, it was noted that Towers, Richard Burden and Stephen Byers had met and discussed the possibility of an alternative on Friday 17 March.

Although they decided to keep the idea confidential at the time, we can now see that these conversations were the very beginnings of a plan that eventually succeeded. In this chapter, we have shown clearly how Hemming was actively looking for any sign of an alternative on 19 March, that he launched his idea publicly on 21 March and that, however much things changed once Phoenix really got underway, he did make serious attempts to start putting a bid together himself. These efforts undoubtedly assisted the birth of the alternative bid, if only in the public eye. Hemming played his part, even if, as he himself said at the time, it was only as 'a doorman who opens the door for someone else to go through.'

Once Phoenix was publicly launched, Hemming stayed out of the details but acted as a spokesman for the consortium, working tirelessly under the media spotlight until 28 April, when a full-time PR company was hired for the bid's latter stages. BMW had apparently become nervous about having a politician involved in the deal, and so Hemming, the local Liberal Democrat leader, had to distance himself and become a 'supporter' instead. As he said to me at the time: 'I am happy to fall on my sword if it helps the chances of success for the Phoenix bid'. Towers himself acknowledged the help of Hemming's enthusiastic public backing when interviewed by me after the crisis. He said: 'You need some external help and it was handy to have people like John to be involved in that because it allowed those people at the centre to more easily get on with their work.'

But we are jumping ahead, because before Phoenix itself was revealed to the world after that 31 March meeting there were a few days when little new emerged on the Rover crisis. The general public had shown themselves to be enraged about BMW's plans with the huge march on 1 April, and various individuals had become passionate about a possible alternative. Yet nothing concrete was immediately forthcoming. The unions still demanded the involvement of the government, with Woodley insisting on 3 April: 'I would say that a government has got to do what is right for its people and its country. They must not be allowed to renege on their responsibility to Rover, to Britain and to its people.'

Responding to many similar challenges, Prime Minister Tony Blair said on that Monday: 'We have strongly criticised BMW's decision to sell Rover. But if governments in the past, of both major political parties, have been drawn towards 'rescuing' a company in difficulties, we see our role now as helping to equip people and business for the new economy, as encouraging innovation and entrepreneurship, as improving education and training and as broadening access to new technology.' Basically, Blair ruled out a Rover rescue package from the government itself.

Union anger turned back onto BMW the next day, 4 April, when a leaked memo suggested that the German carmaker was already organising Rover into separate units in preparation for the Alchemy deal. Terry Pye, a national officer for the MSF union, said: 'We have reiterated our opposition to the breaking up of Rover, but it would appear that BMW are moving with indecent haste to try to get the deal completed. We have told them that we are still looking for an alternative solution.'

On 5 April, pressure mounted on Trade and Industry secretary Stephen Byers when he was subjected to a grilling over his handling of BMW before a House of Commons Select Committee. *The Guardian* reported that Tory committee member Tony Baldry was scathing of the government's ignorance about the impending Rover crisis, but Byers, appearing alone, told the committee: 'We were not given information that BMW were considering breaking up Rover and selling Longbridge.' Committee chairman Martin O'Neil demanded to know why the DTI had not picked up on what he called widespread 'café gossip' in Munich about the shifting position of BMW's board towards Rover. But Byers insisted that he said he had no recollection of remarks, said by BMW to have been made by Professor Samann, that the clock was standing at 'five minutes to 12' – later interpreted as a clear warning that drastic action was about to be taken.

The pressure was on the government, Byers was in the dock and yet no realistic alternative to BMW's sale of Rover to Alchemy had been revealed. Was someone, perhaps in the government, now prompted to leak the Phoenix bid to the press in an attempt to relieve these strains? This certainly appeared to be the case, judging by the tone of the article that appeared in *The Guardian* on 6 April under the headline 'Byers Backs New Rover Buy-Out':

> An alternative buy-out of the crisis-hit Rover car group is understood to have won government backing and will be formally presented to its troubled parent company BMW in Munich by the end of the week. According to top level industry sources involved in putting together a complex new financial package, the trade and industry secretary, Stephen Byers, has been quietly supporting the creation of a consortium committed to mass car production at Rover's troubled Longbridge plant near Birmingham, to be headed by the former chief executive of the Rover group, John Towers. The rescue operation – initially codenamed Project Phoenix ... – will be presented as an alternative to the offer from the Alchemy venture fund ... As well as Mr Towers, the team is believed to involve the Midlands Rover dealership mogul John Edwards. Mr Towers – who resigned as Rover chief executive in April 1996, two years after it was bought by BMW – is known to Mr Byers socially and professionally ... Mr Byers made it clear he would welcome an alternative to Alchemy's plan to turn Rover into MG Cars ...
>
> In the wake of Alchemy's appearance, the millionaire Midland businessman John Hemming, a Liberal Democrat member of Birmingham city council, went public with plans for a counter-bid. The

computing entrepreneur, who at the time appealed for backing for his own fledgling bid, might also join the new syndicate.

Whatever prompted the public launch of Phoenix, the cat was out of the bag, and prominent figures were suddenly talking about it. In his diary for this date, Hemming recorded the way that John Towers asked him to handle the publicity: 'Neither confirm or deny, but say if it is true then it is the dream team.' On cue, Hemming told assorted media on 7 April: 'It seems to me that this is a dream team, a group of people working together for the future of volume car manufacturing in Birmingham.' Woodley, also now known to have played a crucial part in negotiations with Phoenix, told the world: 'This is a deal that is better for the employees, better for the dealers, better for Britain and even better for BMW. We would be disappointed and dismayed if BMW didn't provide serious players like this with the information required to put in a formal bid.'

It was not all good news, however, because everyone was talking about Phoenix facing a race against time to win the battle for Rover. For a start, the Towers' camp had not yet actually prepared the details of its bid. What's more, the BMW-Alchemy negotiations were reportedly going very well and were officially exclusive until 28 April, the deadline set by both sides for an agreement on the sale. Therefore, BMW could not easily allow approaches from Phoenix for fear of damaging its deal with Alchemy. All these factors meant that there was little positive said in the press and on TV and radio about Phoenix.

The only glimmer of hope in public that anyone was taking Phoenix seriously came from Alchemy's Jon Moulton himself. On 11 April, it was revealed that he was furious that one Phoenix partner was former Rover director Nick Stephenson, a brother of Alex Stephenson, the chairman of the taskforce mapping out a future for Longbridge workers. Towers, originally a member of the taskforce himself, had pulled out once Phoenix was born, and Moulton was concerned at the remaining Stephenson link. In a fax to Byers at the DTI, leaked to various newspapers, Moulton said: 'We were assured by Nick Stephenson that he was not part of a rival bid, and on that basis we continued to work with Alex. We have now had confirmed by Alex that his brother was working with another bidder. This is obviously an unacceptable basis for us to continue to work with the taskforce and we will not be doing so.' Moulton was clearly shaken, but still his Alchemy bid was thought by most to be in prime position to take over Longbridge. Phoenix may have gone public, but no-one knew what was in its bid. For a start, it still had to secure financial backing; to do this it had to see BMW's books, and it was not allowed any access to these within the exclusivity period.

There was one other stumbling block, at least in terms of the general public's perception of Phoenix as a serious bidder. That was the fact that Towers constantly declined numerous requests to say anything about his bid at all. And the longer he said nothing, the less any industry analysts believed he stood a chance. Unions did their best for him, at one stage on 14 April threatening BMW with High Court action if it did not allow 'proper consultation' over the sale. Roger Lyons demanded that 'further bids for Rover' should be discussed. Later the same day, on BBC Radio WM's *Ed Doolan Show*, Byers reported that Towers was now talking to BMW and that he hoped he had 'some exciting ideas which are worthy of consideration'. Towers himself continued to say nothing in public.

On Saturday 15 April, Dr Carl Chinn joined Longbridge shopfloor union stewards Carl Lanchester and Ian Robinson as they rallied with scores of their colleagues in Birmingham city centre, thanking the public for their support. At the same time, they pledged their backing for the Towers' bid. Lanchester said: 'We're pinning our hopes on the Towers' bid and are 100% behind him.' Robinson added: 'Towers is our last hope, although we don't yet know what is in the new bid.'

There was at this stage a peculiar twist in the media coverage of the Rover crisis. The *Evening Mail* had published a small reader's letter in its columns on 6 April, from a Mr G E Moore, of Castle Bromwich, which read:

> Mr Moulton of Alchemy tells us that he is not an asset stripper. The history of his company would suggest otherwise. In my view he will sell off the huge stockpile of cars, not necessarily a bad policy, since making cars purely for stock is a dangerous course to follow. He may make a few token MG Cars to justify the new company title, but when the time is ripe he will sell off large chunks of Longbridge for housing development, then shut down the whole shebang …

This jibe from a member of the Birmingham public so annoyed Moulton that he wrote to editor Ian Dowell insisting that this was not the case, and that the only future for Longbridge lay with Alchemy:

> The Evening Mail printed a letter from Mr G Moore on April 6 stating that the history of Alchemy suggests we are asset strippers. There is no such history, and I challenge Mr Moore to produce support for his statement. Alchemy Partners is a provider of capital – nearly always to make things grow.
>
> [*Evening Mail*, Thursday 13 April 2000].

Dowell was fascinated by Moulton's attention to detail. Here was a fully occupied, high-flying businessman, involved in the biggest deal of his life, yet someone who must nevertheless have been reading every paragraph of coverage on the Rover crisis in order to have spotted a few paragraphs on the letters page of a Birmingham newspaper. Dowell told me, his head of news, to call up and ask for a face-to-face interview on what Alchemy really would mean for the future of Longbridge. Dowell wanted to meet this man, see what made him tick and find out exactly what would happen to Rover under Alchemy. I phoned

Jon Moulton, the managing partner of Alchemy Partners, (centre), being interviewed by the *Evening Mail*'s Stephen Dyson (left) and editor Ian Dowell (right). *Picture by Alan Williams*

Alchemy's offices and insisted upon leaving a message for Moulton on Friday 14 April, and was quite surprised when he phoned back personally an hour or so later. Yes, he said, he would like to meet Dowell and myself and was very happy to face a barrage of questions. He revealed that the request was very timely, because he was about to reveal to the world on the afternoon of Monday 17 April the more precise details of his plans. If we would like to meet him after his management meeting at 10.30 that Monday morning, then the *Evening Mail* could have the first full chat with him.

Dowell, of course, jumped at this chance, and he and I spent the weekend planning a series of questions with the help of paper's industrial correspondent Chris Morley and business editor Jon Griffin. Dowell, *Evening Mail* photographer Alan Williams and myself caught the train to London early on Monday, knowing that we were tight for time, as the paper's main edition deadline was only an hour or so after the interview. But Moulton saw us early, and we pumped him for every ounce of information. Candidly, he answered every question without hesitation and at some length, and my rusty shorthand note was really put to the test. Pages one to four of that night's paper went into every detail of what would happen to Longbridge under Alchemy in an amazingly frank question and answer session. The headline was: 'Alchemy – We Put Key Questions to Boss Moulton'.

ALCHEMY

We put key questions to boss Moulton

ALCHEMY Partners boss Jon Moulton today predicted Longbridge would employ "several thousand" workers in five years time - producing aluminium-based cars.

In an exclusive interview with the Evening Mail, Mr Moulton outlined his vision of a hi-tech future for the Birmingham car plant bolstered by a major sales drive in the US.

In the most detailed analysis yet of Alchemy's plans, Mr Moulton predicted that low development costs of £25 million to introduce new products would pave the way for a successful Longbridge.

And he poured scorn on the rival bid by John Towers, suggesting losses at Longbridge as a major car producer were inevitable.

But he admitted that the scale of redundancies would be "significant," pledging "full contractual payments" to workers affected.

He said of the jobs outlook for the future: "We have got some ideas but we can't give you a full answer in exactly where we're going to be in that time.

"What I would say is that we hope to be employing several thousand. It would be a miracle if we reached 10,000 employees."

Mr Moulton predicted:
● A big sales push for the MG Car Company in the US, the first entry

By Editor Ian Dowell and Head of News Steve Dyson

into the market for 20 years.
● A hi-tech Longbridge producing new aluminium-based cars at a cost of just £25 million a model.
● Sales of a large chunk of cars by use of the Internet over the next five years.

ROVER
£25m to make Longbridge a success: Pages 2, 3 and 4

The *Evening Mail*'s front page of 17 April 2000, when Alchemy's detailed plans for Rover were revealed

What reassurances can you give the thousands of Rover workers who read the Evening Mail every night?

Growth. There are things that are going to happen that will make this company grow quickly and successfully. Believe it or not, the development of aluminium products will need more workers and will take more time to make, but will be more profitable because of the raw material costs, the tooling costs and the product development costs, which will be much, much lower. I'm talking about a maximum of £25 million to develop a new product, because it's aluminium based, as opposed to £800 million or more to launch a steel-based... replacement... Lotus Cars is in the same framework and even people like Renault are starting to use aluminium for low volume car production.

Does it disappoint you that your bid for Rover has had such a hostile reception in the West Midlands, virtually from the day it was announced?

Yes, it does because we actually regard ourselves as saving something rather than closing everything.

What do you think generally of the range of Rover cars developed by BMW? Is there any prospect of other models being produced in any volume?

The brand Rover is tarnished, that regrettably is the case. The cars themselves, the 75 is a good car and is selling well, now the prices have come down. The car is obviously too good to be part of the BMW family. The Rover 25 and 45 are reasonably decent cars, not fantastic. The prices and marketing will now be decisive for them. The old Mini is a great car now nearing the end of its life and we've only got it for a few more months although we hope to make the most of that. The *MGF* is a car that's been allowed to go nowhere for quite a long time which may have something to do with the fact that the company's ownership has changed so often. There's definitely scope for rapid development there. Yes there is a prospect for other models to be produced at Longbridge, although I can't go into details.

Do you see yourself as some sort of white knight who could save a sizeable number of jobs at Longbridge?

No, once this transaction has been completed I will be fairly invisible and the management team that already exists will be strengthened and will grow very quickly.

Does it surprise you that Trade and Industry Secretary Stephen Byers has publicly given his support for the alternative consortium headed by John Towers? How can you say that this plan from a former chief executive of Rover is doomed to failure, especially when Mr Towers has not yet revealed any details?

... I was quite cheered by some of what Mr Byers had to say. He said he would give backing financially to people who gave substantial employment at Longbridge and I have now written to him saying that we fall into that category ...Yes, I believe Mr Towers was an MD at Rover although that and being successful are not necessarily connected... If Mr Towers was able to raise his cash and to beat my bid then that's life. But what would be a horrible scenario would be if someone appeared to have a successful bid and then in five months time was faced with all this chaos again... If (Towers) believes he can make anything other than very large losses while keeping a large workforce he must have a calculator that's set very differently to mine.

It has been suggested that your MG Car Company could sell up to 100,000 models a year. Last year, Rover sold only 12,000 MGs. Where will you find the extra buyers? ...
We don't expect to sell 100,000 MGF's. We'll have to have a model range that includes a sports saloon and I can see good volumes for that and therefore in the medium term we may see figures approaching 100,000...

You have been quoted as saying that Alchemy could make 'a great deal of money out of Rover'. Yet in just two years, Rover's losses were almost £1.4 billion. How can you justify your optimism?
It's easy enough. The losses have been generated by the mass market business. With the MGF alone it has shown some profits over the last few years. We are not going to be a mass market producer. If you imagine we're going to have a new sports car model that will probably be an add-on to the MGF not a replacement. There will also be a sports saloon, and if you add these models together we'll soon be nearing units of 100,000 a year...

Do you see the possibility of creating a space for contract car assembly at Longbridge?
Yes indeed we do, it is a strong possibility and one we're talking about with several producers and if that happens it will be very good news for our plans. Longbridge has got a superb paint shop and we would struggle to fill it to capacity in the next few years...

The Rover 'jobs for life agreement' outlaws compulsory redundancies. Will you scrap this deal? How many jobs do you now think you will keep?
... We don't know anything about jobs for life in law...There will be redundancies beyond reasonable doubt... there will be a need for some and they will be significant... we will absolutely ensure full contractual payments are made. The same applies to pension schemes... when redundancies happen, we will try to do things as quickly as we can, whilst fully adhering to employment law.

Did the scale of the march and rally for Rover in Birmingham, involving more than 80,000 people, surprise you?

No. A few weeks ago we actually had some protestors outside these offices in Covent Garden waving their Socialist Worker banners and chanting 'nationalise, nationalise'. But after I sent down a secretary with a box of chocolates for them they stopped their chanting, started eating them and went away... the march...was an outpouring of sadness about the huge costs faced in the region. The march was not very much anti Alchemy but was actually far more 'anti what have the Germans done for us'? I do feel very sorry for what's going on but I hope for people to see what we're trying to do... we want to create an excellent, small growing company... something that is actually on its way up rather than on its way down...

Can you offer any message of hope to the 50,000 workers in the Midland supply chain whose livelihoods depend on Rover?

We will be looking for suppliers but only on strictly commercial grounds... clearly volumes will be lower...

What sort of business does Alchemy see selling on in five years in terms of long term jobs?

...we hope to be employing several thousand. It would be a miracle if we reached 10,000 employees.

If an offer came in within five years, would you leave sooner rather than later?

We plan to have a very successful company in three years time or four years time or five years time... That does not mean we do not plan the company for the long term, because people will pay far more for companies which have a future...

Who do you think might buy the MG Car Company from you?

The most likely route would be a flotation... That would be our aim.

How would you distribute your cars?

We are contractually bound to the existing dealer network and we would use it to its full to distribute our cars. We would also absolutely use the internet...

What will be your marketing strategy for worldwide sales?

How personally will you yourself be involved in the running of MG Car Company, given that you have no direct experience in the industry? We will most certainly be re entering the American market as soon as we can... It has been 20 years since the MG was sold in the USA and yet there are 28,000 members of the MG Owners Club in the USA. I've had a dealer on the phone from California begging for models and he told me that he could have the cash and orders for 1,000 MGF's if I could get them out there… Once this deal's done I will be putting in ten or 20 days a year as a non-executive director. The main man will be Chris Woodwark. What you have to remember is that Rover is a complete operating unit and there are a great number of skilled middle managers already existing there… which is why I don't think there is much credibility in the argument that people say we don't have the experience…

What is your target annual profit for the MG Car Company?
… we will be very lucky if we reached £50 million a year in the short term.

What stage have your talks with BMW now reached?
…I believe we will complete by April 28.

Are BMW effectively paying you to take Rover off their hands?
…Let's just say BMW have provided enough finance to make sure we can deal with the costs of launching the MG Car Company and thinning out the old business.

You have been portrayed as a hard man. One media observer said: 'Some people would say that his main delight was picking the legs off flies when they were ill.' What's your reaction to that?
I'm not really into pulling legs of insects, although I would quite happily pull the legs off one of my competitors who made that statement, another venture capitalist.

What innovations have you got up your sleeve?
The MG Car Company is almost certain to re-enter sports car racing… possibly even entering Le Mans…   [*Evening Mail*, Monday 17 April 2000].

This interview had immediate results. For a start, it set the Midlands and Britain fervently talking again about the fate of Rover under Alchemy. Moulton's revelations in the *Evening Mail* had been well publicised, with blanket bill posters around the region and several advertisements on different commercial radio stations. They contained the close detail both dreaded but desperately wanted by everyone, resulting in a sales increase of several thousand copies that night. On an otherwise fairly quiet news day, most media outlets picked up on the new aspects revealed. The fact that Moulton had come across as so honest with every answer, and that anyone who wanted to now had the whole story of what he planned in front of them, seemed to make the Alchemy deal inevitable.

More importantly, this heightened public awareness and Moulton's blunt jibe at Towers obviously enraged the Phoenix camp. Dowell had made sure that copies of the Moulton interview were faxed to everyone known to be close to Towers, and within hours there was a reaction. Carl Chinn, who had been at the historical 31 March Phoenix meeting and was unofficially acting as an intermediary for the consortium, had an attractive proposition. Would the *Evening Mail* be interested in talking to a very highly-placed source who could provide intricate details of the Phoenix bid, someone who could challenge Alchemy's assertions and who knew exactly what Towers and his team were planning? Perhaps shaken by the thought that the world may now have resigned itself to Alchemy, it seemed that Phoenix was about to fully air its plans and views in public for the first time. Dowell and I took up Chinn's offer and two hours after arriving back from London, with the Moulton interview still on the newsstands, we left the *Evening Mail*'s offices again to meet someone who had a different story to tell. Pages one to four of the next night's paper were filled with my resulting article. The headline was: 'The Rival – We Reveal Phoenix Plan For Longbridge'.

> John Towers' Phoenix Project claims to be able to raise Rover from the threat of ashes – and save thousands of jobs. The bid mounted by the former Rover chief executive is seen as a genuine attempt to keep volume production at Longbridge, whereas Jon Moulton's venture capitalists herald little more than a niche sports car factory. Mr Towers and his team have steadfastly declined to comment about the details of the Phoenix Project, but highly-placed sources both in London and Munich have revealed to the Evening Mail just why the bid may prove so attractive to BMW.
>
> For a start, the Rover dealer network is strongly behind Towers' bid. John Edwards and Peter Beale, bosses of the influential dealer Edwards of Stratford, are publicly on board. This is seen as important because the Alchemy deal was strongly opposed by dealers, who had already threatened legal action against BMW... Other organisations involved include the Mayflower engineering business, headed by Terry Whitmore, and Lola Cars, headed by Nick Stephenson. Also, all the unions representing workers at Longbridge back Phoenix, potentially removing another legal threat against BMW.
>
> 'It's almost a cooperative style bid,' said the London source. '... none of the people in it is looking for a profit out of it, their interests is in keeping things going to help their own businesses. Mayflower want to ensure an ongoing business which then would help its own. Various suppliers are backing the bid because they want to continue to be supplying. Dealers are involved because Rover success means that they continue to sell. And trade unions will back it because it will mean jobs for their members. None of these people are actually seeking profit or cash or assets for themselves. This has to be seen as a strength for Phoenix. I believe there is even a plan for workers to become shareholders.

…'The Phoenix deal would not be painless. I understand they would initially only directly employ those workers involved in the Longbridge assembly operation, some 5,500 people. Phoenix would have to cut costs, and may need to shave between 1,000 and 2,000 workers… But by returning to the volume market, and they plan to make up to 250,000 cars a year, there would be a helpful knock on effect throughout the other wings of what was Rover. Success… would mean that BMW would have a more controllable jobs issue at Swindon body panels plant and at Powertrain (engines)…'

So what are the main differences between the Alchemy and Phoenix camps?
'There is so much more good in the Phoenix bid,' said the source. 'Rover will remain a volume car producer, resulting in thousands more jobs being retained. BMW will have no legal hassles from unions, dealers and even suppliers under the Phoenix bid, whereas Alchemy seems fraught with legal issues.

'Rover has huge assets that are being ignored… the Rover 75 is the best car it has ever produced. Phoenix is considering two options with the Rover 75. The first would be to run it on a sub contract basis at Cowley. The second, more preferred option would be to relocate the facilities to Longbridge, and it is understood BMW would be happy with that. Then there is the 75 Estate. Amazingly, I have heard that Alchemy has cancelled plans for the 75 estate. They don't want it, although there's less than £10 million left to spend on development for it. Phoenix would resurrect the 75 Estate straight away… launching it as soon as possible. They could sell 20,000 Rover 75 Estate a year. At the same time, Phoenix would continue producing the Rover 25 and 45 and the MGF at sensible volumes. BMW are keen to keep the new Mini… Phoenix would continue to produce the old Mini for as long as BMW allowed … Basically, where Alchemy would discard Rover as a brand, Phoenix would keep it – the 25, 45 and 75 would all live on. Once this production has been re-established, Phoenix would then launch new models as MGs, Triumphs and Austin Healeys…'

The source said that any new models would share a platform and costs with another major producer. There has been speculation that such a partnership could be planned with Japanese car maker Honda – a company Towers worked with so successfully when he was chief executive of Rover. But this is unconfirmed. The source in Munich, who has told the Mail he knows BMW is impressed by Phoenix, said: 'John Towers has received very different types of support. There is the outspoken support of people like Dr Carl Chinn and Birmingham councillor John Hemming. Then there is the backstage, but public, support of the dealers, the suppliers and even the unions. And then there is invisible support, people and businesses who have told Towers that they will support him if he wins the deal.

'Alchemy has had the advantage of months… But the great thing about the arrival of the Phoenix bid is that just one month ago BMW did not have a choice. They had a situation that was seriously damaging their business… They were faced with closing Longbridge or Alchemy, so they chose Alchemy. Now there is another option, in Phoenix, and we are all watching with interest to see if BMW will be flexible.

'I know BMW are taking it very seriously, although it's created an awful dilemma for them. I can't see how they can ignore the good things in this proposal… the suppliers are kept on board, saving more jobs – rather than losing 50,000 under Alchemy's plans. The Phoenix deal would not be totally painless. It would still lose jobs… But it would be a hell of a lot less …'

But how could Phoenix hope to be successful, given the timescale? And what about the costs of developing new steel cars, which Alchemy's Jon Moulton told the Mail yesterday could be as high as £800 million, dwarfing the £25 million he claimed was the maximum cost of a new aluminium model? Where is this cash coming from?

The source said: 'The experience and collective knowledge that Phoenix has means it can put a better plan together far faster than anyone else could. Remember we are talking about John Towers here, the ex-chief executive of Rover. And Alchemy keep on quoting April 28. I understand there is more time than that. Whatever happens on April 28, I know BMW never do anything without the backing of the board, and I also know that the next board meeting is not until May 16.

'As to finance, Jon Moulton seems to come out with these figures off the top of his head. A new car is not just the body – steel or aluminium. You have the transmission, the engine, and all the parts to pay for. This is work that suppliers have got to put in. One of the ways of reducing the costs of a car is that various participants share the investment and share the costs. This can result in a steel car at a very low cost.

'Nick Stephenson, the former product and design development director at Rover under John Towers, was well known for developing the MGF model at a cost so low that many in the industry could not believe it. I understand it was not a lot higher than the £25 million Moulton keeps banging on about. Moulton has been saying a lot about things he knows little of. He told the Mail yesterday that he will launch the MG into the USA – but I bet he didn't mention that the MGF is not a legal platform for the USA…'

Yet still the question of where Phoenix will raise its cash is posed by analysts up and down the country.

The source declared: 'I understand the money is absolutely there. And I'm told it is standard financing, not venture capital. There is no public money involved in their sums. And whether Alchemy or Phoenix win, both can rely upon the fact that BMW will be financially supportive of their investment. Sensible, justifiable and auditable costs and activities for the establishment of a new business will be met by BMW.

Towers has pulled together a bid that was quite disparate and disjointed. Phoenix is now a solid plan… Is it too late? That's the big question.'

[*Evening Mail*, Tuesday 18 April 2000].

The article may only have come from unnamed sources, but they were individuals known well to the *Evening Mail*, people we trusted. And the exciting picture they painted in intricate detail made the deal we made via Chinn to keep their identities secret much more than worthwhile. Again, the paper contained the story that everyone wanted to read, and most Midland news outlets re-ran the facts revealed. There was even a positive rewrite of the article in the *Financial Times* the next day. At last, the worried general public in the West Midlands, and the mainly cynical press in London and the world, had a chance to see exactly how Rover's future as a volume car maker could be resurrected under Phoenix.

Speaking after the crisis, Towers confirmed that this leak to the *Evening Mail* had been necessary. Although the canny 52-year-old had until 18 April been keen to downplay details of Phoenix, to allow Alchemy Partners to believe they were unassailable, he had reached the point when the alternative had to be taken seriously. From that day until the end of the crisis, I continued a series of regular conversations and the odd meeting, mainly late at night, with a well-placed Phoenix source. This kept me, and therefore the *Evening Mail* and its readers, closely appraised of developments inside Phoenix, meaning that at least one media outlet saw the true picture. But why was this done with a Midland regional newspaper, rather than with a national newspaper with a wider audience? The main reason must have been the stance that Dowell had decided to take weeks earlier by backing the march against the BMW-Alchemy deal. A vastly experienced and admired regional newspaper editor, Dowell can be like a dog with a bone if he believes the cause is right, and he had shown the paper's true colours by carrying the banner proclaiming 'Don't let Rover die' during the march. The Towers' camp therefore knew that the *Evening Mail* was behind Phoenix. The Phoenix consortium also felt it was important that at least one source of reliable information was available to the workers of Longbridge and the thousands of Midland families anxiously awaiting news. Some observers scoffed at the unnamed sources who went on to spin pro-Phoenix lines in the *Evening Mail* for the next three weeks, but Dowell and I ignored this, because we knew the paper was now following the story with much closer contacts and far better knowledge than any other media. Meanwhile, every cough and spit of both the Alchemy and Phoenix bids was now in the public arena, and the race was on.

Phoenix Rising

In the days before the march, *writes Carl Chinn,* John Hemming and myself had struck up a strong understanding. Both of us were aware fully that each of us had a different role to play, but we were as alert to the fact that our separate roles had to complement one another. I kept John fully informed of my actions and meetings and he did the same with me. In the week before the rally, he worked strenuously to talk with all the people who were battling for Rover and Longbridge and had formed a kind of advisory group, of which I was a member. Then on 31 March, he brought all the interested parties together at the offices of stockbrokers, Albert E. Sharp – now called Old Mutual.

The meeting was highly secretive – because it had to be. At this embryonic stage of an effective, alternative bid it would have been folly to let out any information at all. Because of last-minute phone calls regarding the march, I was late to arrive but quickly I noticed that everyone's attention was focused upon John Towers. I had met John before. He is a strong character with a powerful presence and rightly, he is confident in his abilities. As an engineer, as a manager who had successfully led Rover, and as a man whose credentials in the car industry were of the highest, it was apparent that John was the key to the chances of any new bid. This reality was as obvious to John Hemming. Although it was he who had appointed Jonathan Bartlett of Sharp's to project manage the counter bid and as such was the client, John Hemming wanted the deal to be done. Like me, he felt that John Towers was clearly the best person to achieve that objective and to ensure not only the survival of Longbridge but also its future viability.

There was a detailed discussion informed by the expertise of those present. Amongst them were Duncan Simpson, who attended with the support of Tony Woodley; John Edwards, of the Stratford upon Avon Rover car dealership, and his finance director, Pete Beale; and Dominic King, another representative of Sharp's and now a Birmingham director of the company. His knowledge of financial matters commanded respect, as did the understanding of John Edwards about the need for good marketing of world beating cars such as the Rover 75. Importantly, John ensured the unity of the Rover dealers and, with threats of litigation against BMW, provided another crucial factor in leading the German car company to negotiate with Phoenix. As the meeting progressed, it became clear that it was going to very hard for the unions to prevent the break up of Rover. Given that Land Rover was going to be sold to Ford and seemed to have a secure future, given that there were hopes that Gaydon would also be taken over by the American company and given that Cowley was to be retained by BMW, then it was evident that the issue for us was how we could keep Longbridge open as a volume car producer.

Accordingly, it was decided to adopt a two-strand strategy towards attaining this goal. From amongst our number there would be an inner circle which would include engineers, trade unionists, dealers and stock brokers and which would be led by John Towers. They would be meeting over the weekend and thereafter to work out a strategy for Phoenix and to put together a feasible bid to buy Longbridge and whatever else was possible of the Rover Group and its business. Outside this group would be John Hemming and myself, neither of whom needed to know or wanted to know the details of the negotiations that we hoped would ensue with BMW.

Once this was decided, we left the meeting. Brian Parker and Mike Whitby accompanied us. Meeting in a pub afterwards, both John and I felt that Brian and Mike should have a place in the inner circle because each of them had entrepreneurial abilities that we believed would be advantageous to Phoenix. Later on, John ensured that Brian did become part of the select group. It was a wise move, for Brian was essential to the success of Phoenix through securing the necessary financial backing from Burdale Financial, the UK operation of the First Union Bank of North Carolina. (Brian's involvement is discussed in detail in Chapter Ten.) In so doing, he worked closely with Jonathan Bartlett, whose guidance and professional acumen were vital. Indeed, Brian regards Jonathan as 'the brains behind everything. Without him doing the appraisal of Rover, I wouldn't have been able to go to the States to get the money.' [Telephone call from Brian Parker, 23 July 2000].

Mike Whitby is another highly successful businessman and is deputy leader of the Conservative group on Birmingham City Council. Like John Hemming, Mike eschewed any connection between his actions for Longbridge and his politics. A Black Country chap, he is imbued with a love for our region and is noted for turning around manufacturing businesses that are in difficulties. Although he did not become part of that inner group, Mike did have a significant impact in the battle for Longbridge. As John Hemming stressed, 'he never showed any hesitation in backing West Midlands manufacturing when some other local politicians and commentators expressed hesitation and he was always positive.' [Phone call, 24 July 2000]. Moreover, Mike was available readily to talk to the press, and as someone who did have money and was talented in the manufacturing sector, his backing for Phoenix emphasised the positive credentials of the counter bid.

CHAPTER SIX

The Battle Of Nerves

By Stephen Dyson

Once their rival bids had been fully outlined to the general public, Jon Moulton and John Towers entered into a nine-day phase of calling each other's bluff. On Wednesday 19 April, Moulton told the world again that he hoped to have the Alchemy purchase of Rover sewn up by Friday 28 April. Although Towers was still not saying anything himself, the then Phoenix spokesman John Hemming insisted that: 'Munich is being very positive and giving our bid due consideration'. BMW themselves were giving nothing away, a carefully worded statement reading: 'We are familiar with the details of the Phoenix plan and examining the proposals very carefully. We are checking to see if there is enough substance in them for a negotiation.' No real movement, but at this stage every day that passed with Towers still in the frame seemed a godsend.

The spirits of the Phoenix consortium must certainly have been raised by the car-buying public, who began to put their money where their mouths were in supporting Rover. The opinion poll surveying car purchasing intentions has already been discussed. In the *Evening Mail* on 19 April, Rover dealerships then reported sales increases of up to 200%. The surge followed a promotion which slashed £1,000 off the screen price of a Rover 25, £1,500 from a 45 saloon and £2,000 from the award-winning 75 model. Jason Pickerill, general manager at the All Electric Garage, in Harborne, Birmingham, said: 'This should have been done six months ago. Maybe then BMW would have had a different view of Rover cars.' Doug Clark, of Clark's Motor Services, in Rednal, added: 'The confidence in Rover cars is there from the public, and hopefully it will give Rover a boost.'

It can be argued that price cuts will always attract buyers, but this was not just a feeling that the tide was turning for Rover sales. The official figures went on to prove it, with statistics from the Society of Motor Manufacturers and Traders on 5 May revealing that Rover car sales in the UK had more than doubled in April, rising from 5.72% to 13.48% of the market share. The company climbed to second place in the new car sales chart, selling 22,665 vehicles in that month. And the Rover 25 was the most popular model in the UK – selling nearly 10,000. Yes, there was a good deal on offer, but there also seemed to be a growing feeling that if you needed a new car it *should* be a Rover.

Meanwhile, on 20 April, the stalling from BMW continued. One of the company's spokesmen said that negotiations with Alchemy were 'proceeding swiftly', but added that it was 'still examining' Phoenix. This saw Northfield's Labour MP Richard Burden putting more pressure on BMW chiefs to clarify the situation. He said: 'What I want is for BMW to dismiss claims that the deal with Alchemy will be done next week. I want them to say that they will allow sufficient time to consider the alternative bid by Phoenix.' Burden also made no secret of which side he preferred: 'It seems to me the Phoenix bid is credible and imaginative, and if there was any time Rover should be relaunched, it is now.' On Alchemy, he added: 'Their bid has raised all sorts of fears about volume of production and redundancies. Some of their ideas for the future are interesting, like contract assembly, but some of the specifics they talk about do seem to be a little half-baked.'

The unions flexed their muscles again on the same day, revealing that it was to follow up the legal threat from 14 April, mentioned previously, with the launch of new proceedings. The MSF union's Terry Pye said the action was being taken to win a 'protective award' over BMW's lack of consultation, under the transfer of undertakings regulations. The move came because of what Pye said was frustration at BMW's attitude to talks with unions. 'We meet with BMW,' he said, 'but we never get concrete answers to our questions.'

Then Phoenix, on 21 April, indicated that it had made a breakthrough with BMW in principle, although the Germans still wanted more details before the 28 April deadline. The *Evening Mail*'s London source told me:

> This has turned into an incredible situation. BMW has made it known that it finds the Phoenix bid far more attractive than Alchemy's, yet it is causing impossible problems by insisting on every little detail by next Friday. Phoenix has only had three weeks to hammer together its deal, as opposed to the near six months it has taken Alchemy – and already BMW prefers Phoenix. I understand that Towers can deliver everything by mid-May – possibly by the time the BMW board meets again on May 16. All he needs is those three extra weeks and the deal could be his.

Local MPs and unions again demanded that Towers get this extra time, Burden pointing out that Midlanders wanted to be assured that 'both bids are given fair treatment', and the AEEU's Sir Ken Jackson pleading that Phoenix gets 'a fair crack of the whip'. Officially, however, a BMW spokesman would only say: 'We are assessing both bids,' adding that senior managers had met Phoenix representatives 'to clarify some points'.

The Easter weekend brought with it a break from any developments in the real world, leaving a barren national press with nothing better to do than predict the end of the Phoenix bid. It was, after all, the weekend before the 28 April deadline, a perfect chance for the Sunday broadsheets to pontificate on what they thought was Towers' inability to raise finance for a deal. This was perhaps even more tempting a conclusion to reach given that Towers was still not publicly talking to anyone about his plans. The inaccuracy of many of these London-based reports on 23 April, and the damage they could have caused, is considered in detail in Chapter Nine, although it should be said here that, at best, they cast a negative shadow over the hopes of Phoenix. Many in the financial world judge the pulse of deals and negotiations from what is said in the so-called serious press, and it certainly appeared that BMW now thought it was all over after reading the offerings of the Easter Sunday business sections. Indeed, on 24 April, Easter Monday, a BMW spokesman indicated that Alchemy Partners was now its first choice to buy Rover, that it expected to conclude talks with them soon and that its dealings with the Phoenix bid did not have the status of negotiations: 'We are negotiating with Alchemy, we're not holding negotiations with Towers, we're only holding talks with him. Alchemy was our first partner and we want to conclude negotiations with them as soon as possible. The negotiations should be concluded soon.'

It was pretty damning stuff, but, amazingly, the Towers' camp remained calm, insisting that Phoenix *could* raise finance because nowhere near as much money was needed as the figures guessed at in the media. The £700 million total annual losses BMW had cited as its main reason for disposing of Rover were also challenged. The *Evening Mail*'s Phoenix source said that Towers estimated the actual cash losses, ignoring the write-offs and depreciation used in German accounting methods, were only £170 million a year. The source told me on 24 April: 'Phoenix analysed BMW's results and found Rover's actual cash losses were only £170 million, a situation that could quickly be turned around in the right hands. That's why volume car manufacturing operations at Longbridge are still so viable to Towers.' The source also revealed more details of the Phoenix plans for workers to become shareholders, an idea first revealed in the *Evening Mail* on 18 April: 'All managers and workers would be granted share options from the beginning of the take-over, and these would increase once Rover became profitable.' And the source sniffed at the Sunday newspapers' various guesses of the finance involved in the Towers' deal, adding that, if successful, Phoenix would receive £500 million from BMW to take Rover off its hands and that only another £200 million was needed from private bankers.

None of this vexed Moulton, who on Tuesday 25 April was pitched into battle against Hemming on BBC Radio 4's *Today* programme. Claiming Alchemy was miles ahead of Phoenix in the battle for Rover, Moulton said: 'I don't think we are blowing them out of the water. I don't think they are even in the pond. The rival bid has the great benefit of being derived from a pretty great state of ignorance. We have spent six months working on this company, looking hard at all the options, including the mass production route that Mr Towers' group seem to think is viable. Nobody at BMW, none of the experts we've been working with and not even the civil servants at the DTI believe that the mass production route is viable.' Hemming performed well, retorting: 'I think pretty well everyone in Britain, apart from those at Alchemy, want to keep this bid alive … what we have talked about is initially 1,000 to 2,000 redundancies which, compared to the potential 40,000 job losses, is relatively small.'

Trade and Industry Secretary Stephen Byers suddenly began to turn up the heat on BMW. On the same day as the Moulton-Hemming radio debate, a spokesman for the DTI said Byers would be speaking to senior executives from BMW to ask them to treat the Towers bid with fairness: 'They have previously promised to give the Towers bid detailed consideration. Now is the time to honour that commitment.' If that was not strong enough for some, Byers completely broke cover on 26 April, branding Moulton a 'worried man'. He was annoyed at Moulton's radio claims that government officials had written off the Phoenix mass production plan as 'unworkable'. Speaking to Shaun Connolly, the *Evening Mail*'s political editor, Byers stormed:

> My officials deny they ever said that. They would not discuss other bids with Moulton and say he is misrepresenting them. All the indications are that Moulton is now a worried man. He is worried BMW will look seriously at the Phoenix bid. Obviously he will make comments to support his commercial interests…If BMW need to extend the deadline to give the Phoenix bid consideration they should do so.

Byers was saying this on the day that Towers was due to meet Rover boss Professor Samann, and company spokesman Hubert Bergman then made the most positive comment about Phoenix to date, albeit as a kind of challenge:

> There is not a written deadline, but we need a bid which we can compare with Alchemy partners. John Towers knows the clarifications we need, mainly over the financial backers, and we need it as soon as possible. We are in exclusive negotiations with Alchemy Partners. When negotiations have finished there will be a contract to sign. Then we have a chance to compare the unsigned contract with any other bid. As long as we are in negotiations we are open to any additional bid. At the moment we do not have the information we need to be able to compare the new bid from Mr Towers.

Confused? So were we at the *Evening Mail* to start with, but basically Bergman was saying: 'Tell us your backers Towers and we'll wait', which formed the paper's sub-headline on that day's front page. I phoned my Phoenix source to see if these demands could be met and was told: 'Towers will today give BMW everything it needs to know, but only on a highly confidential basis. It is hoped that this will result in BMW allowing time for the due diligence process, leading to a full investigation of Rover accounts by Towers' financial backers.' The fact that such a meeting was being held at all must have been infuriating to Moulton, who had been promised exclusive negotiations. BMW were playing a risky game, but referred to the Towers meeting as mere 'talks', which it classed as different to 'negotiations'. Riled or not, Moulton remained defiant and declared that

Alchemy was poised to move into Longbridge on Tuesday 2 May after signing its deal with BMW on 28 April.

It was against the backdrop of these claims, counter claims and baffling pacifications from BMW that a controversial meeting was held late on Wednesday 26 April in Warwick. And Towers was in no uncertain mood. Flanked by his corporate finance manager Jonathan Bartlett, of AE Sharp, and two of his backers, Nick Stephenson and John Edwards, he strode into the conference room for some straight talking with Prof Samann and Christian Jon Von Freyend, Rover's finance director. Later that night, my Phoenix source leaked snippets of how a frustrated Towers had blown a fuse during these 'talks', and this formed the *Evening Mail's* front page for 27 April, under the headline: 'Row as Towers Meets BMW'.

> The Phoenix consortium's 11th hour swoop for Rover was today said to be very much alive after a heated confrontation with BMW chiefs last night. Reports suggested that German executives were surprised at the ferocity of former Rover chief executive John Towers as tempers flared during their two-hour meeting in Warwick. A London source said: 'The word is that Towers was irritated by BMW's nit picking over shareholding stakes in the Phoenix plan. They seemed to want to know exactly what level of equity there would be for the Phoenix backers and the dealers. I understand that this caused tempers to be raised and much forceful language was exchanged. Basically, I think Towers was offended by this interrogation and let his feelings be known in no uncertain terms … Towers demanded that BMW stop paying lip service to him. He asked that once the exclusivity period with Alchemy was over that BMW provide him with a letter proving that the Phoenix bid would receive a proper chance to progress. Apparently Samann and Von Freyend were clearly moved and impressed by this passion and told Towers and his team that Phoenix would be given a chance. It was a frank meeting and serious points were made. I understand that BMW were given all the documentation for the banking and financial process which they had wanted clarifying. Towers' team also presented them with a far more detailed business plan, and the issues of the new Mini, which BMW want to keep, and the Rover 75, which Phoenix want in Longbridge, were discussed – and there was little difference between the parties. I am told the meeting was ended on friendly terms and Towers and his team left feeling that a lot of progress had been made on a number of issues.'

The above article was carefully written, intending to inform our readers about what had gone on at the meeting without rocking the boat too much, for fear of losing access to what was going on. Therefore, parts of what my source told me that night were so sensitive that they did not appear in the paper, but can

The *Evening Mail*'s front page of 27 April 2000, after his heated meeting with BMW executives.

be documented now, to show just how precarious the Phoenix bid still was at that stage. Samann and Von Freyend basically gave Towers and Co the third degree, laying it on the line that BMW *must* have every detail about the equity structure and plans behind the Phoenix bid. It was all too much for Towers' patience, particularly since he was trying to present an alternative bid for Rover without even being allowed to see any detailed accounts. I understand he asked various financiers to leave the room before he delivered a quietly controlled outburst that went something like this: 'On the one hand, you are interrogating us on the minutiae of our plans, but then on the other hand, you see entirely happy to sell Rover to people who appear to know two thirds of nothing about how to run a car business.' Samann reportedly said that BMW had to 'adhere to a process', and added it was losing some £2 million a day at Rover. 'Not true!' Towers retorted. 'The losses you quote are an opinion affected by lots of accounting philosophy. The real losses as expressed by cash flow from trading are much less than that.' No one knew then whether these sort of outbursts would sway the Germans one way or the other, but what a daring way to raise the stakes! In actual fact, BMW's response appeared to be encouraging, a spokesman saying: 'Towers has provided some of the clarification we are seeking. We are examining the new information very seriously; Phoenix is not yet out of the running. The window is not closed to him but we need to check the details he has supplied.'

The day after the Towers-BMW meeting was 27 April, the eve of the Alchemy deal deadline, and the bidding war for Rover had now reached fever pitch. For a start, it was revealed that the trade unions' various legal threats against Alchemy had resulted in a planned action for damages of up to £100 million. Papers had been served on behalf of every single Rover employee affected by the sell-off, up to 10,000, each intending to take Alchemy to industrial tribunals. Moulton described the move as 'a big headache and huge liability', but was still determined to press on with his bid. 'It is in the hands of our lawyers who will sort it out,' he told me. 'It has changed nothing. We are still in the final throes of negotiations and expect to be completed by this weekend.' And then, on top of these official legal moves by various union hierarchies, there was also the growing activity of union officials from the shopfloor, motivated by Carl Chinn. Dismissed by some, insulted by others, Chinn and what he termed 'the lads' began to make waves.

The Workers Fight Back

The huge turnout for the rally and march on 1 April revitalised the Longbridge workers and the people of the West Midlands, *writes Carl Chinn*. For several days afterwards, there was a great sense of optimism and a growing belief that together we could change the minds of those in charge of BMW and ensure that Longbridge did not 'die a death by a thousand cuts'. A worker at Land

Rover, P. Condon of Dorridge evoked this feeling of hope in a letter in The Mail on 13 April. He described how he had joined the mass of people waiting to embark on the momentous occasion and taken in the image before him. It was a remarkable sight 'that filled me with emotion and immense pride. Thousands were waving banners, some smiling – some not, but all bearing a look of determination. Determination, that whatever the conclusion may be over the coming weeks, the fight was not over. That fighting spirit must not die!'

Similarly, great numbers of folk rang up Ed Doolan's show on BBC WM and BBC Coventry and Warwickshire to talk about the rally and to back my call for a march on London. Dave Osborne and I did discuss this idea and I know Dave met with other senior trade union officials to see if it were possible to arrange such an event. The consensus was that there was too little time before Easter to organise a mass protest in London, whilst because of BMW's proposed two-week shutdown over that holiday it would be very difficult to do something during that period. Instead it was agreed to have a trade union lobby of Parliament, which did take place.

There is no doubt that a large march in London would have caused major logistical problems and the decision not to go ahead can be understood. Still, the lack of a clear strategy for a continuance of the public campaign immediately after 1 April did lead to an emerging mood of despondency. Of course, much was happening behind the scenes, but this was hidden from the workers and the people of Birmingham and the West Midlands and they themselves knew that they had a vital role to play in keeping up the pressure on both BMW and the government. They wanted to act and to do so they needed a lead. That lead was provided by two shop stewards from Number 3 Paint Shop at Longbridge: Carl Lanchester and Ian Robinson.

Shop floor union leader Carl Lanchester makes his feelings clear at the public forum with the taskforce on 15 April. To the right are Ian Robinson and Phil Sidhu. *Picture by Marc Kirsten*

Carl and myself had kept in touch in the fortnight following the march, during which time I met Ian. Both were fully in tune with the views of the men and women whom they represented and realised that the workers themselves had to do something. They were fearful that if they were not proactive then this would be seen as a sign that they were not bothered about the future of Longbridge. In these circumstances, the worry was that a largely hostile London media would find it easier to influence the government against helping alternative bids for Rover and thus ensure the success of the deal between BMW and Alchemy.

Raised in Aston, Birmingham, Carl is married to Lynne, a proud Black Country wench. Throughout the battle for Longbridge, she gave her chap sound advice, words of caution and firm backing. Because of his determination to act decisively, Carl found himself thrust to the notice of the media. Unused to this spoltlight, he handled himself with assurance, dash and skill. A fervent and fluent speaker, he proved himself also to be a deep thinker and a clever strategist. Carl personified the tenaciousness of the Longbridge workers. No matter what the set back or knock back, he was never prepared to yield. His doggedness had a great influence upon all of us, myself included. Most of all, Carl had the respect and trust of the men and women whom he represented. Whenever he called upon them, they turned up in great numbers to do whatever was necessary.

The younger of the two by twenty years, Ian Robinson revelled in his role as a champion of Longbridge. Staunchly supported and encouraged by his partner, Tina Smith, his mobile phone was always at hand and he became the visible and eloquent link between the workers and the media. In this capacity, he proved himself to be quick-witted and careful. Often he had to respond to events that were fast moving and swiftly changing and he did so with self-confidence. Importantly, Ian was not only fighting for his own job and those of his pals, but also he was fighting for those of his family:

> My dad already worked at Rover and he had been there for I think 30 something years and brought the whole family up on his wages and we had a good family life . . . My brother works at the Rover. He has been there for about 20 years. He works as a pipe fitter. Then my dad got me a form for the Longbridge, which I filled in and then gave back to him. I didn't hear anything for a few weeks but when I did the Rover offered me a job. I was over the moon. I thought that I had won the lottery. I started at the Longbridge when I was 19. When I started there I was still living at home, so when I had my first wages that was great – straight up the pub, but not before my Mom had her £20 housekeeping first. [Letter to Carl Chinn, July 2000].

Ian himself emphasises that in successfully reacting to a new situation in which he found himself sought after by local, national and international journalists, he was helped by the knowledge he had gained through attending courses on trade union law and affairs at the Floodgate Centre of South Birmingham College.

Ian Robinson and Carl Lanchester were vital to victory in the battle for Longbridge. Powerfully aided by their fellows from Number 3 and Number 2 Paint Shops and later by shop stewards from elsewhere at Longbridge, they became the voice of the workers. It was a voice that was passionate yet not aggressive. It was a voice of resolve and hope. Above all, it was a voice which was intelligent and which indicated an innovative response to an industrial struggle. These men could not be branded as militants because their actions were peaceful and intelligent. They did not have recourse to strikes, instead they came up with new initiatives which kept the public with them.

Carl himself had been responsible for the 'Blair dummy', which the lads from Number 3 Paint Shop had carried into Cannon Hill Park on 1 April and which had featured strongly in local and national newspapers. Carl realised that to be heard you had to be noticed and this understanding affected his actions in the second week of April:

Workers from the No.3 Paint shop protesting outside the task force meeting at the Hollymoor Centre, Longbridge, on 15 April 2000. Left to right: Ian Robinson; Billy Singh; Leroy Scott; Atrnik 'Arnie' Jutla; Jaz Dhani; and Andy Cartwright. *Picture by Marc Kirsten*

When we saw how many people were there (at the rally) it was absolutely amazing and you felt proud to belong, you felt you could achieve something and yes, yes we'd got a purpose now and 'yeh we're gonna beat BMW'. And when we marched along to Cannon Hill Park, the feeling was absolutely brilliant and it was a talking point for the rest of the week, 'yeh, brilliant'. But what were we going to do next. And then it just went dead. Everything went dead, I'm ashamed to say . . . It just went flat. Nobody was doing anything. Nobody was saying anything. And people wanted to know what was our next move. What were we gonna do. And they kept coming up to me, 'Carl we've got to do something.' And we used to sit down of a dinnertime and people were willing to help, they were all wanting to do something. So we had the idea of fly posting, but what could we put on these posters? Well Woodley had already put out a trade union brief and on that brief was 'Dishonourable Dishonest' in bold print. So that was the caption that we used, 'BMW Dishonourable Dishonest'. I printed em up, got a load duplicated, give em to the lads and they took to em like a duck takes to water. And they put them posters up everywhere, myself included . . . and people felt they were actually doing something. At this moment in time we didn't know what we was gonna achieve and how we was gonna achieve it. From that, we said we've got to become more visual. So we had the idea of the badges. We sat down again, 'What can we put on the badges'. There was all sorts a things bandied about . . . Look I says, 'It's got to be Dishonourable Dishonest' and Dishonourable is a bloody big word to get on a badge. But we found a bloke that knocked up badges and Gary Tedstone got 2,000 of em knocked up. We had a whipround, we formed our own fighting fund . . . and they paid for the badges. We got them knocked up and we distributed em out and people loved em. They wore em. [Tape recording by Carl Lanchester, 17 July 2000].

The wearing of the badges led to the management to call Carl and other shop stewards into the office. They were threatened with disciplinary action if the badges were not removed. Carl phoned the Works Committee to alert them to this situation and they asked to see the badges. Contact was then made with Tony Woodley, 'and he said, "tell the lads to wear em". He says, "tell em to take em off when BMW stop acting dishonourable dishonest and come back to the negotiating table."' In Carl's opinion, 'that was the start'. But he and his pals were aware that they had to go one step further. They had to make their presence felt in Birmingham. They agreed they would go into the city centre and say thank you to the Brummies and hand out leaflets and badges. The plans were not made public for fear of the Socialist Workers becoming involved – for if that had happened 'it wouldn't have been a shop floor fightback'.

Rover workers marched from Broad Street to the Bull Ring to thank the people of the West Midlands for their support. Ian Robinson hands a letter of gratitude to Carl Chinn. Others pictured, left to right, are: Phil Sidhu; Andy Cartwright; Greg Hepburn; and Gary Burford.
Picture by Alan Williams

I was the only outsider who knew about the intentions of the workers. Their plans boosted me. I still wanted to fight openly for Longbridge, but since the march I was unsure as to how I could do so. It seemed as if everything had been shifted into closed rooms and that the public campaign had been sidelined. Carl's lead allowed me once again to become a fully active participant. I knew that without the support of the workers I could do nothing on the streets that would gain the eager notice of the media. And it was on the streets where the workers of Longbridge and the people of Birmingham and the West Midlands had to clamour for Phoenix.

Over this period of quietness in the public campaign, I had continued to speak regularly with John Hemming and to talk with the press when necessary. Then on Friday 15 April, it seemed as if every journalist involved in the Rover story was ringing me and John to get hold of John Towers, after it was revealed that the Phoenix Project had sent its bid to BMW. The intention was to buy both Longbridge and Cowley, to keep Rover as a volume car producer and to safeguard as many jobs as was possible. The new offer was welcomed by union leaders and Labour MP Richard Burden, who played an active part in Phoenix. Neither John Hemming nor myself would give out the mobile phone number of John Towers, but later in the day I managed to speak to the man upon whom the hopes of tens of thousands of people now rested. John Towers told me that he would not speak to the press. He explained that his approaches to BMW were at a very early stage and he did not want to divulge anything that might prevent further and deeper involvement with the German company. Moreover, he was loath to alert Alchemy to any of his thoughts. John maintained his silence until victory was won. His tactic was vindicated and can be seen now as wise and correct.

Yet if John Towers did not wish to talk with the press, he did authorise me to do so on this occasion. He briefed me as to what I should mention and I made my first appearance on the Annie Othen Drivetime Show on BBC WM and BBC Coventry and Warwickshire. I told her, and later BBC News 24 and The Mail, that the Phoenix bid was solid, and I highlighted the fact that John Towers 'is a man of integrity and honour and he realises how many livelihoods and futures are at stake . . .' From my own perspective, I believed the Towers bid would maximise the number of Rover jobs and help retain Longbridge as a volume car manufacturing centre.

Early on the evening of Friday 15 April, Carl Lanchester rang me to let me know more details of the march through Birmingham city centre. I told him that I had alerted Paul Fulford, on the duty news desk at The Mail, and that a photographer would be following the Longbridge workers from Broad Street; and I also advised him that Ian Robinson should ring BBC WM and the local independent radio stations BRMB and Heart FM to alert them. The next morning, as soon as the lads 'hit Broad Street with the Blair dummy, with all our banners, with all the whistles, with a megaphone – it was off, we were off. They loved it and we loved it . . . And I've got to say it, the police, the public were absolutely brilliant.' [Tape recording made by Carl Lanchester 17 July 2000]. From Broad Strcct, thc workcrs madc thcir way across Centenary Square and Chamberlain Square and down New Street to the Bull Ring, where I met them. There could have been no better place for the culmination of the march. The Bull Ring is where Brum began, it is the working-class heart of the city and it is overlooked by our parish church of St Martin's.

It was a cracking sight. Two of the lads carried a big banner stating 'Thank You Brum & West Midlands Rover Longbridge' and as they chanted and whistled the shoppers and traders clapped, cheered and shook their hands. I spoke to as many of the paintshop lads and women as was possible. There was big Phil Sidhu, who was always there whenever the call came and who stood out not only because of his height but also because of his resilience, and there were plenty of other South Asian Brummies who were prominent over the coming weeks. There were also Black Brummies such as Kevin Beckford and Leroy Scott, two other chaps who turned up whenever they had to; there were many female workers, including Jackie Davis, Yvonne Faulkener, Maggie Sanderson and Colleen Rai; and there were Scots Brummies of the ilk of Bill Mitchell, who carried a placard which declared 'The Score on No. 10 Door. 10,000 Longbridge, 40,000 West Midlands, 4,000 Dagenham, 2,000 Ship Builders. This Space For You? & Still Blair Doesn't Care!'. Then there were John Tuck, Billy Bishop, Andy Cartwright and other English Brummies who never once hid away. And, of course, there were Black Country chaps such as Ray Grove. A quiet and shy man, Ray told me he had never done anything like this until recently. His active part had begun with him handing out leaflets about the rally on Saturday 25 March and he was committed to doing whatever was necessary despite his shyness.

Rafiq Muhammed of Small Heath had worked at Longbridge for 19 years and he emphasised how much all of the Longbridge workers were depending upon the success of the bid of John Towers: 'although we don't know yet what is in the new bid we are very hopeful it will be accepted. Mr Towers is our last hope – I've already been looking for a new job but can't find one. If the bid is not successful it will be devastating for my family.' [*Evening Mail*, 15 April 2000]. Another of the lads, Atrnik 'Arnie' Jutla from Smethwick, carried a doll upon the head of which was a photograph of Stephen Byers and around the neck of which was a bib with the words 'Baby Byers'. At that stage of the battle, many of the workers felt let down by the Trade and Industry Secretary. It is fair to state that this view changed in the following weeks. Myself, Carl Lanchester, Ian Robinson and most of the other workers came to appreciate how much effort and personal and political commitment Byers put into the Phoenix Bid. Various informants did confirm his robust support for maintaining Longbridge as a factory of volume car production. These sources also suggested that Stephen Byers was having to contend with the views of some other cabinet ministers who were not convinced by the viability of the Phoenix Bid and preferred a purchase by Alchemy. Whether or not this was the case, Stephen Byers did show himself to be determined to back British manufacturing in the Battle for Longbridge.

That appreciation of the vital part played by Stephen Byers lay in the future. For now, he was seen as a minister of a government that many workers believed had abandoned them. As we stood in the Bull Ring, Ian Robinson received a phone call from someone who told him that Stephen Byers was attending a meeting of the Task Force at Hollymoor Estate, near to Longbridge. A contingent of the lads made their way there and when they arrived the television crews and press photographers that were covering the event fastened upon them. Once again, the actions of the paint shop workers drew the notice of the nation as they watched the various news bulletins on terrestrial and satellite TV and read the Sunday newspapers.

The achievements of that weekend raised morale not only in the paint shop but also throughout Longbridge and Birmingham. The following Thursday, 20 April, Carl and Ian went with all the other shop stewards to a meeting called by the trade unions at Gaydon. They arrived back at the plant too late to give a report to the workers and it was agreed that this would be done the following day, Good Friday, on the Rover car park. Carl informed Bob Turner of the Works Committee of their intentions and he arranged for the meeting to be held in one of the function rooms of the Rover Social Club.

Early on Good Friday morning, Carl rang me to tell me the arrangements. Once again I informed the news desk of The Mail, whilst Ian Robinson communicated with local radio and regional television. As Carl indicated, we did have some apprehension for 'when you call a meeting like that you can never tell how many's gonna turn up. And when I saw the press there

Rover workers joined by Carl Chinn before setting off in their cars for a cavalcade around the Longbridge plant to demand more time for Phoenix. Trevor Taylor is on the right of Carl, Jaz Dhani is behind him. To the left of Carl is Terry Riley. Atrnik 'Arnie' Jutla is on the far left, nearest the front.
Picture by Loretta Brennan

and the cameras I thought, "I hope to God everybody turns up here". And sure enough they did. The cars started to roll in. And I was holding me breath till then. I thought there's got to be a good turnout. And it was. It was a cracking turnout.' The television cameras were allowed in to film the start of the meeting and then were asked to leave so that Carl could report back. He told the workers that the shop stewards had been informed that the future looked pretty bleak and that John Towers and his consortium was the only chance. He added that once we left the meeting he wanted all of us to get into our cars, fill them with those who had no transport and drive in a convoy around the factory. I was honoured to be asked to sit on the platform and to speak. For my part, I affirmed the need not to give up hope, to keep on fighting, to carry on making our voices heard and to maintain the pressure on BMW and the government. Outside the meeting we piled into our cars, all of them Rovers, and as The Mail reported that day, 21 April, we:

> formed a 100-strong car cavalcade . . . which drove around the plant at 5mph in support of Phoenix. As the cavalcade drove around the plant, drivers of cars festooned with posters created a crescendo of noise as they tooted their horns. Bystanders waved and gave them the thumbs up signal. The protest reached a climax just before noon as the cars continued to circle Longbridge creating a deafening blare of horns outside the main Q gate where workers and supporters cheered and

Rover workers rally outside Q Gate during the cavalcade including, from left, shop stewards Martin Glaze, Tom O'Hanlon and Noel Moloney. *Picture by John Cassidy, Newsteam*

The cavalcade around Longbridge by workers. Standing up in the car are Paul Siniarski (left) next to a colleague called Ralph. Driving the car is Dave Billingham. (Dave Linton was also in the car, but cannot be seen.) *Picture by John Cassidy, Newsteam*

clapped.

The aims of the cavalcade were simple: to show the full support of the workers for John Towers and to gain attention for that support. We achieved what we set out to do. I told The Mail that we wanted BMW to give the Towers bid the time it needed; Carl stressed that 'there is only one option and that is Towers'; and Ian brought to the fore the fact that the workforce increasingly was pinning its hopes on Towers. These views were reiterated by Iqbal Mucadem from Sparkhill, a Rover worker for twelve years, who explained 'that even if we lost 2,000 jobs at least Mr Towers knows what he is doing because of his involvement in Rover Group'. And Paul Brown from Newtown made plain the financial worries of the workers: 'We are 100% behind Towers. I have got a £50,000 mortgage and two kids to support, with Towers at least we will survive. All of us were energised by the success of the cavalcade and before we went off, I met with Carl and Ian to discuss our next move. We knew that there had to be one, for over the next fortnight Longbridge would be shut down and it was crucial that the factory and its workers were kept in the limelight. If it were not, we were certain that Alchemy would be in control. It had been announced in the meeting that some of us would go to Munich if we had to and that was one option we talked about. We also chatted about the possibility of a huge cavalcade of Rover cars leaving Longbridge and making its way slowly down the M40 to London and Westminster. Such a move would lead to traffic jams and we were aware that this might mean that we alienated some of the general public. But against that was the chance to take our fight to London, to gain extensive media coverage and to thrust the strength of our feelings right at the heart of power. We made no firm decision about what we should do, but we agreed that we would speak again on Saturday and that I would keep in touch with the lads from Ireland, where I was off to research a book about the Irish in Birmingham. I never got a chance to do my research, for within days I was back in Birmingham as our campaign heightened.

CHAPTER SEVEN

Munich

By Carl Chinn

Throughout our involvement with each other, Carl, Ian and myself met almost daily and in between, we phoned one another regularly. Our minds were in a constant flux with thoughts as to what could we do and what should we do. We had no preconceived notions about our actions and were unfettered by belonging to a formal organisation. This freedom gave us the opportunity to take our own initiatives and to do things that were unexpected and radical. But we could only act in this unrestricted and unpredictable way because we knew that we were not on our own. The paint shop workers had one will – not to let people in powerful positions think that they were going to be silent and to allow Longbridge to 'die a death by a thousand cuts'. Crucially, the deeds of the paint shop were matched quickly by those of other sections of the Longbridge workforce. Their collective actions gave strength to the Works Committee, the members of which had put forward strenuously the case for Longbridge since the beginnings of the crisis.

Buoyed by the cavalcade, all of us were hopeful that BMW might extend the deadline of 28 April. Our expectations were dashed over the Easter weekend by the reports in the business sections of the Sunday newspapers which mocked the chances of John Towers and Phoenix and which asserted that the deal with Alchemy and BMW would be done by the end of the working week. That Saturday 22 April, I took our Rover car on a Stena Line ferry to Dublin. The intention was for me to spend the Easter weekend with Kay and our two youngest kids at the home of Kay's Mom and Dad, Mick and Aggo, in Finglas on the north side of Dublin. Then on the Tuesday I would head off on my own to Roscommon, Mayo, Galway and Sligo to carry out my research. But from my arrival, it was as if I was constantly on my mobile speaking with Carl, Ian, John Hemming and Stephen Dyson about a situation that appeared to be deteriorating rapidly. Things looked really rough for Longbridge and by late on the afternoon of Sunday 23 April, Carl, Ian and myself concluded that we had one last throw of the dice left and that was to confront the BMW management in Munich itself. Of course, union officials had done this in a forceful manner, but we believed that the warnings of the senior trade unionists could be reinforced by the words of those who could speak directly for the shop floor workers and for the people of Birmingham and the West Midlands. We were never that conceited to feel that we alone could be responsible for any change of heart by BMW's directors. We always knew and stated that we were part of a much wider picture and that our actions were just one element in that picture.

It was agreed that I should phone Tony Woodley and advise him of our proposition. Tony was as low in his spirits as were we. He had worked tirelessly and ceaselessly to keep the Rover Group intact and bring about a sale to Phoenix and now all his valiant attempts appeared worthless. Tony told me that we might as well go over to Munich as things were looking so bad that anything might help – and he indicated that he would speak to Bill Morris and try to get us taken over in Rover's own plane.

Obviously, this means of transport was only a possibility, so early on Tuesday 25 April, I rang Birmingham International Airport to get a price on a return ticket to Munich. The amount shocked us for it was over £600. There was no way that we could afford that, but we were certain that we had to go to Munich on the Thursday, the day before the deadline. Ian, Carl and another shop steward, Brian Crockett, had already discussed the possibility of the four of us driving to Munich and once we knew the airfare this possibility again loomed. Along with Stuart Hughes, Brian was another person upon whom you could count and who was ever ready to become involved in whatever way was necessary. But soon we dismissed the thought of a trip by car because the drive to and from Bavaria would have taken us too long. I had heard nothing from Tony Woodley about going over in the Rover plane and so it was imperative that we found a way to raise the cash we needed. Ian decided that he would ask for assistance from various companies whose businesses would be affected adversely by a running down of Longbridge. One of them did help us. It was All Electric Garages of Harborne, Birmingham. Both John Leek, the chairman, and Jason Pickerill, the general manager, were keen to do something and gave us £300. (Later, after the crisis, I bought my Rover 75 from this garage.) Thankfully, John Hemming was also forthcoming and donated £150.

Even with this money we were still well short of our target. Our Dad then rang me and said that he had been in touch with Zip Travel of Moseley and when owners Bill Jackson and Kay Massey knew why we wanted to go to Munich, they had agreed to book everything for us and forego their commission on each ticket. This was a total of about £150. It was another smashing gesture. Then Our Dad offered to pay the whole sum on his credit card and we could pay him back later. We took up the Old Man's proposal, for by now we knew that in a couple of weeks we could give him back his money. Carl and Ian had been in touch with Adrian Ross, the convenor at Longbridge, who said the unions would pay for their flights. Adrian had added that he wanted to come to Munich with us and that he thought that it was wise that the delegation should include shop stewards who represented other parts of the Longbridge workforce. It was a good thought and the correct thing to do, and it was right and proper that Adrian himself should head our party. Zip Travel also went without the commission for this group.

In between speaking to Carl, Ian, John Hemming, Stephen Dyson and Our Dad, I rang the office of Professor Milberg in Munich. I was told that he was ill and so I inquired if I might speak to someone else in authority. I was asked why I made such a request and after explaining about the visit, I was informed that someone would ring me back later. As promised, I was contacted by a secretary who told me that everyone in authority at BMW was on holiday and as a result we should not visit Munich. I replied that we had booked up our flights and that if we were not met by anyone when we came to BMW's headquarters then we would walk into the city centre and would hold high the Longbridge banner. Following this conversation, I spoke with a lady in the office of Manfred Schock, the trade union representative on the executive board of BMW. I was informed that he would be in meetings throughout Thursday and would not be able to talk with us.

On the evening of 25 April, I flew on an Aer Lingus plane back to Birmingham. Our Dad and Our Kid picked me up and dropped me to the Rover club where I met Carl and Ian and was introduced to Adrian Ross. We discussed our strategy, went through the statement that we would take to Munich, and finalised the arrangements for a rally that was going to be held the next day in Cofton Park, just down from Q Gate. This had been suggested by Carl and Ian over the Easter weekend and they had gained the support of Dave Osborne and Adrian Ross for it to happen. Once agreement had been gained, Carl got cracking.

> And then we had to put it all together and one of the first ideas to publicise it was when Lynne said that the Blues and the Albion were playing at home (Bank Holiday Monday). So I phoned you, got the phone numbers of the grounds and they put it over at half time at both grounds. And a lot of people heard that. We got a lot of posters knocked up – Ian, myself and Lynne went out on the Monday night to the social clubs, the pubs, shops – all around Longbridge so people'd see em. And on the Tuesday when Adrian Ross came back from Wales, we brought all our stewards into the Works Committee office, we phoned up people, told em that there was a rally. We printed up a load more posters and myself, Ian, Crockett and Harry Hickman took to the road with a megaphone and we ended up in Northfield and as soon as we hit Northfield the news people surrounded us. And this was the start then of that big interest by the media in this little band of people that was running about. And that is where we met Dick Howell up there . . . and he joined us and old Dick stayed with us then right through to Munich.
> [Tape recording made by Carl Lanchester, 17 July 2000].

With money that had been raised or given, Carl bought whistles, flags, paint and sheets 'and our house became bit of a workshop. We had Lynne painting. I had the kids painting, Our Sarah, Our Robert and Our Sarah's chap, Sam Corfield.' The results of this hard work and that of others was evident at the rally. In spite of the heavy rain, over 3,000 people had turned up by 12.30pm on

Wednesday 26 April. Amazingly the clouds had cleared by the time the speeches began and it stayed sunny until we broke up. There was a banner proclaiming 'We Will Not Lie Down', another shouting out 'We Ain't Going Away' and one more urging 'Give Towers More Time'. This was matched by a banner that translated that message into German, 'Gib Towers Zeit'. Kay's sister, Brenda Hemmrich, lives in Germany and speaks German fluently and she had given us the correct terminology.

Terry Reilly and Harry Hickman were two of the many shop stewards who ensured the success of the rally. They had spent a couple of days in the Works Committee ringing people at home and telling them of the need to be present at the event. In fact, throughout the shutdown the paint shop stewards kept in touch via telephone and had a list of names they had to ring if they had to gather supporters. Terry also sorted out the generator, speakers, mixing desk and radio mike for the speakers, using the equipment he has for his wife, Christine – a member of the Starlighters, a group of singers and entertainers. Christine's dad, Ronnie Harper, had worked at Longbridge for 40 years and had been a shop steward in Powertrain and his home overlooked the factory.

Amongst the crowd was Derek Robinson. Speaking from a lorry, his latest successor, Adrian Ross, explained that he had just become convenor at Longbridge and he did not intend to be the last. It was poignant affirmation of belief in the factory's future and it was greeted with great applause. A Welsh

Rover workers at a mass protest in Cofton Park on 26 April in support of the shop floor union delegation about to fly to Munich. *Picture by Steve Murphy*

chap, Adrian worked hard at maintaining contact between the shop floor and senior trade union officials and at liaising effectively with Richard Burden. His links with key figures were important, as was his firmness of purpose.

Carl also addressed the rally, as did I. For my part, I declared that BMW had thought that we would lie down and surrender and on 1 April we had showed that we had not given in. But after the great rally, it was obvious that BMW had thought that we had gone away. Well, we had a strong message for them, 'We ain't going away!' Suddenly, the crowd starting chanting these words and over the next couple of weeks they became the rallying cry of all the Longbridge workers. I reiterated that Rover would not die and asked the people what should we do now that BMW had pushed us into a corner. With one voice, they called out, 'Fight! Fight!'. And I finished by proclaiming that if BMW did not listen to us on the next day then tens of thousands of us would go to Germany to march through the streets of Munich.

This rally gained us great publicity on the television. Anil Chandra and Harry Hickman were interviewed by a number of stations and both ably put forward the case for Longbridge. Harry stressed that the workers wanted the Phoenix bid because under Alchemy 'they're talking about big job losses. There's a lot of youngsters with mortgages going to lose their jobs and it's going to have a big effect on the West Midlands. So we all want the Towers bid to succeed.' John Towers knew all about making cars and he could build Rover back up again. No-one else could do that. [Carlton Television News, 26 March 2000]. Ian Robinson agreed with these sentiments and warned BMW that 'people aren't going to go away . . . We're going over to Munich tomorrow and we'll be knocking on their front door saying to BMW, "if you want to regain some credibility take the John Towers consortium bid"'. [BBC Midlands Today, 26 April, 2000].

After the speeches we walked en masse to Q Gate where people signed petition forms which we would take to Munich and then we dispersed. Later that afternoon, I received a call from Manfred Schock's secretary telling us that he would make the time to meet us and that we would be able to speak to a pair of senior BMW managers. The change of heart had come about through the intervention of Tony Woodley. Then I went to the offices of John Hemming in Moseley where I met Carl, Ian, Adrian and two of the other shop stewards who were going to Munich. These were Paul Parsons, representing the West Works, and Noel Moloney from the CABs. Paul is a hard-working man who is dedicated to his family and his city and was prepared readily to act for the well being of both. He has an imposing presence and is a vigorous speaker who made sure that those for whom he acted had a strong voice. Noel is quieter, but was just as determined and as focused on achieving victory as were the rest of us. Thoughtful and analytical, he is a man whose advice is valuable because it is so well-considered. Noel also capably represented his fellow workers.

John Hemming was very helpful in laying out a statement which had the Rover badge in colour upon it and which looked good. It read:

Rover Longbridge Delegation

We, the undersigned delegation members, urge the board of BMW to allow a reasonable time scale for the Phoenix bid for Rover to be put in place.

We believe that BMW should respond favourably to the Phoenix bid, which seeks to keep Longbridge open as a volume car producer and minimise job losses. Not only is the bid better for Birmingham and Rover workers, but it is also significantly better financially for BMW and its Shareholders.

As representatives of Rover Longbridge workers and of the people of Birmingham and the West Midlands, we urge BMW to recognise the devastating effects that any running down of Longbridge will have on our region. We are determined to fight for the future of volume production at Longbridge and for the future of our city and our region.

Below the statement were our names, the date and the mobile numbers of both Ian, Carl and myself. We had a large number printed off thanks to John Hemming and his secretary Emily Cox, who also contacted the German media on our behalf.

On the same day as the rally and these preparations, The Mail recited how Alchemy's Jon Moulton, who had read about his activities in various press cuttings, had personally phoned Carl Lanchester. Carl told the paper's industrial correspondent Chris Morley:

> He congratulated us on the press coverage we had achieved and said he would like to keep in touch, but I don't feel any warmer towards him. I told him: 'What we were looking for is someone who could offer hope and the only hope we have is John Towers.' I said: 'A drowning man grabs any branch he can hang onto,' and he responded by saying he knew what I was saying and that over the last few months we had been kept in the dark. But it is no good sympathising now, he should have done that ages ago. I did laugh with the bloke, but he is a businessman... He may make me redundant and it is my job to fight that. [26 April 2000].

By this date, many of the workers were calling Carl, Ian and myself 'three men and a flag'. This had arisen because it had been reported that Alchemy had felt that they would have nothing to worry about from public opposition to their buy-out if all that was involved was 'three men and a flag'.

Early on the morning of 27 April, I met the last member of the delegation at Birmingham Airport. This was Dick Howell, a shop steward from Powertrain. Dick has worked at Longbridge since 1969 and an intense feeling for the factory and its products courses through his veins, as mentioned in Chapter One. A keen trade unionist, he had been a shop steward since he had been asked to take on such an office a couple of months after he started his employment. During the troubles of the late 1970s, Dick was a firm advocate of Derek Robinson and was prominent in a march that supported the convenor after he was sacked. Like all the workers, Dick was horror struck at the thought of the running down or closure of Longbridge and fought vigorously to stave off those unwanted possibilities. In common with the other shop stewards in the delegation, he was a man whom I admired for his concern and drive. None of them wavered from the task that they had set themselves.

There was much media coverage of our departure and Paul Parsons summed up our opinions when he said that 'We've got to be hopeful going over there, 'cus I don't believe we would be going over there if we didn't have a chance. I mean, our main aim is to give BMW an insight into how we feel and we feel that the Phoenix bid is the right bid for us and hopefully they'll listen.' [Carlton Television News 27 April]. When we arrived at Munich Airport, we were greeted by a top news team from BBC Midlands Today that was made up of reporter, Colin Pemberton, and cameraman, Ian Johnson. They had flown out the night before and teamed up with their BBC network colleagues to deliberate over tactics and the logistics of how best to cover the story. These people included Jonathan Charles, the BBC's European business correspondent, Jonty Bloom, the BBC radio business correspondent, their producers, the network cameraman and the engineers who were to operate the satellite outside broadcasting vehicles which would feed filmed material and live reports. It was agreed that the pair from the Midlands would interview our delegation when it arrived, follow us in a taxi and overtake us to get a tracking shot. They would then join the national news crew awaiting our arrival at BMW's main entrance.

Everything went to plan as we came out of the airport behind the Longbridge banner. After our interviews, we got into a courtesy taxibus that BMW had sent for us and which was used regularly to pick up Rover executives, and we set off for our meetings that were scheduled to begin at 12 noon. It was now 11am and so we should have arrived at BMW about a half an hour later, giving ample time for network news interviews before we went inside. But as Colin Pemberton noted, they never got their shot of overtaking us for the taxibus was well ahead and could not be caught. Their own taxi did catch up with a vehicle similar to our own. It had no-one inside other than the driver and Colin Pemberton joked that 'the party had been kidnapped'. Keen to keep in touch with his network colleagues, he rang them to advise them that we should be arriving shortly.

The Midlands Today duo duly arrived at BMW to find a quiet scene outside the 4-cylinder building. 'Did everything go OK?' enquired Pemberton. 'They're not here yet,' replied a suddenly anxious network producer. 'What!' was the exclamation from Pemberton. 'Where the devil are they then?'

Mobile phones were whipped out and Carl Chinn's and Ian Robinson's numbers punched into key pads. Chinn was engaged . . . did that man ever stop talking! . . . and Robinson's was switched off. Where could they be? Pemberton speculated on the likelihood that they had gone to see their shop steward counterparts around the rear of the HQ building in the manufacturing plant itself. But surely they would still appear for a brief interview and shot of them going into the main building?

As time went by there was not a sign of them and they still couldn't be reached by phone. Perhaps they HAD been kidnapped, mused Pemberton. His earlier joke now seemed a ludicrous contender as an explanation.

It appeared that the network news team had been told by the BMW Press Officer, while the shop stewards were en route from the airport, that the Directors had no knowledge of the visit. The Press Officer said they had not been informed of any visit, there was no appointment and the company did not know any names in the party except for one . . . Carl Chinn. Nonetheless, the Workers Director on the board was prepared to see them at short notice out of courtesy said the spokesman. [Letter from Colin Pemberton to Carl Chinn 26 July 2000].

BMW did know of our visit but when we arrived at the factory we were taken to the back entrance. Justifiably, the shop stewards were angered at this slight and we remonstrated with the representatives of BMW. We were told that

Carl Chinn, Carl Lanchester and Ian Robinson are pictured about to leave for Munich on 27 April. Their banner reads 'Gib Towers Zeit' – or 'Give Towers Time'.
Picture by Loretta Brennan

Adrian Ross, Paul Parsons, Carl Chinn, Dick Howell, Carl Lanchester, Ian Robinson and Noel Moloney pictured outside BMW's headquarters in Munich. *Picture by Michael Dalder, Reuters*

we had greatly upset the senior management of the company because of the media attention we had attracted. Fuming with rage, Carl and Paul resolved to walk the long distance to the front of the building. As they reached the gate, they went to unfurl the 'Gib Towers Zeit' banner when two cars pulled across them and a security guard jumped out of one of them and ran at the lads. He grabbed Carl and threatened to call the police. Carl retorted that he was on the public highway and was not a hooligan. The situation was tense, but I persuaded Carl and Paul to come inside and have our meetings – but only on condition that when we left we did so proudly through the front door. The BMW people consented and we were taken to a training room for apprentices.

Our discussions with Manfred Schock went well. We exhorted him to back Phoenix, all the more because he was a worker director. He assured us that he would do so because as a trade unionist this was the option that he favoured as it would secure more jobs than would Alchemy. We also emphasised the need for BMW to open its books to Phoenix so that the consortium could make a proper offer for Rover. Once again, Manfred Schock conceded that this was something that he favoured and he added that BMW was prepared to give Phoenix the same financial incentives that it was offering to Alchemy.

After a half an hour, we were joined by Bodo Donauer, the personnel director of BMW, and Uwe Mahla from the press office. Our presentation to them was tough though polite. We stressed that if Alchemy won, then the battle would not end as we were fighting not only for Longbridge but also for our city and our region. Events beyond our control had pushed us into a corner and we knew only one way out – to fight. We brought to their notice the large fall in the sales of BMW cars in the United Kingdom and the potentially disastrous loss of respect for the company in our country. This could be regained only if BMW acted honourably towards the workers and gave Phoenix a proper chance. We acknowledged that the German company had to make a business decision, but given that now there were two bids on the table it was crucial that they listened to those who wanted to keep Longbridge open as a volume car producer. Finally, we warned that if BMW did not listen to our concerns then we would be back with thousands more workers to march through the streets of Munich. We added that trade unionists at BMW's plant in Munich had confirmed that they would help us.

The two men listened to us courteously and attentively and informed us that they understood our worries and would pass them on to the BMW board. They let us know that they did not believe that Phoenix had the necessary financial clout, but we impressed upon them the fact that this was not the case. They confirmed that if Phoenix could convince BMW of its financial backing then more time would be given and that the bid would receive the same guarantees as those given to Alchemy. After a short while they left and Manfred Schock entered into a long discussion with us. He was reiterating issues we had covered earlier. I began to fret that we were behind schedule to meet the press because of this extended chat and suggested we leave. We did so in fairly good spirits, thinking that we had made our point and that Manfred Schock was on our side. But as Carl made plain, as we came through the front door we were hit by a 'bombshell'. It seemed that the BMW people had taken advantage of our continued conversation with Manfred Schock to rush out a press release before our departure. It contradicted not only the spirit of our meeting but also what had been said, for it stated that the lack of financial details from John Towers 'does not constitute a basis for entering into negotiations with the Phoenix consortium. The negotiations with Alchemy Partners will continue in a straightforward manner.' [BMW Group Media Information release, 27 April 2000]. The media was as much in a quandary as we were.

> What was going on? It was a puzzled pair of shop stewards who Pemberton interviewed live for Midlands Today that lunchtime. In the afternoon, the stewards had just enough time to go into the centre of Munich and take their message to the people in the heart of 'BMW city'. They unfurled their banner once again and marched vocally through the Marienplatz, equivalent to Birmingham's Victoria Square in front of their Council House. Midlands Today's cameras captured the moment for history. Many ordinary Munich folk approached the stewards to hear their explanation of why they were there. What was happening to Rover had not been a big story over there. People seemed sorry about Rover jobs but saw it as a necessary business decision by BMW. [Letter from Colin Pemberton, 26 July 2000].

On the plane home we raised our spirits and Carl, Ian and myself decided that now we must take our fight to Number 10 itself. All of us were bucked up when we came out of Birmingham Airport and were cheered by a contingent of Rover workers called out by shop steward Pete Logan. Carl pronounced to them and the press that whatever had happened 'we ain't going away'.

The next morning, Friday 28 April, I appeared on Ed Doolan's show to talk about our trip to Munich. Ed was doing an outside broadcast from the BBC's Futureworld exhibition at the Gas Hall, next to the Museum and Art Gallery in the centre of Birmingham. Ed interviewed me just after 9.30, but it was difficult to be upbeat. On the previous night all the television reporters had made it plain that they were certain that Alchemy would be signing the deal with BMW. That interpretation was as marked in the London-based newspapers on the Friday morning. Words like 'inevitable', 'no hope' and 'imminent deal' were on the lips of almost all the reporters. It looked as if it was all up, although I maintained that we would continue to fight even if Alchemy won. We would not go away and we had made this clear to the BMW management.

Our chat finished with the 10am news and during the interval both Ed and myself took off our earphones and so did not hear the bulletin. Instead we began to talk with some of the crowd which had clustered about the podium from which Ed was presenting and amongst which were a few Rover workers. Ed has no doubt that what happened next made that programme 'one of the most moving, memorable and extraordinary' in his 30 years of broadcasting.

> As the news came in that Alchemy had left the scene, it took a moment to sink in. Stuart Linnel (a presenter with BBC Coventry and Warwickshire) phoned the show, sensing, like a true pro, that as we were on an outside broadcast . . . we may well not have heard the 10 o'clock news bulletin. We reacted immediately. Carl started crying of course. It doesn't take much, and this was, after all, very special. Looking up at the huge, hushed crowd that had gathered, I started to notice grown men who had come to the show before going on shift, all in their work clothes, weeping unashamedly. The tears were catching and soon about a quarter of the crowd was crying with sheer relief. We weren't out of the woods, but for the first time since this wretched plague infested our industrial heart, we could see a ray of light. 'Your thoughts Carl?' I said automatically. I had no idea what the reply was. He was too emotional to be articulate for a moment or two. And we didn't much care. We had won. We didn't know it yet, but it felt good. [Letter from Ed Doolan to Carl Chinn, 28 July 2000].

And it did feel good. I told Ed that I had to go up to Q Gate to be with the workers and as I came off the podium, people were grabbing hold of me and one lady gave me some tissues to dry my eyes. Then my mobile rang and for the next twenty minutes I was doing interviews over the phone with BBC Radio 1, Sky News and others. I tried to rush through Centenary Square to fetch my car, but I had to go slowly because of the folk who were coming up to me and shaking my hands and patting my back. Then just before I set off to Longbridge, I phoned Kay in Ireland, where her Mom and Dad were as overjoyed as we were. Next, I spoke to Our Mom and Dad and arranged to meet them at the factory and after that I rang Our Kid. He had also been in tears when the news broke and told me he'd been trying to ring me during my chat with Ed because he had realised that we had not heard the bulletin. Speaking next to Ian Robinson, he informed me that he had been doing the same as Our Kid.

At Q Gate on that Friday 28 April, the scenes were wonderful. Scores and scores of workers had turned up, Ray 'John Bull' Egan was there, local people had come along and as each car drove past horns were sounded, arms were raised and thumbs were thrust up. As newcomers arrived, they were greeted with chants of 'We ain't going away! We ain't going away!' A 'jubilant' Terry Riley told *The Sun* that 'It's absolutely superb news'. His happiness was shared by Pete Logan, a Rover worker for twelve years, who had total faith in the Phoenix bid: 'John Towers is a former Rover executive – and when he was here we had a profit bonus. This company used to make huge profits. And it can still be profitable.' Adrian Ross, the Longbridge convenor, was as elated as those whom he represented. In particular, he was delighted that this was the first time in weeks

Rover workers celebrate Alchemy's exit outside Q Gate at Longbridge on 28 April. *Picture by Edward Moss*

Rover worker Dick Howell celebrates the news that Alchemy was pulling out of the Rover deal on 28 April. *Picture by Edward Moss*

he had seen people walking around with smiles on their faces. [*The Sun*, 29 April 2000].

The thoughts of other shop stewards were the next day reported in *The Guardian*, another newspaper that was sure that Rover now faced oblivion. Alan Bradshaw of the MSF proclaimed that 'the fear has now gone . . . Alchemy were being paid to dissolve most of this site and most of the workforce with it. We believe we can carry on producing mass-production quality cars. And we have the British public behind us.' And Dick Howell said that BMW bosses had to trust Phoenix. He was pleased that Alchemy had pulled out but was keeping his feet on the ground for 'We have a long way to go because we need a couple of new models'. [*The Guardian*, 29 April 2000].

These men were not stupid. They are clever and capable and they knew that victory had not been won, but as Noel Moloney spelled out: 'We may not be out of the woods but we can move forward. BMW have not seemed enthusiastic about the Phoenix bid but the tables have been turned.' [*The Sun*, 29 April 2000]. Equally, we were all aware that BMW might just walk away, but as was maintained by Chris Markham, a shop steward with the TGWU, 'closure is not an option for these lads'. [*The Birmingham Post*, 29 April 2000]. And for the workers, the Alchemy takeover had been regarded as bad as closure. That is why there had been no support for the venture capitalists and why everyone was overjoyed at their withdrawal. It is to be wondered why neither *The Sun* nor *The Guardian* took on board the sound and realistic assessment of the workers. It is also a puzzle as to why *The Sun* carried such an offensive headline as 'RIP Rover', which this book explores in detail in Chapter Nine. Thank God that the predictions of the London press were wrong.

The world was watching

The Munich visit by Chinn and the Longbridge shop stewards was on the eve of the BMW-Alchemy talks deadline, *writes Stephen Dyson*. Everyone, therefore, was watching BMW for any sign of the completion of the deal. Although Chinn and 'the lads' held what seemed to have been a morning of cordial meetings with various executives, the BMW press officers on duty had obviously become quite agitated by the fact that a pack of TV cameras and press photographers had wanted to cover the arrival and were waiting outside for the departure of the delegation. Perhaps unsure of how the story would be covered, a company spokesman rushed to the gates to get BMW's version of event in first. The resulting press release was headlined: 'Visit of British Union Representatives in Munich,' with the sub-heading: 'BMW: Phoenix Bid still not financially backed.' The text read:

> Munich. On the occasion of a visit, a delegation of the British unions has turned over a petition, demanding to sincerely consider the bid of the consortium of the former Rover head John Towers. During this visit BMW made clear, that despite a demand of BMW the financial backing by the

consortium has not been provided yet. On the occasion of the visit of the unions, BMW has once again repeated this fact and pointed out, that this docs not constitute a basis for entering negotiations with the Phoenix consortium. The negotiations with Alchemy Partners will continue in a straightforward manner. [BMW Group Media Information release, 27 April 2000].

The statement had obviously been hastily put together, as it was awkwardly phrased and contained a few repetitions within just four paragraphs. Yet it triggered an instant response from the Western world's media. Without hesitation, as if they had been waiting for a 'final' signal, everyone pounced on this press release and began to announce that Phoenix had now failed. First, the Reuters international news agency ran a two-paragraph newsflash, announcing just the bare bones of this BMW announcement. This was followed by radio and TV news bulletins carrying the same words, and then the UK-based Press Association, the bible of so many media outlets, ran a full story on the breakdown of Phoenix efforts and the imminent success of Alchemy. It was, after all, the eve of the Alchemy deal deadline, and so it was in some ways quite reasonable to have expected a decision from BMW, which to many this seemed to have been.

I was at my desk as usual that day, running the *Evening Mail* newsroom, and Chinn was in constant touch by mobile telephone about each new development. We had time in later editions to add a paragraph of the BMW press release to the paper's page 2 picture story, which had described the union's Munich visit. However, we decided *not* to develop this into a new front page lead heralding Towers' failure, instead holding our nerve with the 'very much alive after a heated confrontation' story outlined in the previous chapter. Once the final deadlines had gone, I stood alongside business editor Jon Griffin watching the various reports continue to build up, and we became increasingly despondent. Remember, we had been working on the story for a month and a half now, and felt personally involved. But something did not feel quite right about this media reaction to me, as it seemed to be based on too much of a U-turn from what BMW had said overnight following the Towers-Samann meeting. I called the Press Association's industrial correspondent Alan Jones, an experienced and widely respected journalist I had met at various conferences over the years, and suggested to him that the story did not ring true. I asked him: 'Are you sure BMW actually mean what everyone thinks? We're in touch with Chinn out in Munich, and the feeling is that this was perhaps a panicked reaction to the union activists' visit.' Jones was interested to hear this opinion, but had spoken to more senior press officers at BMW himself, who had assured him the statement was sound.

On my way home, I called the *The Birmingham Post*'s business reporter James O'Brien, and told him of my misgivings over the knee-jerk reaction of the media to BMW's statement. But he too said he had crosschecked the development with a BMW contact, and was also working on the basis that Phoenix now had the odds overwhelmingly stacked against them. Then I called Chinn, who had flown back to Birmingham and was exhausted after an adrenalin-filled day, and we discussed the bleak scenario at some length. 'I'm getting too close to this, Carl,' I told him. 'I'm a journalist and should just be covering the story, not feeling as if I'm on the losing side. If Phoenix really has gone, I'm going to have to sort myself out and start reporting the inevitable.' Towers himself was maintaining his low profile, still not talking in public to anyone. But much later that night, I managed to speak to my Phoenix contact and asked him exactly what the feelings were like in the Towers' camp now. 'It's looking pretty slim,' he confided. 'Not at all optimistic.' That was one of the most depressing moments for me, hearing that even people close to Phoenix now thought the game might be up. Just before he hung up, my contact did add a vague line of hope, saying: 'Of course, there's always the chance that Moulton might just walk away at this point, he's done it before in other deals. But don't raise your readers' hopes on that.' By that stage, I was too down in the dumps to pay much attention anyway, and I climbed the stairs for a pretty sleepless night.

By the next morning, 28 April, every single national newspaper referred to the failure of Phoenix. As already mentioned, the London media deserves and gets its own critical chapter later on, but, just to set the scene, these were the sorts of headlines splashed across the newsstands that Friday. 'BMW Scuppers Rover Job Rescue', announced the *Daily Mail*. 'BMW Dashes Union Hopes of Rover Talks With Phoenix', *The Scotsman* lamented. 'BMW Will Sell Rover to Alchemy Within Days', decided the *Independent*. At least O'Brien of *The Birmingham Post* did not totally write-off Phoenix. Although his article did calculate that 'Alchemy Partners moved closer to taking control of Rover last night', he also prominently quoted consortium spokesman John Hemming as saying 'our bid is not dead', under the headline 'Last Throw of Dice for Towers Bid'.

Despite this faint glimmer of hope, even the *Evening Mail* must now, surely, have to consider a front page that would not have made pleasant reading down at Longbridge, despite people like Griffin, industrial correspondent Chris Morley, editor Ian Dowell and me hoping for Phoenix success. Griffin dolefully began the task, as we all braced ourselves for an announcement that the Alchemy purchase had gone through, something we all feared could come any moment. But then, at around 8.15am, while Griffin's story was still being formed on his screen, what even we were beginning to think was impossible happened. The Press Association, returning a favour, called me and said to watch out for some breaking news, because Alchemy had just released a statement revealing it had walked away from the Rover deal. What? Yes, Moulton was gone. His parting comments in a statement, headed 'Alchemy and BMW Terminate Rover Talks', read: 'Alchemy partners and BMW have ceased negotiations as they were unable to agree upon certain contractual matters, some of which arose yesterday. Alchemy Partners thanks BMW for its cordial negotiations and wishes Rover and its employees well.'

'Alchemy Deal Off', screamed the *Evening Mail*'s front page for the rest of the day, in the latest dramatic twist to the Rover saga, throwing the crisis on its head again. Did this turn of events mean that the 27 April BMW statement in Munich, responding to the energized presence of Chinn and the shop stewards, *was* just a panic-stricken press officer, overreacting during an Easter week when no-one more senior was around, simply releasing an abridged version of an earlier press release? Or had BMW wanted to distance itself from Phoenix, with an Alchemy deal really on the cards at that moment in time, only to find that this floundered at the last minute? And why had it floundered? BMW sources blamed Alchemy for failing to take responsibility for redundancy costs, while Moulton's team accused BMW of vastly increasing those costs at the last minute. Exactly what caused such a bewildering state of affairs will probably never be known. But what was certain was that Alchemy was no longer in the bidding.

And didn't the workers celebrate. Despite the Easter shutdown, the main Q Gate entrance at Longbridge was quickly alive with joyous crowds, where cheers and determined chants erupted. 'We ain't going away!' they shouted, as passing cars honked their horns, and Chinn and some of the other Munich veterans arrived to join in. Rob Torkington, aged 43, a Rover worker from West Heath, said: 'It is good news because it puts the Phoenix bid more in the running to succeed. I think that everyone at Rover is going to be delighted that the Alchemy bid has failed because it really meant the most job cuts.'

The unions and interested politicians were slightly more circumspect, knowing that this was not the day for them to celebrate but to work towards the next goal. The MSF union's Terry Pye said: 'The only game in town now is to get BMW to look at the Towers' bid. We have been working for this day but if BMW does not get its alternative buyer we could end up losing the lot.' Duncan Simpson, of the AEEU, said: 'So much for the claims of Alchemy that it was a done deal. We cannot say we are disappointed, because we have been opposing the Alchemy takeover, but we now need to know what are the implications of this and for that we need urgent discussions with BMW.' And the Labour MP for Northfield, Richard Burden, said: 'There is now no excuse for BMW not to divulge to Phoenix the information they need and start negotiations with John Towers in earnest.'

The caution and pressure was well placed, because BMW's reaction to Alchemy's pull-out was uncompromising and blunt – giving Phoenix a chance, but at the same time threatening closure if the deal did not work quickly. 'BMW and Alchemy have terminated their negotiations,' read the German carmaker's statement. 'No agreement was reached on the sale of Rover Car operations … BMW Group will now pursue alternative routes to bring to an end its involvement in Rover Car operations. Those routes include the sale of Rover Car operations or its closure. A decision on which of those alternatives will be implemented will be taken during the course of next month.' It was first thought that this meant Towers had 30 days more time to convince BMW that his bid was feasible. But 'during the course of next month' actually meant convincing the Germans well before the next supervisory board meeting in Munich on 16 May, and even that was only 18 days away. And if Phoenix failed, Longbridge would be closed.

That prospect was still such an alarming one for so many thousands. Longbridge shop steward Josephine Wardell certainly had more than most to lose from any closure. She had been an engine assembly worker at the plant for six years, her husband, Des, had been there for 37 years – and his father had worked at the plant before him. The couple's two sons, Darren, aged 28, and David, 26, both worked at the Land Rover factory in Solihull, along with their daughter's fiancé. Mrs Wardell, of West Heath, said:

> The motor industry is a way of life in this area. The thought of Rover cars not being built in Birmingham is too much to contemplate. The whole area relies on Longbridge. It's not me and my husband I worry about the most, but the younger generation. They have got mortgages to pay off and families to look after. I have got two grandchildren and it also their futures that we are fighting for. Whole families rely on Rover and this area would be left devastated … Round here you just can't walk into another job. I am optimistic about the future – nothing is certain yet, but John Towers has a proven pedigree in the car manufacturing business. [*Evening Mail*, 28 April 2000].

But was Towers up to it? 'I do not believe he has got the legs to do it,' sighed Moulton, his rival, almost as a parting shot. 'To do the deal would be a spectacular achievement.' And so the pressure on Towers mounted.

CHAPTER EIGHT

Rover's Fate In Towers' Hands

By Stephen Dyson

The dramatic turn of events on Friday 28 April 2000 triggered the beginning of the most stressful period of the Rover crisis for John Towers and his consortium. Up until now, Phoenix had only been seen on the horizon as the would-be white knight – keen, willing and very popular because of its desire to maintain volume production and jobs. Yet, in most experts' minds, Towers was not in with much of a chance. Now, with Alchemy walking away, things were different. Thousands of Longbridge workers, all their families and friends, hundreds of thousands of other Midlanders and, indeed, the whole country, waited with baited breath to see whether Phoenix really had the substance to save Rover. The eyes of the world, and consequently the critical analyses of the media, were firmly on Towers. Many national newspapers had that latest event in the Rover saga on their front pages the next day, 29 April, although almost all of them were still very negative about the chances of Phoenix. Conversely, the *Evening Mail's* page one story the same day on the new battle for Rover remained expectant, after my conversation with my Phoenix contact late on the Friday night.

Not that anyone close to Phoenix now thought it was going to be easy, as I found out when I asked how the Towers' camp had reacted to the latest news. 'His (Towers') main concern is that thousands of Rover workers' hopes are not raised too high, because he knows his bid is still racing against time,' was the first thing my source told me, although he went on to explain how resolute the Phoenix consortium was despite the huge trials it now faced. He insisted that 'no horses will be spared in his (Towers') dash to the finish', but added that there was some uneasiness about the time factor, as Phoenix needed to prove its bid was serious or it could be dismissed within a week. The bankers, who had agreed in principle to back Phoenix, had read all the reports about why BMW felt it needed to ditch Rover, and were also about to read the negative statements about why Alchemy had rejected the deal. Towers now needed to persuade these bankers that he could make Longbridge viable, a huge presentation challenge in itself. Now Alchemy had gone, BMW were about to allow Towers to see the full books for the first time, enabling him to start convincing people with real numbers that the business would have a supportable cash flow. But this persuasion had to come quickly. My Phoenix source added: 'Businesses like BMW, and even the government, have entire backrooms of assistants doing the work. Almost everything that happens for Phoenix is done through Towers.' It was a huge task, but it was thought that if anyone could do it, Towers could, the man who was, after all, a former Rover chief executive with immense experience and knowledge of the business.

The *Evening Mail's* resulting page one story on 29 April, the day after Alchemy's departure, appeared under the headline 'Towers: Three Great Challenges'.

> Phoenix boss John Towers was today determined to pull off his Rover coup – but faces three great challenges along the way. BMW has given him one week to seriously impress them with his business and finance plans before a fuller board discussion on May 16; his bankers have to be persuaded that volume car production at Longbridge is viable, despite huge negative vibes created by a chaotic sell-off; and his team must be ready to fight off what some analysts have predicted may be a sudden return to the negotiating table by Jon Moulton, the boss of venture capitalists Alchemy.

One unnamed BMW executive underlined the urgency of the task in hand on 29 April, telling *The Birmingham Post* that Towers had been formally invited to come back to the table to talk, but that 'he has also been told we need a clear indication of where his financial backing is coming from, what the business plan is and how it could be sustained'. The executive said the next few days were critical, because 'if he does not come up with the money next week, the end could be quicker than you think.'

And while he was insisting to BMW that Phoenix had the money, at the same time as proving to bankers that Rover was actually worth it, Towers also had to keep glancing over his shoulder in case Alchemy tried to return. 'I think Jon Moulton will be back,' motor industry analyst Paul Teuten, of Ernst and Young, told the *Evening Mail's* Jon Griffin. 'This is a negotiating tactic. It is quite common for venture capitalists, at the end of a period of exclusivity, to try to call the other side's bluff to get better terms.' Indeed, Moulton never did close the door for good, even at this early stage telling the world 'there is very little prospect of the deal being revived'. Note the carefully chosen words 'very little prospect' rather than something more definite, like 'no prospect'. Moulton was waiting in the wings.

Over that Bank Holiday weekend, as another torrent of scepticism appeared in London newspapers, a BMW courier delivered a huge proposed sale and purchase agreement to Phoenix, a document that was described to me as 'several inches thick'. This had to be combed on a line-by-line basis by Towers and his team in preparation for their first official negotiations with BMW, due on

Tuesday 2 May. Not a word could be missed during a weekend of frenzied preparation activity. Phoenix bankers, who would be seeing the full BMW books for the first time, had to be more than happy with every pound Towers planned to spend. And BMW executives would be watching their confidence levels like hawks.

I had been tipped off that the meeting between Phoenix and BMW was due to take place at 11am on the Tuesday, at the London offices of BMW lawyers Norton Rose. As already explained, Towers had at this stage remained silent in public, releasing no statements and appearing before no press conferences, so I rushed down to London to await his arrival and to record what was hoped to be his first formal words to the world's press. With me was *Evening Mail* photographer Alan Williams, himself hoping to grab the first picture of Towers in action for Phoenix. As we taxied across from Euston station to the Norton Rose offices, I called my Phoenix contact to make sure the meeting was still going ahead and to check a question that was persistently being asked in the press: did Phoenix need Government cash? 'Yes, I understand the meeting will start by 11am,' my source said. 'No cash whatsoever from the Government has been requested.' We got to the entrance of Norton Rose at 9am, not wanting to miss any early arrival, but were obviously not the only journalists to have been told of the whereabouts of the meeting. The Press Association was already there, and within the hour ITN, *The Times* and various freelance photographers joined us. Not a huge press pack, but half a dozen or so hungry hacks, stomping feet in the cold morning air, eyes darting this way and that lest we miss the moment.

John Towers and various Phoenix partners and advisers sweep into Camomile Street in London for the BMW meeting on 2 May. Brian Parker is on the far left. *Picture by Alan Williams*

And then they arrived, swinging around the corner of Camomile Street like a scene out of High Noon – updated for the 21st Century with pinstripe suits and briefcases. There in front, with a purposeful stride, was Towers, flanked in quickstep by consortium members Nick Stephenson, John Edwards and financial adviser Brian Parker, followed by various assistants. Being local journalists, Williams and I spotted Towers immediately, and a gripping picture of Towers in the flesh, about to do business with BMW, was captured for that night's *Evening Mail.* He appeared professional, smartly dressed, with intent eyes and determined jaw – a sight for Longbridge workers' sore eyes. Towers only stopped to speak for 20 seconds, and said: 'We have had quite a lot of information thanks to BMW and have been busy with this all weekend. We are

The world was watching as John Towers arrived for talks with BMW on 2 May.
Picture by Alan Williams

Stephen Dyson talking to Alchemy's Jon Moulton by mobile phone outside his offices near Covent Garden on 2 May. *Picture by Alan Williams*

quite enthusiastic, although there are a number of points to sort out. We are looking forward to a very productive meeting.' It was enough. He had now spoken in public; an act that many observers considered was a significant step forward. If Towers was out in the open, he must have felt Rover was finally within his grasp. Five hours later, as he left, Towers was again pictured and this time his words were broadcast on every national TV and radio news bulletin on that night of 2 May: 'We've been through a heck of a lot of very detailed stuff and it's been extremely positive. What we've done is to identify the few remaining items that our teams are going to have to work on for the rest of this week, and it's all going in the right direction.'

While Towers was in the meeting, I heard that Moulton had appeared in various national newspapers, hinting that Alchemy was trying to reopen negotiations with BMW. I caught a black cab to his offices in Covent Garden and badgered various secretaries into letting me speak to him. Although he declined to come downstairs to see me on this occasion, he did confirm to me on my mobile phone that: 'We have been in gentle contact over the weekend. We have left a door open.' He also made what I considered to be a strong hint that things might change after the local elections on 8 May, the mention of which suggested that politics were perhaps temporarily holding Alchemy back. As it turned out, however, the venture capitalists did not return to the Rover equation after the elections. Indeed, Rover boss Professor Werner Samann insisted that Alchemy could not, declaring that day that 'Phoenix is the only possibility to continue Rover Car Operations in the desired sense...', although he repeated the warning '...otherwise a closure is unavoidable'.

Just before midnight on 2 May, my Phoenix source phoned me to outline just how positive the BMW-Phoenix talks had been. 'I understand they went very well,' he said. 'BMW executives acted as if they clearly wanted to create a deal.' Keen for something a bit stronger for the next day's paper, I asked: 'Exactly how well did the talks go? How sure is Towers of success? What percentage rating would he now give his chances?' The source replied: 'I reckon Towers is now 80% sure of securing the deal.' As soon as *Evening Mail* editor Ian Dowell heard this figure, he decided to run it on the front page all day on 3 May, to give Longbridge workers and all his Midland readers a real sense of hope – something they were still not getting from the London media. The headline read: '80% – That's How Phoenix Rates Its Chances of Pulling Off Rover Coup'. It was the sort of stance that could have resulted in egg on the paper's face, because no-one else in the world was giving Phoenix such a chance. Thinking back to that day now, Dowell certainly knew when to back a winner.

My Phoenix source also revealed that Towers had been told that his purchase plan must be watertight by Friday 12 May, just over a week away, to give BMW time to consider it privately before various board meetings after that weekend. 'There's just ten days to complete everything,' he said. 'There will never have been a financial deal like it completed in this space of time. The timing is still awfully tight, but it almost certainly will be done. The motivation created by the time pressures is very powerful.' He revealed that the Phoenix team had now broken formation and was shooting off in different directions, concentrating on their individual disciplines to make the deal work. The source went on to dismiss national newspaper reports that banks had refused Phoenix the £200 million finance it needed. He said: 'I understand the bankers have now seen BMW's books and that BMW has seen details of the bankers, and there is no problem. It's just the small print – and a lot of it.'

Earlier that day, *The Birmingham Post* had published a full interview with BMW's Professor Samann by business reporter Jim O'Brien, and the vibes in the German executive's quotes were more than encouraging.

> I am confident the Towers consortium is able to acquire the money, maybe through the banks or involving additional partners who are prepared to put in some money ... I am confident and everyone supports the Phoenix consortium. In my opinion Mr Towers and his colleagues will be able to run the Rover business successfully ...BMW promised to allocate him the Rover 75 saloon and maybe the Rover 75 estate as well, taking then from Oxford to Longbridge ...Our proposal is a total package including the BMW money, the Rover 75 and the estate version.
> [Wednesday 3 May 2000].

Samann's quotes were brave, and were obviously designed to create a more positive image for Towers' chances. Never before had a BMW executive spoken so positively about Phoenix, and it was also the first time the Germans had confirmed they would allow the successful Rover 75 model to be switched to Longbridge, along with the as yet unfinished estate version. The upbeat news continued later that day, when it was revealed that BMW had whisked Towers to Longbridge for a surprise factory visit – enabling the former Rover boss to see exactly what he was about to buy. It was the first time Towers had been at the plant since he had left the company four years previously, and he was taken on a tour of the car assembly and paint shop areas. He had requested the visit to ensure that machinery and production methods were still up to scratch and to examine the potential for future development. During his tour of Longbridge, Towers met several workers, who later told me how his physical presence had lifted the morale on the shop floor.

'He was delighted,' one said. 'He kept on saying that the site was in an excellent state and he was impressed with the quality of production.' Before Towers arrived, workers had been briefed by managers not to make a fuss over the Phoenix boss and to carry on working as normal. It remained quiet for the first few minutes, but then, reportedly, 'there were smiles and suddenly one chap broke off from what he was doing and walked over to shake his hand.' Other workers started doing the same, and then 'a ripple of applause started, which seemed to follow Towers around the plant.' This reaction was described as spontaneous, making it obvious that the whole of the Birmingham car plant was behind the Phoenix bid. One worker added: 'It was marvellous to see the man at the centre of things in such a buoyant mood.' Dowell and I constructed a front page story around these quotes for the next day, 4 May, intending to boost the confidence of Longbridge workers, the Phoenix consortium and any bankers or BMW executives who wondered just how Towers had been received. Dowell went away into his office to design the entire front page around the story, and came out with a strong cut out image of Towers pictured against the background of a Longbridge production line with the huge headline: 'All Brum is With YOU Mr Towers'. It was another gamble by the *Evening Mail*, but Dowell felt that if the word from the Phoenix camp was that it was 80% certain of a deal then it was something worth shouting about. Speaking after the crisis, Towers told me that the workers' welcome had indeed been warm and that this response had further boosted his confidence. 'It felt great to be back,' he said.

On 5 May there was more news that must have further gladdened the hearts of Towers and his consortium: Rover's sales had more than doubled during April, figures that have already been recorded earlier in this book. The other front page news of that day was about Labour's heaviest poll defeat since entering government, with Conservatives taking around 600 council seats across the country. In Birmingham, the electoral meltdown saw Labour's council majority fall from 35 to 15 seats – with many outgoing veterans like former city council leader Sir Richard Knowles blaming the 'Longbridge factor'.

Then BMW again lifted hopes for Rover on Saturday 6 May by confirming it had seen the financial details behind the Phoenix rescue bid. Finance had until then reportedly been the main sticking point in negotiations, at least in the eyes of the London media, who still doubted whether it was in place. *Evening Mail* reporter Mark Cowan, working that Saturday, chased BMW all morning, repeatedly demanding an answer to the question of whether they had seen the money or not. Eventually, the qualms were dismissed. Spokesman Juerg Dinner said: 'We can confirm that we have got details of the financial package from the Towers group.' At work as duty editor that day, I immediately ran the story on the front page, under the headline: 'BMW: We've Seen The Money', the first paragraph reading: 'BMW today boosted hopes for Rover by confirming it had seen the colour of the money behind the Phoenix rescue bid.' Dinner pointed out that BMW would now have to check out all the information provided and would continue talks with Phoenix all weekend and throughout the next week. He added: 'Obviously, the more material that we get the better picture we can get. However, we do not currently see any reason to get back in contact with Alchemy.' This last comment was important, again contrary to what some London newspapers were still predicting.

The Birmingham-based *Sunday Mercury*, the sister paper of the *Evening Mail*, was also getting strong, positive vibes on that Saturday afternoon, and on Sunday 7 May ran what turned out to be the most accurate headline of the day. 'Towers Deal Could Be Signed Within a Week' sang out its front page, with the sub-heading 'Optimism all round as rescue plan comes together', above a decisive article by reporter Simon Mowbray.

Despite these encouragements, I personally found that weekend quite nerve-wracking. My Phoenix source was no longer able to shed any fresh light on the state of negotiations, with Towers and every member of his consortium seemingly locked away in meetings from dawn until the early hours of every day. I *thought* things must be going well, but hadn't that been the case between Alchemy and BMW less than two weeks previously, before that process was suddenly shelved? Carl Chinn called regularly to ask: 'Have you heard anything, Steve?' (Even he, as a well-connected Phoenix supporter, was now out of the information loop during this delicate stage.) 'Not a sausage, Carl,' I replied on the Sunday evening, and so we nervously discussed what the next news would be, and when it would arrive. Many other people – friends, family, colleagues and even Longbridge workers like Carl Lanchester – called that weekend to ask how I thought things were going. Dowell, my editor, was also keen to know of any progress, having positioned the paper so definitely behind what Towers was trying to do. But I had nothing new to report.

This void of information went on throughout Monday 8 May, with both BMW and Phoenix sources unaware of any new developments. All I had been told by my Phoenix contact was that if anything major did now happen, for better or for worse, he was sure that Towers himself would contact me to let me know. Towers and his consortium had seen how Dowell's *Evening Mail* had at some points stood alone in its accurate reporting of the Phoenix bid's progress, and they knew that Longbridge workers and their families were now turning to the paper every night to find out what was really happening. 'Keep your mobile phone switched on and next to you,' my source warned. 'Towers has your number and will call when the time is right, whatever happens, because he feels he owes it to the paper and its readers to keep them in touch with any success or failure straight away.' The wait seemed endless. I hoped it would be worth it.

A Visit to Number 10

In a rapid and amazing turnaround, our downheartedness upon our return from Munich had been swept away by our exhilaration at the news of the Alchemy pullout, *writes Carl Chinn*. On that joyous Friday evening of 28 April, many of us had met in the Rover Club to be interviewed by radio and television crews and our mood had been upbeat and confident. Later that night, I flew back to Dublin, but like everyone else I was bitterly upset and angered by the negative stance that was taken by the London press over the weekend. It seemed that they were intent upon burying Longbridge beneath a pyre of doom. Each time it looked as if there was still life, then they caught hold of something else grimly fateful to chuck on the heap in an attempt to put away all hope of a future for the factory.

Throughout that holiday weekend I spoke regularly with Carl, Ian, John Hemming and Stephen Dyson about our proposed trip to lobby Parliament and Number 10. We knew that everyone had to keep up the publicity pressure because of fears that BMW might close Longbridge. Interestingly, we learned later from a source close to the German company that on the day after our visit to Munich there had been a meeting of the BMW hardliners. They had come to the conclusion that they had two options: to plan for closure behind a smokescreen of talks with Phoenix; or to enter into meaningful negotiations with the consortium led by John Towers. We were made aware that it was decided to speak constructively with Phoenix because the hardliners were worried about the continuance of the public campaign for Longbridge. They had taken seriously our insistence that we would not go away and that we would do everything possible within the law to fight to keep the factory open as a volume car producer.

Our firm sense of purpose was affected also by rumours both in the press and amongst informed observers that some government aides and senior figures in the government were against the Phoenix bid. It was said that these people feared that if the John Towers bid were successful, he would be unable to make Rover profitable and the company would collapse before the next general election. According to this scenario, Longbridge would close and tens of thousands of men and women would be thrown on to the dole. In these circumstances, it was feared that Labour would lose its chances of victory in Birmingham and the West Midlands. Moreover, it was murmured that the anti-Phoenix group believed that our city and region needed to move away from a reliance on car manufacturing. Consequently, a running down of Longbridge might be beneficial in the long term in that it might stimulate a change in our economic base. It was said that this aim would best be served by reviving the Alchemy bid. If Alchemy could be persuaded to come back in and did win, then it could be proclaimed that proper jobs had been saved and that the Task Force would lead a shift into new sources of employment.

Such political and economic considerations were perturbing, and it was with these worries in their minds that a large number of workers joined the May Day Parade in London on the Holiday Monday. They were given pride of place at the head of the trades council-led march. Pete Logan, Noel Moloney, Carl Lanchester and Ian Robinson led the chants of 'We ain't going away!'; whilst Paul Parsons and Tom O'Hanlon proudly carried the Longbridge banner. A TGWU shop steward on the Works Committee, Tom was yet another representative of the shop floor who did his duty to his fellows. Because of the trouble caused by anti-capitalist rioters, the trade union march was unable to proceed into Trafalgar Square but speeches were given. Indeed, Ian rang me on his mobile to let me hear Adrian Ross address the crowd and to allow me to pass on my support to the workers and my apologies that I could not be with them. Once again, the positive and resolute actions of the Longbridge men and women captured the interest of the media – as did their next move. This was thought up on the coach home from London when Carl and Ian met a chap called Bob. They were sitting at the back planning:

Rover workers led by convenor Adrian Ross about to leave by coach for a May Day rally in London. Behind the little girl is Works Committee member Bob Turner. The little boy is Cameron Robinson, Ian's son.
Picture by John Reavenall

as we always did. And we was banging it about, about going to London and Bob says, 'You need an angle' . . . and I mentioned something about a banner, something to do with Blair's baby. And he says, 'That's what you need.' He says, 'Take a young child with you. A baby.' I said, 'Well where are we going to get a baby from?' And no sooner we said that, Andy Cartwright was sitting next to us and said, 'I got one.' And there it was. Next thing you know we'd got Gemma and little Pearce knocking on the door of Number 10. [Tape recording by Carl Lanchester 17 July 2000].

Mersade Cartwright, aged six, pictured with a certificate she received in a colouring competition at a Rover Future event weeks before the crisis. With her is dad Andrew, a Rover worker, little sister Tiaadelia, mom Gemma and brother Pearce, who later joined a workers' delegation to Downing Street to see Tony Blair. *Picture by Alan Williams*

In an inspired decision, Andy's wife, Gemma, was asked if she would join us on our trip to London. She agreed readily. Gemma is an outstanding young woman. She has a keen mind, a fast learning curve and an ability to put forward her case strongly yet without any hint of aggression. She is another person whose important contribution to the battle of Longbridge should not be forgotten. Nor should that of her chap, Andy, who had worked at Longbridge for eleven years and was one of the thousands of workers who could have sat back and let events overtake them. That they did not is a tribute to their collective sense of reponsibility to ensure that children such as Pearce should have a future.

By the time that I returned from Ireland on the Tuesday evening, all the arrangements had been made for our trip to London the next day. Ian had done sterling work in ringing the Metropolitan Police, finding out the details as to how we could lobby Number 10, and liaising with Adrian Ross. It had been agreed already that all those who had flown to Munich should go to London – Carl, Ian, Adrian, Paul, Noel, Dick and myself; whilst we ought to be accompanied by the members of the Works Committee. Once again, this was the correct thing to do. Individually and jointly, these men made their contribution to victory. They ensured a connection with senior trade union officials; they provided a legitimacy to the workers' campaign because they were a long-established and official body; and they gave a unity to that campaign by bringing in workers from across Longbridge.

The Works Committee consisted of seven men: Adrian Ross, the convenor; Joe Clarke, who has been mentioned several times in this book; Bob Turner, another representative of the TGWU, who arranged many important things without seeking publicity for himself and who had a commonsense approach to matters; Aelwyn 'Ollie' Thomas, of the AEEU, whose contribution to the life of Longbridge was longstanding and deep and who was prepared to persevere until victory was gained; Tom O'Hanlon, of the TGWU, who was quick to add his weight to the public campaign and was keen to show his unshakeable faith in Longbridge; Martin Glaze, of the AEEU, who was measured in both his approach and thoughts and was full of sensible insights; and Dave Dutton, of the MSF, who quietly but surely ensured that the voice of MSF members was heard and who was perceptive with his comments. Finally, our numbers were made up by Pete Logan, who was fervent in his desire to keep people in jobs and was a stalwart defender of Longbridge; and Tony O'Keefe, who impressed me with his powers of observation and strength of will.

On the train down on Wednesday 3 May, we were accompanied and filmed by a news crew from Channel 5, and when we arrived in London we were met by a senior official of the MSF. Because Richard Burden had arranged for us to meet the West Midlands Group of Labour MPs, we headed for the Houses of Parliament where Ray 'John Bull' Egan awaited us. It was marvellous how he gave his all for the campaign and the media was fascinated by him, as described in Chapter Ten. Although we went into the Palace of Westminster, we did not get a chance to talk with the MPs as it was fast approaching the time we needed to be at Number 10 and so we headed off. When we reached the bottom of Downing Street, our group was split up. Only a few us were to be allowed inside. Obviously, there had to be a representative from each of the unions, so that meant that Bob Turner, Olly Thomas and Dave Dutton would go in. The delegation had to be headed by Adrian as works convenor and it also included Gemma, Pearce and Tony. I was the last member. Although I was happy to have stayed outside, the other shop stewards insisted that I should be in the lobbying party.

To cries of 'Rover! Will not die!' and 'We ain't going away!' we were led by Richard Burden to Number 10 where more members of the press met us. Then we went inside. We had been told that we would not be meeting the Prime Minister, Tony Blair, but as we approached the staircase to go upstairs, he came out of side room. He seemed a little surprised to see so many people in the hall and was informed by an aide that we were 'the Rover workers'. We introduced ourselves. I came last and after giving my name I added that I did not work at Longbridge. Tony Blair replied that he knew who I was as he had seen me on the television. I wondered about that as I could not imagine that the prime minister of the United Kingdom sat and watched TV or if he did that he would have noticed me. I felt that it was likely that my involvement in the public campaign had been brought to the Prime Minister's notice by his aides.

Adrian rose magnificently to the occasion and read out our statement in full:

> We, the representatives of the Longbridge workforce and of the people of Birmingham and the West Midlands wish to make it clear that:
>> The government should recognise that the Phoenix bid is the only acceptable option for the future of Longbridge because it will maintain the factory as a volume car producer and will minimise job losses.
>> The government should be actively backing the Phoenix bid for jobs and security at Longbridge.
>> The government should give Phoenix the same financial backing that it has undertaken to give BMW.
>> The workforce of Longbridge and the People of Birmingham and the West Midlands will never accept the closure of Longbridge as an option and within the law will fight wholeheartedly to maintain volume car production at Longbridge.
>> Finally, we urge the government to enter into discussions with Trades Unions, the CBI, and other interested parties to develop a coherent strategy for strengthening British Manufacturing.

As soon as Adrian finished, Gemma and the shop stewards drove home to Tony Blair that we would never accept the closure of Longbridge and that we wanted the government to come out firmly in favour of Phoenix. The Prime Minister listened to us politely and thoughtfully. He said he wanted the best for the workers and that the government would do what it could, but that the whole matter really was down to business decisions. Then he was ushered away and we were shown to a room upstairs. We were accompanied by Richard Burden, Gisela Stuart, Labour MP for Birmingham Edgbaston, Dennis Turner, Labour MP for Wolverhampton South East and Ken Purchase, the Labour MP for Wolverhampton North East. The purpose of our visit was to meet John Cruddas, a government adviser on industry. We were introduced also to Geoffrey Norris, another adviser to the government on industrial matters. He took no part in the conversations and sat on a window sill – although it was apparent that he was listening carefully to all that was discussed.

John Cruddas sat down amongst us and was attentive to our comments. At one stage he looked at me and questioned me about what we planned next. I replied that we did not know as yet. We would report back to the other shop stewards and then collectively we would decide on a course of action. But one thing could be guaranteed, there would be more action. Ollie Thomas emphasised this by affirming that 'we ain't going away'. Dennis Turner then declared that our aims and objectives had the full support of the West Midlands group of Labour MPs. I had spoken to Dennis on the march on 1 April, when he had made plain to me his personal and political support for keeping Longbridge open. Since then, Dennis had maintained a high profile in fighting for jobs in the West Midlands and had shown himself to be an MP in tune both with his principles and his people. So had fellow Midland Labour MPs Ken Purchase, Peter Snape, Gisela Stuart, Estelle Morris and Robin Corbett.

It was important for us to have such powerful backing. All of us had taken note of the rumours about the apparent anti-Phoenix bias in certain personalities associated with the government, but it must be made clear that the local Labour MPs were unswerving in their commitment to Longbridge and the workers. Similarly, Liberal Democrat MEP for the West Midlands, Liz Lynne, put pressure on BMW to release information to Phoenix and assured us that, if it were to be needed, she had ascertained that the giving of state finance would be cleared with the European Competitions Commissioner, Mario Monti. However, no Conservative MP made an approach to us to offer backing and no Tory MP outside the West Midlands convinced us that they believed in the future of the factory as a volume car producer. Indeed, we were assured by sources that the majority of senior Tories also favoured Alchemy.

Despite the fact that she had never been involved in something such as this before, Gemma Cartwright was assured and purposeful during our visit. She told the Prime Minister that her son was one amongst thousands who would lose out in life if Longbridge were to close, and she emphasised that 'we were representing all the young families at Rover and all the people in the Midlands who are affected by the crisis'. As Gemma pointed out, Mr Blair's 'children may have a future but what is going to happen to children like Pearce and the other children of the workers'. For her the fear was that 'if Longbridge closes it would be devastating for the Rover workers and Birmingham would become a ghost town. We would be forced to bring up Pearce on social security. We are in the middle of selling our house and this couldn't have come at a worse time.' On her return home, Gemma explained to the *The Birmingham Post* that 'we didn't feel we got what we demanded and we feel let down by Tony Blair's reaction'. Let down or not, our visit to London had captured the gaze of the press and kept Longbridge in the limelight. Above all, it had given us the opportunity to make plain our feelings to the leader of the nation.

Rover shopfloor union leaders show the world it is 'business as usual' while the Towers bid progresses. Pictured from the left are: Carl Lanchester, Brian Crockett, Richard Martin and Adrian Ross. *Picture by John Reavenall*

CHAPTER NINE

The London Bias That Nearly Killed Rover

By Stephen Dyson

The Rover crisis had all the makings of a big story for the national press. There was perceived German treachery; potentially tens of thousands of jobs losses; vociferous union leaders calling for action; intransigent politicians refusing to get involved; a plan to produce sleek sports cars; an underdog who promised to save the British motor industry; so much intrigue, secret meetings and public awareness; and all against the colourful and historic background of Longbridge, evoking memories of Red Robbo, strikes, rallies in the park and classic motor cars like the Mini.

Despite these rich ingredients for a good read, so much of the London media's coverage was riddled with regional prejudice, anti-industrial snobbery, factual inaccuracies and, on occasions, unbelievably insulting stances. Such treatment did nothing to help Rover, did so much to lower the morale of thousands in the Midlands – and probably went some way towards hindering the progress of the Phoenix bid. This chapter will consider the vast array of foregone conclusions that Towers, his backers and Rover workers were faced with from so many different newspapers. First and foremost, however, *The Sun* must get the focus it deserves.

On the day that Alchemy pulled out of negotiations with BMW for the purchase of Rover cars, there was obviously some relief among workers, who now hoped that Phoenix would at last be given a chance – by the media as well as by BMW. No one expected the reaction of the nation's most popular paper, whose journalist Paul Gilfeather instead really stuck the knife in under the headline 'R.I.P. Rover'. (On this occasion, because they were so deliberately placed, I have reproduced *The Sun*'s capitals, italics and bold typescript as they appeared in that article.)

FIFTY thousand jobs were doomed last night as all hope of rescuing car firm Rover vanished. In a day of industrial disaster for Britain, the Alchemy group **SCRAPPED** its deal to take over the company from BMW … workers **CHEERED** as the news broke – because they believed the rival Phoenix bid for the firm would resurface, saving more jobs than the Alchemy plan. *But last night the cheers had*

*turned to tears as the bleak reality sank in at thousands of Midlands homes –
there will be* **NO** *Rover rescue and many families are set to face life on the dole.*
[29 April 2000].

It was difficult to work out *The Sun*'s reasoning behind such a damning
assumption. On reading this front page, despairingly, I immediately assumed that
someone within Phoenix had told the paper that there was no realistic chance of
success. Or that BMW executives had leaked that they were never going to
consider Towers' bid. Faced with such an unnerving headline, I at least
anticipated that the unions, the car dealers, the workers or *somebody actually
named* had drawn this gloomy picture. But upon studying every word in detail, I
discovered that there was no such justification at all for such a condemnation.
The entire article appeared to have been based on an 'unnamed Government
source', who had allegedly told *The Sun* that it 'had been accepted at Downing
Street that Rover would be shut'. This source was quoted as saying: 'The picture
of cheering workers at Longbridge is one of the saddest sights of my life ... It
looks certain that Rover will close.'

That was not enough for the tabloid that bills itself as 'The People's
Paper'. In a second article on page 4, on the same day, it quoted another
'Whitehall insider' as saying: '...although the Germans are likely to entertain
Phoenix, ultimately they won't do a deal.' Then came 'a source close to BMW's
failed negotiations with Alchemy', who remarked: 'The writing is almost certainly
on the wall for Rover now. The workers are waiting for the cavalry to come over
the hill – but Phoenix are more like a couple of cart-horses.' All this
unsubstantiated misery was printed under the big banner headline, across pages
4 and 5, 'The Tragedy of Longbridge'. Worst still, some of the characters already
mentioned in this book who did so much to keep the spirit of Phoenix aloft were
pictured on the same page 5. Carl Chinn, Longbridge union convenor Adrian
Ross, shop steward Carl Lanchester and the now almost legendary John Bull
character, alias Ray Egan, were among those shown cheering, elated, almost
dancing together – with *The Sun*'s caption, 'Rejoicing in vain', mocking them from
underneath. There were so many Longbridge workers I spoke to both during and
after the crisis, and *all* of them mentioned *The Sun*'s infamous edition of 29 April,
with its hideous 'R.I.P.' front page, and each one of them did so with distaste. *The
Sun* probably lost many readers thanks to its offensive approach on that day.

But that was not the first time *The Sun* had written Phoenix off. On 25
April, the paper had published a grainy picture of a Rover 25 car with an MG
badge on its grille – under the headline 'Secret Snap That Dooms 5,000 Jobs',
with the subheading 'BMW sale to Alchemy is a cert'. Reporter John Scott's
confident article was very conclusive:

A picture of a newly-produced MG 25 today proves that up to 5,000 jobs
are doomed at Rover's Longbridge plant. The car – which looks just like

a Rover 25 with MG badges – was built there in secret last week. And it is a clear sign that Alchemy's bid for Rover is a done deal… the secret prototype shows (BMW has) already decided on Alchemy, which plans to produce MG motors under the MG Car Company name… *The Sun*'s discovery of the prototype MG is the final nail in the coffin for Phoenix. [25 April 2000].

No one was actually quoted as saying that this was the end for Phoenix, but *The Sun* itself decided that that was what the picture meant. The newspaper went on to predict the failure of Phoenix at least twice more, firstly with the introduction to a story headlined 'Phoenix Bid Not Enough To Save Rover':

The Phoenix plan for Rover looks likely to turn to ashes because ministers won't plough taxpayers' cash into the deal, Government insiders revealed last night …ministers fear the plan relies on state handouts – in which case Birmingham's sprawling Longbridge plant is doomed. A senior government official said: 'It doesn't take a rocket scientist to work out the sums.' [1 May 2000].

There was no mention of the fact that Phoenix had been reported as *not* wanting any Government cash. And five days before Towers' deal was clinched, *The Sun* ran another story headlined 'Where's the Cash?', with the sub-heading: 'Phoenix bid totters as BMW demand details':

Hopes of the Phoenix consortium saving Rover faded last night after BMW bosses demanded: 'Show us the colour of your money.' The plan to rescue 9,500 jobs at Longbridge looked in doubt when BMW chief Werner Samann said Phoenix had consistently failed to reveal how it would bankroll a takeover. [4 May 2000].

This article was accompanied by an even more extreme judgment in *The Sun*'s editorial comment of the same day:

The Phoenix bid for Rover is never going to rise from the ashes. The bid is a no hoper. *The Sun* has said that from Day One. So why is Trade Secretary Stephen Byers even giving it the time of day? He is allowing Longbridge workers to be cruelly deceived.

This insistent, self-satisfied opinion enraged many people, not least countless Longbridge workers themselves who wondered why their future was given no chance by the paper they loved to read. Other Midlanders were also enraged, including *Evening Mail* editor Ian Dowell. His paper had welcomed debate throughout the Rover crisis, giving equal treatment to all opinions whilst attempting to allow Phoenix, which appeared to have a feasible volume production solution for Longbridge, a fair crack of the whip. Dowell was appalled at *The Sun*'s relentless barrage of criticism against Phoenix – especially following Alchemy's exit, when in the eyes of thousands of workers the Towers' consortium offered the only hope of retaining most jobs. In the newspaper industry, it is quite unusual for publications to openly criticise each other – and it is particularly rare for a regional evening paper to go for the throat of a national redtop tabloid. But Dowell is not an everyday newspaper editor and, after the last straw of the above 4 May comment in *The Sun*, he sprang into action, deciding to run the following angry comment piece under the headline '*The Sun* Never Shines on Rover':

> Twice now *The Sun* newspaper has demanded the death sentence on Longbridge. With a heartlessness that can only be construed as contempt for the working man, *The Sun* front page on Saturday, after the collapse of the Jon Moulton deal, was simply 'R.I.P. Rover'. In an editorial, it slated Trade Secretary Stephen Byers for backing John Towers' attempt to rescue the plant and said venture capitalists Alchemy had been Rover's only hope... The London-based *Sun*...claims Towers is unable to raise the cash for a successful takeover, but the *Evening Mail*, much closer to the action than our London rivals, knows that the former Rover chief executive has his finance in place and simply needs his team to complete a thorough examination of BMW's books. Doesn't *The Sun* care about the increasingly buoyant campaign for survival? Doesn't *The Sun* care about the prosperity of the West Midlands? Or the car industry in Britain? Doesn't *The Sun* care that as many as 50,000 jobs are hanging on the outcome? Someone should tell *The Sun* that the good Brummie doesn't like to be on the dole. That he is a fighter to the last. And that he doesn't like newspapers who recommend murder. [*Evening Mail*, 4 May 2000].

The general public in Birmingham and the West Midlands must have loved reading this tirade, as did journalists in the region.

One was Chris Morley, the *Evening Mail*'s industrial correspondent, who himself later wrote a cutting article after the crisis on what he saw as the vindictiveness of the national press. Printed in the *Journalist*, read by thousands of members of the National Union of Journalists across the country, his 'Gripe' column was headlined 'Capital Offence':

> The national press shows a terrible snobbery when reporting regional affairs like the threat to close the Rover plant ... As the story of Longbridge's fate weaved from hope to despair and back again, there were no voices in the nationals to proclaim why Rover should be saved. When the idea of a rescue bid from former Rover chief John Towers was raised there was almost universal scorn. *The Sun*, a supposed paper for

working people, was the worst. Twice it demanded a death sentence for Longbridge. Its headline 'R.I.P. Rover' was almost as insensitive to regional feelings as had been its blunder over the Hillsborough soccer tragedy that caused widespread fury in Liverpool. Not only was it offensive, it turned out to be wrong. [July 2000].

It was the last six words of this quote, '…it turned out to be wrong', that summed up just how bad *The Sun*'s coverage of the Rover crisis became. We all know *The Sun* is a racy, tabloid newspaper, and that it has to write and portray news in a popular style. Hence, headlines such as 'R.I.P. Rover' and phrases like '…the final nail in the coffin for Phoenix' would have been perfectly acceptable – if the paper had *known* that what it was writing was, at least roughly speaking, the truth. But for these tabloid tools to have been employed time and time again in what turned out to be a series of abysmally inaccurate reports was, for many, unforgivable. *The Sun* editor David Yelland must thank his lucky stars that at least one of his journalists *did* give the Phoenix idea half a chance in the paper, good old motoring editor Ken Gibson …step forward for a quick bow! Yelland, to give him his one due on Rover, even allowed Gibson to be openly joyous at Towers' success in a well-displayed column the day after the deal was clinched. (Ken, funnily enough, once worked for the Birmingham *Evening Mail*.) But it was too little, too late, against an overwhelming tide of narrow-mindedness.

I did, in the course of writing this chapter, feel that I ought to contact Yelland to give him his chance to reply to this criticism. On phoning his office, I was asked to address my queries via his personal assistant Rebecca Rogers by email, which I did, introducing myself, outlining what the book was about and then asking: 'In the interests of fairness, I wanted to give David Yelland an opportunity to explain *The Sun*'s stance, and also to ask him where the paper stood now, retrospectively, on Rover. Basically, does Mr Yelland admit that *The Sun* got it wrong?' I added that I was happy to either speak to Mr Yelland personally or to receive a response by post or email. The reply from Rebecca was short and swift. In an email marked 'Re: Rover Questions', she said: 'Mr Dyson, I have put your query to the Editor and I'm afraid it is a no this time to your request. Many thanks. Rebecca Rogers. PA to the Editor.' I replied, reiterating my desire to be fair, and also tried to call Yelland again through his office, finally sending him an email too, but to no avail. Yelland obviously had nothing to say to me about the way his paper had treated Rover, Phoenix and Longbridge workers. I did, however, ask Towers himself, after the crisis, how he had felt when assaults like the 'R.I.P.' front page hit the newsstands. With a twinkle in his eye, he commented: 'The day I wake up and am disturbed by what a paper like *The Sun* says about a serious business issue is the day I will become concerned.' This was a sensible attitude. But I know that Towers and other Phoenix consortium members *were* shaken by such coverage at the time, especially when it was mirrored, albeit in diluted form, by so many other newspapers.

Only the London *Evening Standard* matched *The Sun*. This tabloid publication started with a harsh editorial comment printed the day after news broke that BMW wanted to sell off Longbridge:

> … Longbridge just does not have a future. To pretend otherwise is to pour good money after bad … it is impossible to see Longbridge clawing its way back. It is desperately tough on the thousands who will be thrown out of work, but in reality they are lucky the plant has survived this long. Let us hope the Government, which has already foolishly promised some aid, now has the courage to walk away. [15 March 2000].

This was the sort of opinion piece that began doing the rounds from that day, summing up the honestly held, south of Watford view of so many in the London-based media.

But there was much worse to come from London's evening paper. Exactly one week before the BMW-Phoenix deal was signed to save Rover and tens of thousands of jobs, the *Evening Standard's* celebrated columnist and renowned art critic Brian Sewell was given the space to vent his exasperation on the subject, under the headline 'Don't Throw Money at Rover'. It was a 1,200-odd-word article, quite eloquently rambling on about the disastrous history of British motor manufacturing, but injecting several doses of spite specifically aimed at Rover, the Midlands and Towers for good measure:

> …Rover, a half-drowned rat, a half-dead duck… What on earth did BMW think they could do with Rover?… Midlands management, Midlands complacency and ghastly Midlands taste have for decades been running the whole native British car industry into extinction… The Midlands now call, yet again, for Government intervention… Politicians, however, should not provide life-support for those that are brain-dead… Rover has for years been brain-dead… It matters not at all to whom Rover passes, though why anyone should trust an ex-Rover executive to rescue it is beyond the sane man's comprehension, for it was such executives who brought it to its knees… Rover could still be rescued, but not by or for the Hyacinth Buckets of Birmingham. [2 May 2000].

'Ghastly taste', 'brain dead', 'Hyacinth Buckets' – what drove such a gifted writer to pour such scorn on fellow human beings in the *Evening Standard*, itself read by so many workers? I thought it was only proper to give Sewell the right to reply and he, unlike Yelland of *The Sun*, was more than willing to be interviewed. 'Why,' I asked him, 'were you quite so scathing about Rover and the Midlands?' His answers were every bit as articulate as his original article, and are worth recording. Sewell said:

I'm absolutely unrepentant. I have since a boy been passionate about motor cars, but over the last 50 years I have watched the British motor industry commit suicide. It wasn't competition that caused this, it wasn't the Japanese, it wasn't the resurgence of the German car industry, it was its own damn fool complacency. In the late 1940s, Rover cars were rock solid, streamlined, splendid vehicles, a car in which I learned to drive. Real quality. They then developed the 3-litre version, and its quality was terrific, wonderfully made, real craftsmanship. Then the 3.5-litre, an absolute whiz. I owned two of these cars in the late 1950s and early 1960s. Then Rover lost it. In 1972, I bought a Range Rover, and it had a wonderful engine and gearbox but everything about it, its bodywork, fell to pieces. My second Range Rover was more solid, but mechanically fell to pieces. Something was going wrong. Then Rover management spoilt the image of its next generation of cars by putting in an Austin engine. I ask you – a 2-litre, four cylinder Austin Ambassador engine in a Rover. It took the glamour away. I've heard some bloody idiots, managers who stood there saying 'there is a market for the Morris Marina out there', then saying 'there are people just waiting for the Allegro'. The people at the top were so bloody complacent, and the management they appointed were responsible for a calamitous decline. So I have no reason to repent. [Sewell's phone conversation with Stephen Dyson, 17 July 2000].

I then asked: 'What about the feelings of workers who read your article, Mr Sewell, are you not sorry to have offended them?' He replied:

You can't blame the workers, and I have not blamed them. It is always the management that is really at fault. They will hide behind the excuse of trade unions, Red Robbo and all that, but it was up to them to talk to the workers, to be honest with them, to work together, and they always failed.

My final question was: 'Do you now, given the success of the Phoenix bid, regret what you suggested about its chances?' Sewell, to his credit, replied:

If Towers and his team pull Rover through to make it once more a significant player in the British motor market I would be the first to cheer, eat my hat or whatever they want me to do. I'm not a meanie, but I've seen so many millions of pounds go into Rover. But if Towers succeeds, I will join in the celebrations.

My respect for Sewell has grown because he was prepared to stand up and explain his outlook. Nevertheless, I strongly feel it was at best insensitive, and at worst mischievous for him to have been quite so cutting and cynical in his notorious *Evening Standard* article in the midst of the Rover crisis. His well-read column that contained so much contempt about past failures, published at a time when so many people were considering the potential for future success, certainly did nothing to help the British motor industry. London bankers and BMW may have read his high and mighty words of wisdom, and this could have added to their anxiousness about Phoenix.

Although *The Sun* and the *Evening Standard* carried what I found to be the worst bias, there were plenty of other one-sided articles in the London-based national press. Scoffing at anyone's chances of saving Rover, the respected Jason Nisse, writing in the *Independent on Sunday* on 19 March 2000, sniped: 'No one has ever turned lead into gold, so why should we expect such a transformation for the leaden footed?' By 23 April, David Parsley, another eminent byline in a Sunday broadsheet, wrote off Towers' chances in detail under the headline 'Alchemy to Win Rover After Towers' Secret Talks Collapse':

> Alchemy, the venture-capitalist group, looks set to secure Rover this week after its rival, the Phoenix consortium, failed to strike a deal to take over the ailing car maker in a secret meeting with BMW... Towers is expected publicly to concede defeat when Alchemy meets BMW on Friday. The news will come as a blow to thousands of Rover workers... [*The Sunday Times*, Business section, 23 April 2000].

The words almost sound hollow now, but such a statement in a valued newspaper like *The Sunday Times* was exceptionally powerful. Many in the media and business world I spoke to shortly after they had read this article consequently felt sure Phoenix was dead. Such feelings were amplified by the influence of the *Financial Mail on Sunday*, the esteemed pull-out of the middle market *Mail on Sunday*, which joined in with its own style of despondency the same day. Its front page story of several hundred words talked in detail about how Jon Moulton's Alchemy was going to save Rover by forming a production partnership with Volkswagen, while Phoenix was simply dismissed: 'The rival consortium effectively ran up the white flag this weekend.'

As the 28 April deadline for the Alchemy-BMW agreement approached, other nationals jumped on the bandwagon. What could have been the good news of a rival bid with a slim chance was now discarded as impossible. 'Alchemy Poised to Win Rover', said the page 1 headline in the *Daily Telegraph* on 26 April. 'Hopes Fade for New Rover Bid', echoed the *Daily Mail* the same day, on page 15. The already pilloried *Evening Standard* and *The Sun* joined in again, almost as one, with 'Rover Sale to Alchemy Virtually a Done Deal' and 'Rover Bid is Nearly a Done Deal' on pages 7 and 9 respectively, also on 26 April. Not much joy for Rover workers, whichever newspaper they bought, nor for bankers, who may for all anyone knew even have been reconsidering previously promised funds for Phoenix on the strength of such negativism.

And then, as already touched upon in a previous chapter, came 28 April itself, the deadline day, when paper after paper virtually announced Alchemy's victory. The headlines of the *Daily Mail*, *The Scotsman* and *The Independent* for this day appeared in Chapter Seven, and they were added to by 'BMW Snubs Phoenix Bid For Rover' on page 2 of the *Daily Telegraph*, 'BMW Snub Rover Talks' on page 2 of *The Sun* and 'BMW Snub For Rival Offer' on page 2 of *The Guardian*, (could it be possible that the headline writers of these so different newspapers were actually checking with each other to make sure they had the same line – on the same page? Or were they all using the same single source that told them all that a 'snub' was on the way, and they all just swallowed this line? Surely not.)

But the story did not end there, as we know, because on the same day that these latest preconceived headlines appeared, Alchemy walked away, making the newspapers that carried them look, at best, rather silly. But still most of the London media persevered with their gloom. 'Rover Faces Oblivion as Deal Fails' sang *The Guardian*'s page 1 on 29 April, 'Rover Faces Closure Next Month' chorused *The Times*, again on page 1, and 'Rover Faces Axe as Deal Collapses' chimed the *Daily Telegraph* on its front page. Not as blatant as *The Sun*'s 'R.I.P.', but just as negative, just as dismissive of Towers' chances. So determined were these London experts, it seemed, that they continued with their pessimism right to the end – when they could be bothered, that is, because their interest and nose for the news that was about to break in big style had diminished to such an extent that no stories at all appeared in some papers on certain days. 'Byers Blamed by BMW as Phoenix Bid Faces Collapse' managed the *Daily Mail* on page 16 on 5 May, and 'Rover Rescue Bid Nears End of Road' supposed the *Daily Telegraph* page 29 on 6 May. Didn't any highly-paid London journalists think the Phoenix bid had actually done fairly well, to have carried on despite the persistent chants of the doom merchants? Was it not time to back the good guy? It seemed not.

Even on 9 May, the truly amazing day itself, when the most dramatic industrial story since the height of the miners' strike of the 1980s climaxed, there was so little to commend what the London-based nationals said. Those talented hacks and hackettes from what was traditionally known and widely respected as Fleet Street knew, well, not much more than nothing. To take just one London newspaper, and to be fair let's take the gentlest, here's *The Guardian*:

Components suppliers are said to increasingly believe that the Alchemy option is more viable than the Phoenix plans. The mood on the West Midlands taskforce appointed by the government to deal with the impact of job losses is said to have swung away from the Phoenix consortium. The taskforce met yesterday and a member said: 'Hard-headed businessmen fear Phoenix is just not a goer.' ...Many industry experts believe that Phoenix's plan to build 200,000 Rovers a year is not viable –

and that BMW might return to its original plan: selling the bulk of the Rover car business to Alchemy Partners, the London-based venture capital firm which ended talks with the German car maker last week. [9 May 2000].

Journalists can make mistakes, of course, because they are only human. But so many inaccuracies, so many predisposed opinions against Phoenix, so many pages of so much doubt over Towers in so many newspapers, from tabloid to broadsheet ... it just didn't feel right, given the actual result.

Why was there such fatalism throughout most of the London media? Putting the more responsible journalists aside, who perhaps, if they were now to be honest, simply jumped on the bandwagon of error, where did the more malicious stories and the most cynical, yet anonymous, quotes come from? Who was the unnamed Government source in *The Sun* on 29 April, whose analysis created the 'R.I.P.' approach? Was there someone in the cabinet office who was really so determined that Phoenix should not succeed that he or she actually gave *The Sun* those quotes? Was it a minister or a senior civil servant who spoke? Or were some of the 'insiders' simply businessmen associated with Alchemy, trying to place mischievious stories in a bid to put BMW and the world off the Phoenix consortium? Or were they, more disturbingly if this was the case, merely journalists themselves deciding on a standpoint en masse and inventing their own quotes? These questions can never be answered, and it would therefore be wrong to make any general assumptions or to throw in any conclusive guesses. But it did seem that London generally was against Rover, perhaps because of its history, or maybe because, in Government circles, there was bad advice and certain ministers thought it better to get rid of the problem quickly rather than have it dragging on until the next election, (thank goodness Trade and Industry secretary Stephen Byers and Northfield MP Richard Burden were not in this category). And the London media picked up this anti-Rover feeling, fuelled by whomever, and by the end there was no stopping the prejudice of the majority.

A few newspapers, like *The Mirror*, the *Daily Star* and *The Express* for example, were perhaps not as damning, but they lacked either the knowledge or the courage to hold out much hope for Towers. Only one national newspaper was truly fair on at least two occasions during the crisis, and it must have been something of a blessing to Phoenix that this was the serious-minded, widely respected *Financial Times*. On many days the *FT* had been very sceptical, if balanced, but on 19 April and then even more so on 29 April it really did give the idea of Towers rescuing Rover a chance. The first occasion has already been mentioned in Chapter Five, when the *FT* picked up and reran the facts about Phoenix revealed in the *Evening Mail* on 18 April. Then, on 29 April, the day of *The Sun*'s 'R.I.P.' front page, the *FT*'s Midlands Correspondent Jonathan Guthrie filed a story that made his paper stand alone among the national media's pessimism. Under the headline 'Phoenix Bid Rises From Dust Thrown Up By Alchemy Pullout', Guthrie painted the following altruistic picture of hope about the Towers bid for *FT* readers:

If the Ealing Studios production company still existed, it would make a film about the Phoenix Project. The plotline? A disparate, plucky bunch of Brummies join forces to stop German industrialists and City bean-counters destroying their beloved car factory ... the emergence of the Phoenix project as the only apparent hope Longbridge has to avoid closure is an extraordinary development. The huge support the consortium has gathered in the West Midlands is also a token of how distant the workings of central government have become to many people in one of its traditional heartlands. The public imagination has been captured by the visceral determination to fight cuts at Longbridge articulated by Carl Chinn, lead campaigner for the group ... The response from Westminster has looked anaemic in comparison ... (Chinn) has emerged as an eloquent, powerful and popular leader ... Byers, trade and industry secretary, has won fewer garlands locally. But in reality he is understood to have been in close contact with John Towers ... (Towers) could soon be back.

Such journalism may have restored a little faith in London newspapers, but Guthrie's reason was, in reality, lost in a sea of determined gloom.

I suppose the fact that the national media, in general, got it so wrong brings at least *some* comfort, albeit retrospectively, to the Longbridge workers, who must at the time have felt pretty buffeted by the London-led stories and unfair comment. But for many, the national media coverage of the Rover crisis was the saddest part of the whole affair. Any loyalty Rover workers, their families and friends once had for many London newspapers plummeted during those 56 days, when the majority demonstrated through headlines and articles that they cared not a jot for the community of Longbridge. These people now know more than ever before that 'what the paper's say' can be so, so warped. Dowell's *Evening Mail*, journalists like the *FT*'s Guthrie and the news outlets in the Midlands that kept a torch alight for Longbridge can hold their heads up high. So many in the London media can never do so in this region again, for their unswerving bias nearly killed Rover.

CHAPTER TEN

Saved For A Tenner

By Stephen Dyson

Iwill always remember the moment of 8.25am on Tuesday May 9 2000. I had been told by my Phoenix contact, as mentioned at the end of Chapter Eight, to keep my mobile phone switched on and next to me for when Towers himself was ready to talk of success or failure, and I had done so. But no one expected anything to happen that particular morning. The word was that the arduous BMW-Phoenix negotiations would drag on until Friday 12 May, as Towers continued his last ditch effort to persuade the Germans and his bankers that he could make a go of Rover. And so I had turned up to work as normal, and was sitting in between the *Evening Mail*'s deputy editor Tony Dickens and Dave Whaley, then my right hand man on the news desk, putting together the beginnings of that day's news pages.

Whaley's computer then began to buzz intermittently, a sign that we had learned from experience meant a call was coming in to a mobile phone lying too close to the screen. Seconds later, my mobile rang and as soon as I answered I knew who it was, and so did Whaley, who had read my eyes. 'Steve,' crackled the voice of John Towers, whom I had first met back in 1994 at a Land Rover launch when he was managing director of Rover. 'We've done it,' he said, almost too calmly, catching me completely unawares. 'Sorry John,' I replied, 'what do you mean? What's happening?' He said: 'We've done it, we've bought Rover.' I began to bluster: 'When … er, how … exactly what does this mean? Can we meet? Can you tell me all the details?' Towers sounded tired, and said: 'Sorry, Steve, I'm heading north now. There's a press release about to be issued, but I wanted you to know.' I needed more, and asked: 'What time did it happen, John?' He replied: 'It's just happened. We just signed all the papers a few minutes ago. Look, I've got to go now.' It was my last chance: 'When can we speak, John?' His last words, for then, were: 'Later, Steve. Call me later. I've got a lot to do.'

Talk about holding the front page! I instantly told Dickens, duty editor of the day with Ian Dowell at a meeting up north, and he changed the whole running order of the first edition of the paper due to leave our desk within half an hour. Then Whaley and I triggered numerous reporters into action. The adrenalin started to pump, throughout the office, as everyone raced to get the full story told. We needed quotes from the unions, the workers and the politicians, we had to speak to Alchemy's Jon Moulton, prepare a background piece on Towers, and take photographs of celebrating workers down at the main Q Gate entrance to Longbridge. But to start with, the breaking news had to make the first edition of the paper.

I had just started to write the front-page story myself, using what Towers had told me, when Carl Chinn rang. His voice tense with emotion, Chinn asked: 'Steve, is it true? Our Kid's just caught something on the news. Has Towers done it?' I replied: 'Yes, it's true, they've done it! I'm writing the first sentence of the front page story now.' It was almost too much for Chinn, who had lived and breathed the crisis from day one. 'Oh, Steve,' he exclaimed, his voice trembling. 'That's great news. I'm on my way to Q Gate now. I'll see you later.'

At 9.15am, 50 minutes after Towers had rung, BMW's statement on the sale was faxed through to the *Evening Mail*, just in time to help us add more detail to that first edition story. It was headlined 'BMW sells Rover Cars to Phoenix', and carried the sub-heading 'Negotiations successfully concluded and contracts signed'. The press release was a lot longer, but so much clearer than the one issued after Chinn and the union shop stewards had visited BMW on April 27. It read:

> The successful sale of Rover Cars to the Phoenix Consortium has prevented the closure of the Rover plant in Birmingham. This is the result of the negotiations between the BMW Group and the Phoenix Consortium led by John Towers that were successfully concluded this morning. Prof Joachim Milberg, Chairman of the Board of Management of the BMW Group said: 'After intense negotiations, we have managed to find a buyer for Rover whose aim is to continue to run Rover and who will therefore prevent the loss of thousands of jobs in the Rover plant in Birmingham, in the supplier industry and in the retail business.' The BMW Group and Phoenix Consortium signed and completed the purchase contracts in London today. The symbolic purchase price is £10. Phoenix will be taking responsibility for the development and distribution of Rover Cars. In addition, Phoenix will acquire the MG brand and other Heritage brands. Prof Milberg said: 'Rover customers can be certain that they will continue to receive the expected high quality of customer services in the future too.' The Phoenix Consortium will take over production in Birmingham of the Rover 25 and 45, the *MGF* sports car and the current Mini, until the start of production of the new Mini. Furthermore, it was agreed to shift the production of the Rover 75 from Oxford to the Birmingham plant. Phoenix plans to start production of the Rover 75 Estate at a later point in time. The BMW Board has thus taken the first important step towards implementing the reorientation of the company. On March 16 2000, the Supervisory Board of BMW approved the Board of Management's resolution to withdraw from

Rover. To avoid a closure, the sale of Rover always took first priority for the BMW Group. After negotiations with what was then the only interested party, Alchemy Partners, had collapsed because of new demands that were unreasonable, negotiations with the Phoenix Consortium, which had been formed in the meantime, were started, these successfully concluded today. As already announced the BMW Group will be investing in production of the new Mini in Oxford rather than in Birmingham. The new Mini will be launched in the early summer of 2001. The completion of the new BMW Group engine plant in Hams Hall in the Midlands will proceed as planned. [BMW Group Media Information release, May 9 2000].

It was a lot of information, and needed a lot of interpreting. But it was such good news for Longbridge workers, for the car component industry and for Birmingham and the Midlands. 'It's a Deal!' shouted the *Evening Mail*'s front page that day, with the sub-heading 'Longbridge saved as Towers gets Rover ... for a tenner'. Every radio and TV news bulletin began to blare out the news, with most programmes interviewing any experts they could grab hold of in between. Nationally, it was a huge story. Locally, in the Midlands, it was incredibly good news – for tens of thousands of workers, and hundreds of thousands of families and friends. It was also a fine turn of events for Prime Minister Tony Blair, rescued from what was possibly the gravest industrial crisis of the Government's time in power. Trade and Industry secretary Stephen Byers, who was known to have worked so hard behind the scenes for Phoenix, was jubilant, commenting: 'Three weeks ago when I got John Towers and BMW together and facilitated their meeting I was widely criticised. Today's news proves it was the right thing to do.' Blair, whatever any advisors may have told him previously about Rover's likely fate, agreed, saying: 'After all the attacks directed at Stephen Byers, he rolled up his sleeves and got on with doing what the Government could. This is an example of the new role of Government amid massive economic change that is seeing jobs being won and lost across the industrialised world. We resisted calls for some form of renationalisation, but nor did we stand idly by.'

Local MP Richard Burden, who had also beavered away with Byers for the future of Longbridge, was ecstatic. 'This is excellent news,' he said. 'A vindication of the work many of us have been putting in. It is a conclusive answer to all the negativity we have seen in certain parts of the press and certain parts of the country. Thousands of jobs will be saved as a result of this. This creates a sure future for Rover to build success upon and go from strength to strength.'

The unions revealed how they had burned the midnight oil until 2.20am with Phoenix on legal issues, helping to smooth the way for the deal. The TGWU's Tony Woodley said: 'I am exceptionally tired but absolutely delighted.' Rover workers gathering at Q Gate were just as happy, one employee, Richard Martin, saying: 'This is a great day for Rover. I always thought Towers would be successful, he's a shrewd businessman and he wouldn't have got involved unless he thought he could do it. His success has also got to be down to the people of the West Midlands who backed us all the way.' Even Alchemy's Jon Moulton was positive, stating, with a hint of irony: 'I am very surprised. I think, above all, I wish Mr Towers good luck – he'll need it.'

As soon as the *Evening Mail*'s main edition was under way, I raced down to Q Gate, where Towers was expected to arrive for a press conference at 2pm. It was midday when I arrived, the sun was shining and the scenes were unforgettable. There was one character who will always be remembered that day – for this was the last of numerous appearances he had made at nearly all Rover demonstrations during the crisis. It was John Bull himself, the historical personification of the English people. Sporting his huge, exaggerated moustache and false sideburns, he had taken to the streets time and time again in a crisp white shirt, big black bow tie, union jack waistcoat, white breeches, black boots, black dapper hat and long red tails. Always carrying aloft his lollipop man-style placard reading 'Save the Rover, save British jobs, no surrender', the very sight of him had never failed to lift dampened spirits. A frequent visitor to Longbridge, he had also joined the 1 April march to Cannon Hill Park and had even taken his individual campaign for Rover to the Houses of Parliament. And now, on victory day itself, here was colourful John Bull in all his splendour at Q Gate, all smiles, waiting to proudly present the eventually victorious John Towers with a glass of champagne.

Ray Egan, the man behind the John Bull mask, had became the colourful symbol of the Rover workers' fight to stay in work, appearing in hundreds of newspapers and on dozens of TV news bulletins around the world. Actually born in Liverpool, Egan made Birmingham his home for the majority of his life, moving to the area when he joined West Midlands Police in 1961 and working the beat in Handsworth, Ladywood, Winson Green, Smethwick and Solihull. Now retired, the 62-year-old former agricultural worker first began his John Bull

John Towers is given champagne to toast his victory as he enters Q Gate on 9 May. *Picture by Trevor Roberts*

The colourful John Bull, alias Ray Egan. *Picture by Steve Murphy*

role some eight years ago in a patriotic attempt to promote Hereford cattle at the Royal Show. The married father-of-two is simply a fan of all things English, and in an interview with *Evening Mail* journalist Diane Parkes after the Rover crisis he explained just why he could not resist joining the fight for Longbridge:

> As soon as I heard about Rover I thought: 'I have to get down there and support them.' I used to be a long-distance lorry driver and often used to carry goods in there so I had links with them going back quite a while. I heard about the march and thought that I wanted to be a part of it. I think John Bull is a way to fly the flag and add some colour to the whole thing ... I became very good friends with many of the people down there. They call me Bully. I am so happy to have been a part of it all. I will never forget that march. [24 May 2000].

Surrounding John Bull at Q Gate on 9 May were scores of workers in various groups, some just talking, all smiles and excited gesticulations, others dancing, singing, chanting, carrying the likes of Chinn shoulder high for the cameras. As one set of workers went back inside to the shop floor, so others appeared, using their break to celebrate to the world. John Hemming was also there, up on a grass bank on the edge of Cofton Park overlooking the gates, being interviewed by the press, enjoying the atmosphere. He deserved this moment of glory.

The *Evening Mail*'s victory edition on 9 May, sold by Gordon Heale. *Picture by Alan Williams*

Every Rover car that passed Q Gate received a roar of approval from the workers, and most honked their horns in support. Every BMW car that passed was booed and sworn at, the mood was so high. As I stood talking to various workers, the various regional correspondents of the London media arrived, as unobtrusively as they could, and waited in the shade for Towers to arrive. None sought or received any welcome or acknowledgment from the workers, all of whom were buying *Evening Mail*s from paper seller Gordon Heale as fast as he could be resupplied. Like the national press, I stood somewhat awkwardly amidst these celebrations. Chinn was there and spotted me, loudly introducing me to 'the lads' who raised a cheer and many came to shake my hand. This was nice of them, as I'd been close to the crisis. But it was not my job, my life, my home, my family and my future that had been on the line. I was not a Longbridge employee, and at times on that triumphant day, as the expectant crowds of workers waited for their first glimpse of Towers, I felt a little intrusive.

But then, shortly after 2pm, the cheers really started and anyone's uneasinesss dissolved as Towers arrived in a lime green, W-registered Rover 75. Next to Towers was fellow Phoenix member Nick Stephenson, and in the rear of the car, in support, was Woodley of the TGWU union. All three appeared touched by the sincere warmth of the Longbridge crowds. Such was the hero's welcome that the car could not even get through the gates for three or four minutes, so many workers wanted to see Towers in the flesh. After accepting a glass of champagne from John Bull, he was allowed through to the circular exhibition hall, but was again encircled by an ever-growing crowd of keyed up workers. His hand was shaken, his back patted, Towers' eyes welled up with emotion. The *Evening Mail*'s Jon Griffin, writing in the next day's paper, summed the scene up so well again:

> This was history in the making, a day of genuine raw emotion for the tens of thousands of Midlanders whose livelihoods depend on the survival of Birmingham's world-renowned car plant … Just two weeks ago, Mr Towers had been written off across the world as a no-hoper in the race for Rover as rivals Alchemy Partners prepared to hail a famous victory in the annals of UK car manufacturing. But now television crews and reporters from across the globe gathered on a perfect Spring afternoon to greet the man every Longbridge worker wanted to see back at the helm. [10 May 2000].

Once he managed to get inside the hall, I fell into step with Towers on his way to the podium. Optimistically, I ventured: 'John, well done! When can we talk about how the deal was done?' Towers was still moved by his welcome from the workers, and had to get his head together for the press conference. 'Not now. Can I ring you, Steve? Later tonight.' Moments later he was sitting down on stage, with four of his fellow consortium members, three union leaders and a politician alongside him. They made quite a sight before the press, did those nine

John Hemming enjoys a moment of victory outside Q Gate on
9 May. *Picture by Trevor Roberts*

Phoenix faces the press on 9 May. Pictured from left are: Adrian Ross, works convenor; John
Edwards; Duncan Simpson, of the AEEU; Northfield MP Richard Burden; Tony Woodley, of the
TGWU; John Towers; Nick Stephenson, Peter Beale; and Brian Parker. *Picture by Alan Williams*

smiling faces, all from such different backgrounds. They were: Adrian Ross, Longbridge Convenor; John Edwards, the Stratford Rover dealer who had become such an important part of Phoenix; Duncan Simpson, of the AEEU; Northfield MP Richard Burden; the TGWU's Tony Woodley; Towers himself; Phoenix member Nick Stephenson; Peter Beale, the finance director at Edwards and now a Phoenix member; and financial wizard, Brian Parker.

'It's quite an emotional day today,' Towers said. 'We, the Phoenix consortium, came from a position which did not show a lot of prospects during the early days. Many of you were extremely sceptical about the eventual outcome. But there has been an outcome largely more beneficial for the company, its suppliers and dealers and all the stockholders. I'm extremely proud to have been part of that process. We are equally delighted to have had the support of a whole range of people, people in Government, people out of Government, people in the region. It is a very satisfactory outcome for us and it is an emotional day.'

Towers told the assembled media that Phoenix had a plan that would see Rover turn around its losses, that it would have a positive cash flow within 14 months and return to profit within two years. He explained that this would be helped by a 'debt free, cash free balance sheet' provided by BMW as part of the deal. He said: 'We forget a lot of things in the reporting of the condition of this business. We forget that not many years ago, this business was making money, small amounts of money, but nevertheless making money. Our aim is to create stability, a positive position for the business to let people know what excellent products we have.' Towers added that marketing costs could be cut by 50% and yet sales could be increased by more inventive promotions. There were many other questions, most repetitive and quite a few covering details the *Evening Mail* had already revealed. Towers confirmed that fewer than 1,000 workers would lose their jobs under Phoenix plans, receiving up to £25,000 redundancy each, and that Longbridge would manufacture around 203,000 cars a year. He refused to criticise BMW directly, saying only: 'BMW found themselves in a untenable position … hindsight is a wonderful thing.'

On the future, Towers told the press conference that Phoenix had bought the Rover 25, 45 and 75 models, the old Mini and the MG*F*, the spares business and the vehicle financing business. Phoenix also had options on the possible future purchase of Powertrain, the engine plant at Longbridge, and the body panels operation at Swindon, although these would continue to be run by BMW for the time being. He told the packed hall that the most important thing to begin with was the 'care and maintenance' of existing products, and then that 'collaboration' would be needed with another major player for new models. 'In a business of this size,' he said, 'you have to do something different. That difference will be collaboration. It is not an emerging issue. It is one we will have to tackle in the future.' Towers was asked who a future partner might be, and whether it was going to be Honda, a former Rover collaborator in his days as chief executive. He replied: 'I have a significant relationship with Honda and therefore

Honda tends to be the name that comes to mind. It doesn't have to be – there are a number of people who would be entirely suitable.'

Prominent Phoenix partner Stephenson, a director at Lola Cars and former product and design development director at Rover, added to this speculation after the main press conference. Surrounded by a dozen or more journalists who kept pressing him for the names of potential future partners, he said: 'Honda is a distinct option for us, and there are other manufacturers that I believe would be interested in speaking to us. It could be a very long list … everybody will be banging on our door. But Honda would be a very obvious candidate for us to talk to, simply because of the history of the relationship with Rover.'

Towers also promised the assembled journalists that Rover workers would each be given a stake in the new business, in the form of shares. Around one third of Techtronic 2000, the holding company set up by the Phoenix consortium to handle Rover finances, would be given to an employee trust. It was hoped this would motivate workers more than ever before. After the press conference, Phoenix partner Beale explained that although financial and tax issues still had to be explored, the shares offer was for real. 'We are committed to do it and we will do it,' he said. 'Workers will be shareholders in the company. We feel for this company to succeed, it is important for all stakeholders to have an interest in making it succeed.' It later became clear that a similar stockholding of shares was also to be given to Rover dealers.

Techtronic 2000, which now owns Rover and is handling all these future shares, has never been discussed in detail in public by Towers or any of his partners. There is, after all, no obligation for them to do so, as Techtronic is a private company. What is known is that it has four directors – Towers, Stephenson, Edwards, who owns one of the largest Rover dealer networks, and Beale, his finance director. Each partner reportedly invested a 'six-figure' sum in the business (ie: more than £100,000, but less than £1 million each). The company was pledged some £450 million of finance from BMW and another £200 million was made available by Burdale Financial, the asset-based lending division of the First Union Bank of Carolina, America's sixth largest. Although now it seems that Rover may not immediately have needed this money, the fact that it was offered was so important in persuading BMW that the Phoenix plan had financial clout. Without it, Towers may never have clinched the deal and so it ought to be recorded here that, when all the British banks appeared reluctant to provide finance, Phoenix turned to local financier Brian Parker to help find the money.

Parker, *inserts Carl Chinn*, is a 51-year-old Brummie born and bred. He grew up in Summer Lane, a neighbourhood that epitomised working-class Birmingham. From his earliest memories, he spent much of his time in the Bull Ring helping out his granddad, Wally Chapman, who was a trader. Brian recalls skinning rabbits beneath his grandfather's barrow and learning from the quick banter and fast thoughts of the market men and women. He left school at fifteen with no qualifications and went to work for Triumph at Meriden, where he tested motorbikes. After a time in the United States, he became an apprentice at Lucas but because of his love for playing golf, soon his life was changed radically. He met a lot of influential people on various courses and picked up the intricacies of the financial world by paying attention to conversations in the clubhouse. Before long, he started to make deals himself, quickly establishing a reputation for his sharp mind and knack for spotting a good deal, and becoming a wealthy man. Like all the people involved in the battle for Longbridge, Brian was pushed foward by the highest of motives. His role for Phoenix was fully revealed in an interview by Simon Mowbray of the *Sunday Mercury* days after the deal was signed:

> I first got involved about six weeks ago after Birmingham's Liberal Democrat leader, John Hemming, formed the first consortium. As things progressed, John Towers, who I have known for quite a while, asked me if I thought I could secure the necessary financial backing to get Phoenix off the ground. I told him I could and then spent all my time trying to do a deal ... we couldn't get the money from a British bank because the deal was viewed as too sensitive ... Burdale had confidence in us right from the start and also offered us the best deal ... I knew the money was available for us about three weeks before we signed the deal with BMW, despite reports to the contrary from London.' ... A reluctant hero, Brian ...has not invested any of his own cash in the Rover deal ... 'I am just delighted that I was able to contribute in some way because so much was at stake. I am a Brummie and proud to be so. Longbridge is a part of this great city and we had to fight for it.' [14 May 2000].

Parker's importance to Phoenix was shown by the fact that he sat on the stage with Towers and others during the press conference on 9 May. Following on from his role in helping save Longbridge, Parker became a non-executive deputy chairman of the supervisory board for Rover. Interestingly, Brian Parker had worked with Carl Lanchester at the meat market in Birmingham and at Bywater's on the Coventry Road. They had been mates in those days and had lost touch. Since the Phoenix victory they have re-established contact.

Once that press conference had ended, *resumes Stephen Dyson*, I hung around outside the exhibition hall at Longbridge, hoping to catch hold of Towers again. The *Evening Mail* had fully staffed the meeting, of course, but having been so close to events for the past few weeks I felt the paper should have its own, exclusive chat with the main man behind the rescue. My wait was in vain, and I eventually drove home, and stayed up late for the phone call Towers had told me he would try to make. It didn't come, and I went to bed a little deflated that I had nothing for the next day's paper that was different from any other media. The next morning, 10 May, I climbed into my car at 5.55am and as I reversed off the drive my mobile began to ring. 'Steve, sorry I didn't phone you last night,' said Towers, speaking on his mobile phone whilst travelling from his home in leafy Warwickshire to Longbridge. 'I got home, went for a walk, and was then so tired I fell to sleep! I'm driving to work now and have got time to speak.' This was now my chance to find out exactly how the deal with BMW was finally struck. Towers didn't let me down, and the pressures he told me he had faced in his determination to save Longbridge from virtual extinction were in the *Evening Mail* just hours later. He said:

> I knew it was possible. I knew our option was far, far better than what else BMW had on the cards for Rover. So many people were so fired up, so charged and ready to battle for survival ... We had to try for a better outcome. I took a view that, irrespective of any personal position in life, what was planned for Rover was going to have such a dramatic and awful effect on our region. You just cannot distance yourself from these sort of issues. Some people would argue that I'm in a comfortable position and didn't need to put myself through all that pressure. And yes, your quality of life and family is affected, but what others sometimes miss is the realisation that you can't live and exist and enjoy and work in the region and allow something like this happen, and at the same believe it's nothing to do with you. Of course it is. It wasn't just me who was affected by such thoughts – for a start there was the whole of the Phoenix consortium and everyone who was connected to it. And, amazingly, there was the British public who showed exactly what they thought through April's car sales figures ... we were sort of written off before it started ... The popular assessment which came from so many so-called experts every day was that we were not even in the frame. I think as we approached the final Alchemy deadline and did not seem to be getting too far, things didn't look good. But batting against that kind of issue all the time, against those sort of overwhelming odds, that actually produces good spirits ...The exact moment I knew we had clinched the deal was at 2.30 yesterday morning, and for the first time for days I allowed myself to relax. I stretched out on a table in BMW's solicitors' offices in London for ten minutes before I did anything else ... There was a huge mixture of feelings yesterday. There was a lot of terrific emotion during the day and I found myself in the peculiar position of trying to temper that. It was so difficult not to get drawn in, but so important because there is such a lot of hard work to do. [10 May 2000].

And it was for this hard work that Towers now prepared himself. The one last question I asked him during that early morning conversation on 10 May was: 'What message do you now want to give to your workers, John?' His answer, which actually formed the beginning of the above article because it was so emphatic, was: 'I must thank all the workers for their support. Now I want them all to concentrate their minds, because for every single one of us, every single minute of every single day we are at work at Longbridge, there is only one objective – to make it happen.'

The victory of Phoenix in winning the chance to turn Rover into a viable business was remarkable. Just how did they do it, against all the odds? What was certain was that it had very, very little to do with anyone outside the Midlands, bar one or two individuals like Byers. Although Towers and all those involved with him now prefer to distance themselves from any criticism of London-based politicians and bankers, I know there was once a hint of bitterness within the Phoenix camp. The deal was landed in spite of what I understand was a reluctance for it by some in the government. At one stage before the deal, various sources even hinted that, at times, elements of the Labour government appeared to be actively working against this local bid, meddling politically and through anonymous but damaging quotes to the more gullible media. As one observer reported:

> When the rival Alchemy takeover plan sensationally collapsed at the end of April, BMW was rubbishing the Phoenix proposals and even ministers were privately sceptical. Mr Towers believed until very late … that the DTI was secretly against him. A meeting with Mr Byers ended in acrimony last Friday. Mr Towers and Mr (Tony) Woodley were left fuming – the latter admitted he rang Mr (Geoffrey) Robinson (Labour MP and former Jaguar executive) to accuse the government of still backing Alchemy. A close confidante of Mr Towers disclosed: 'John left thinking the government was deliberately putting obstacles in our way. It did not look good.' [*The Guardian*, 10 May 2000].

Towers has always refrained from discussing any government inflexibility there may have been and, indeed, has been at pains to highlight the help given by Byers. The Trade and Industry Secretary himself told the *Evening Mail*'s Jon Griffin on 2 August 2000 that: 'I was criticised in some quarters for openly backing John Towers and the Phoenix takeover. But had Jon Moulton and Alchemy Partners achieved the takeover, I think it was clear that there would have been literally thousands of job losses at Longbridge and tens of thousands in the component sector. I felt that was unacceptable.' [This quote was cut from an *Evening Mail* article on 3 August, but I kept the original]. Despite the now accepted support of Byers, there were certainly some individuals in and around the government who were not so helpful. There was also so little help from the City of London, with Britain's high street banks clearly shirking from making any sizeable investment in the country's industrial heartlands.

So, again, why and how did Phoenix succeed in raising Rover from the ashes? The main reason behind this achievement was the determination of so many local people – Midland businessmen, Midland workers, Midland media and Midland personalities leading popular Midland support. To be specific, I'm talking about people like Towers, whose reasons and motivations have been outlined in this chapter. I'm talking about Stephenson, Beale, Edwards, Parker and other Phoenix main-players – selfless Midland businessmen who felt there was something worth saving at Rover. I'm talking about committed union leaders, from the likes of Tony Woodley at the top to Carl Lanchester and Ian Robinson on the shopfloor – all their individual roles have been described earlier in this book. I'm talking about some politicians – Richard Burden, Stephen Byers and John Hemming are all worthy of the mentions they have received. And I'm talking about the few in the press who were prepared to go out on a limb for a better future at Longbridge, people like Ian Dowell and Ed Doolan, again already discussed.

Then there was Carl Chinn, whose role I've only delved into in passing so far in my parts of this book. A passionate, open-hearted Brummie, Chinn was as wounded as if he had been a Longbridge worker himself when BMW's original plans were confirmed on March 16. He flung himself into supporting the workforce's need to express its feelings, acting as a go-between for Longbridge and the Birmingham public. At the same time he was there at the birth of Phoenix, using all his contacts, skill and imagination to publicise the worth of Towers and co. He spent long, long hours at meetings, at rallies, in Munich, at No.10 Downing Street and on his mobile phone coordinating workers, press, Phoenix, unions and anyone whom he thought would help. Chinn's actions were so zealous that he faced ridicule from some press and cynicism from some political circles, at times risking his reputation – but that did not ever come close to stopping him. Chinn triggered a Midland stance that will be remembered, a peaceful uprising that proved to BMW, the government and the world that Longbridge was not going quietly. He was an integral part of something special, a spirit of true common purpose, a kind of brotherhood rarely seen in Britain these days. The general public was quick to acknowledge this, as Anthony Warburton wrote in a letter to *The Birmingham Post* on 12 May 2000:

> I think that now is the time for all of us to remember the efforts of one man who, after March 16, concentrated and expressed the disgust of Brummies everywhere more than anyone else. I refer, of course, to Carl Chinn… (Referring to the 1 April rally) To anyone who was in Cannon Hill Park there was no doubt who was the hero of the hour. If there is any justice in the world, Carl Chinn will be publicly honoured for his courage and leadership, the sooner the better.

Yes, there were many people behind the success of Phoenix, and it is warming to remember each of their roles. But there is another set of individuals owed a mention here, although this will not be as welcome to many readers as those listed above. I am talking now about the executives at BMW who decided to alter course. Not the most popular heroes, the bosses at BMW, not people who will easily be remembered for *helping* the Rover crisis. But, in fairness, they did, and they should receive some recognition. Because whatever mistakes BMW made earlier in the year 2000, and it made some big ones, and however obnoxious some of its original decisions may have been, various executives did at least have the stomach to change their minds. Whether this was Professor Werner Samann, Professor Joachim Milberg, or even a member of the controlling Quandt family, we shall never know. It may have been all of them. But certainly someone in Munich in some position of power finally listened to Towers, to Byers, to Burden, to Woodley and to Chinn, Carl Lanchester, Ian Robinson and the workers. BMW had wanted to extract itself from Rover so badly – that can be seen by what many now consider to have been such an ill-judged and premature plan to dispose of Longbridge to Alchemy in the first place. And once that original course of action had been selected, the German company could surely have just stuck to its guns; there were not, after all, many people in London who would have blamed them for too long, were there? Who knows what would have happened then. What is certain is that if BMW had not had the humility to sit down, to eventually pay attention, to finally agree to compare Phoenix with Alchemy, to ignore the advice of much of the national press and possibly some at Westminster and, ultimately, to make a complete U-turn, then Phoenix would, beyond doubt, have failed. As it was, at the end of the day, BMW regained some of its reason and showed its humanity, allowing an ardent group of businessmen to have a crack at saving Rover, even funding the symbolic £10 sell-off to the tune of £450 million plus huge restructuring costs. For that good deed alone, albeit at the last gasp, BMW should be remembered. It was a mad, mad 56 days, was the Rover crisis. But sanity prevailed, thanks to the resolve of so many people.

Workers' Joy

In the days following our visit to London, *writes Carl Chinn*, our spirits were raised as it became obvious that the odds against Phoenix were dropping. Still, there were a few wobbles and the weekend of 6 and 7 May was the most difficult time because of the continued antagonism of much of the London press towards John Towers and his consortium. But by the Monday morning our fears were allayed by the positive news we were getting from Stephen Dyson and other local reporters. Because we were gaining in confidence, Carl, Ian and myself had decided that it was now time to let the business negotiations run their course. We continued making our opinions known to the press and did have a fall back position if things did not work out for the best for Longbridge. As it turned out, we did not need that fall back position.

Just before 9am on Tuesday 9 May, Our Darryl rang me. Excitedly he

Carl Chinn celebrates the Phoenix victory on 9 May with Rover worker Clive Lake.
Picture by Alan Williams

Longbridge is saved! Carl Chinn celebrates with convenor Adrian Ross (left) and John Bull, alias Ray Egan, (rear, in top hat). Others include Terry Reilly (front right), and, to the rear, Brian Crockett, Carl Lanchester and Stuart Hughes. *Picture by Steve Murphy*

Carl Lanchester and Carl Chinn are held aloft by celebrating workers on 9 May. Supporting Chinn to the right is Wagon driver Paul. Phil Sidhu is carrying Lanchester. The chap in the industrial pinafore at the front is known as 'H'. To his left is Atrnik 'Arnie' Jutla, to his right is Billy Singh. Jaz Dhani is on the far right front, next to Ian Robinson and then Pedan Junghi. *Picture by Alan Williams.*

told me that he had been listening to BBC WM and that a news flash had come through that Phoenix and BMW had signed a deal. I shouted out in exultation and Kay came running in to find out what was going on. Joyfully, I told her and then said 'Tara' to Our Kid and immediately contacted Stephen Dyson. He confirmed the news and said that he was writing the first sentence of the front page story for that day's paper. Steve was as chuffed as I was. He had been a brick throughout the crisis. A proud Brummie, he is an astute newspaperman and a sharp observer. My phone calls to Steve had been important to me. Although I had spoken to John Towers a couple of times early in the campaign, I was not privy to the inner circle's thoughts. Through his London source, Steve was fully informed. When I, Carl and Ian were down then a phone call to Steve perked us up again. He did his city proud.

As was reported in that afternoon's Mail, I was elated and ecstatic and was certain that 'the people of Birmingham and the West Midlands have shown they can take on the big firms and win. They have demonstrated that they are not prepared to surrender'. After talking with Steve, I rang Ian who was at home

Rover workers celebrate the deal signed by Phoenix with Carl Chinn on 9 May. Far right is
Clive Lake, next to him is Anil Chandra. *Picture by Mike Simmonds*

because he was on nights that week. We arranged to meet at Q Gate. Then I
contacted Carl, who was on days and was at work in Number 3 Paint Shop. That
morning I was due to chair a session at an Urban Renaissance conference which
was to be held in Balsall Heath and which had been organised by social
entrepreneur and community activist, Dr Dick Atkinson. When I arrived, I told
Dick that I had to be with the workers at Q Gate and would he mind if did not
stay long. He understood, but asked me if I could say a few words at the
beginning of the conference and introduce David Blunkett, the Education
Minister. I agreed and then chatted with a French lady called Marie, who had an
important position at Rover and was overjoyed at the deal. In fact, everyone in
the large marquee was happy and chatting gaily. As intended, I spoke about how
in the midst of harsh environments, urban working-class people had formed
viable neighbourhoods from within, after which David Blunkett took the floor.
He made all of us laugh when he said that he was really glad that the good news
had broken that morning before I introduced him.

      The day Alchemy had pulled out had been special because it had been
our first ray of hope, our first chance to cheer. But the celebrations on 9 May
were even more special because we could relax and enjoy everything simply
because we had won. So many people had achieved what we had set out to do –
keep Longbridge open as a volume car producer and minimise job losses.
Television crews, newspaper journalists and radio reporters were everywhere and

so too were the workers, their families and their supporters. People were chanting 'We ain't going away!' and as a new group arrived, each person was greeted with tight hugs and pumping handshakes.

Worker Damjil Ladwa of Moseley, Birmingham definitely felt like celebrating. He explained to The Mail that 'this has been stressful for everyone and the pressure and uncertainty has affected my family. At one stage I just wanted to get away from the news'. For engine assembly worker Ray Burns, the cloud had been lifted 'from all of us'. He and his wife, Dawn, had been deeply worried that they would have to put off their plans of buying their own house. They wanted a garden for their six-year old son Damian to run in but had been afraid that they would not be given a mortgage because of the uncertainty over Longbridge's future. Now they could go out and find their dream home. A broadly smiling Ian Robinson was pictured with his three-year old son, Cameron, on his shoulders. The youngster was cheering as his dad told The Mail that 'it's absolutely brilliant news . . . Although it's come earlier than expected BMW have made the right choice. There have been some highs and lows over the past few weeks, but now a big weight has been lifted off people's shoulders. This is the only way we could secure the majority of the jobs and car production. When I started at Longbridge, John Towers was the managing director and he

Carl Chinn leads Rover workers with preparations for a concert in aid of charity, to thank Birmingham for its support. Pictured with him from left are: Paul Parsons; Carl Lanchester; Gemma Cartwright; Ian Robinson, with little Pearce Cartwright on his shoulders; Karl Walker; and Stan Astly. *Picture by Trevor Roberts*

did a good job. And I know he will do the job again in the future'.

As it approached half past twelve, there were hundreds and hundreds of folk milling about, shouting and applauding the cars that went by pipping their horns. And, of course, there was also ever steady and ever present Ray 'John Bull' Egan, the man whose garb and placards symbolised the victory. He'd been there since 7am: 'I don't know why, I just felt something was going to happen. The heart of this great manufacturing city is even stronger.' Then at 12.30, as the dinner hour started, the men and women of Number 3 Paint Shop marched out en masse with placards and banners. They were headed by Carl Lanchester. It was a bostin' and thrilling sight. They came across the road and onto Cofton Park where Ian and myself were standing. The three of us were picked up shoulder high as the great crowd began to roar out 'We ain't going away! We ain't going away!' The atmosphere was fantastic and later, when I was interviewed by ITN News for the lunchtime bulletin, it was almost impossible to hear the questions because of the chants of the workers. I didn't care. This was the day the workers had waited for and they had the right to call out to the world their rapture and pride.

Unfortunately, I missed the arrival of John Towers as I had to be on air at 2pm but I know that it was a wonderful occasion. That night Carl, Ian, Adrian, myself and others met at the Rover Club to be interviewed by Sky News. Afterwards, we threw about the idea of a big do to celebrate the victory that Saturday night. Thanks to Bob Turner, we had the use of a one of the function rooms at the Rover Club and a disc jockey was arranged. We had a cracking night. The paint shops had done a whipround and paid for beer tankards to be inscribed and presented to John Hemming and Ian Dowell of The Mail in recognition of the part they had played in the Battle for Longbridge. Because of prior commitments, neither John nor Ian could be there, but The Mail's mug was given to Stephen Dyson and I accepted John's on his behalf.

Next, Kay was given a beautiful bouquet of flowers for her understanding and support and I was handed a decanter and whiskey tumblers. Upon the decanter were the words, 'We Ain't Going Away'. It was one of the finest thing I have been given ever and it has pride of place in our house. There were four more presentations. Lynne Lanchester and Tina Smith were given flowers for the same reasons as Kay, and, unbeknown to Carl and Ian, their pals had bought each of them a tankard that was inscribed with the relevant name and the words 'from all of Number 3 Paint Shop. We Ain't Going Away.'

That night we talked about what had happened and how victory had been achieved. All of us knew that we had played our part but we knew also that it was just that – a part. Longbridge could never have been saved if it had not been for the coming together in a common purpose of so many different individuals and organisations with no formal connection. There was John Hemming, who had stood up and cried out that Longbridge could be saved and who had battled incessantly against the odds and to whom much is owed; there was Richard Burden and the other members of West Midlands group of Labour MPs, who had worked arduously for the right result; there were union leaders such as Tony Woodley, Duncan Simpson and Terry Pye who had striven might and main for the best deal for their members and for British manufacturing; there was Stephen Byers, whom we all recognised now had done as much as he could and had shown clearly his desire and determination to keep people in work and to back manufacturing; and there were the councils of Birmingham and Bromsgrove which had done whatever they could whenever they could.

Despite all the lobbying and private and public pressure exerted by these people and ourselves, victory could not have been gained if there had not been an alternative buyer to Alchemy. That is why John Towers was essential. With John Edwards, Nick Stephenson and Peter Beale, he provided hope and a solid business approach. His fortitude, business acumen and tactical prowess must be admired. So too should the skill and dexterity of Brian Parker, who gained the necessary finance for Phoenix. Yet, in acknowledging and highlighting the importance of all these folk, the powerful effect of the public campaign should not be diminished. No-one can deny the positive impact made by The Mail, whose editor, Ian Dowell, never flinched from putting the case for Longbridge and who inspired all of us with his strength of will and leadership of the superb coverage by his journalists during the Rover Crisis.

Then there were the people of Birmingham and the West Midlands who had turned out in their tens of thousands to support Longbridge and had made their views known through letters to the newspapers and in other ways. They never wavered in their conviction that they would fight for manufacturing and Longbridge. And, of course, there were the workers. Since the late 1970s, the rights of workers have been weakened and the manufacturing working class has been on the back foot. But in the Battle for Longbridge, the men and women of the factory showed that they would not be cowed. They neither bowed their heads nor bent their knees in submission. They stood noble and tall. Carl Lanchester, Ian Robinson, Paul Parsons, Dick Howell, Noel Moloney, Adrian Ross and many more of their kind are people whom I am honoured to have known. No man could wish for better comrades. If I do nothing more in the rest of my life, I can say this: the best and proudest thing I have done is to have marched and fought with the men and women of Longbridge.

POSTSCRIPT

The Flight of Phoenix

By Stephen Dyson

Another book could be written about how Rover has fared since the Phoenix takeover. So much has happened, with various new directors, new sales figures, surprise strategies and continuing London cynicism, that it is tempting to at least devote a chapter or two to post-BMW events. But this book was always set to focus on the Battle for Longbridge – the 56 rollercoaster days, from 14 March to 9 May, from planned carve up to John Towers' rescue. What I can do is provide a précis, a collection of historical facts, mainly collected from the *Evening Mail*, to show in brief what happened during the summer of 2000.

    • 11 May: Harold Musgrove, the former chairman and chief executive of Austin Rover from 1982 to 1986, urged anyone who cares about Rover to 'Buy British'. He said: 'We should give Phoenix and Mr Towers every support, every congratulations. The people of Longbridge do deserve to be protected while they recover from the appalling mess that BMW brought about …This is the British motor industry we are talking about. … Support them.'

    • 12 May: New official figures revealed that Rover had enjoyed a runaway sales success in certain European countries during April, continental sales going up from 24,326 to 37,643 – a rise of 54.7%.

    • 15 May: Towers stated that he was to scrap BMW's unsuccessful attempt to drive the Rover brand up with premium prices. 'The concept of premium pricing has got to go. The Germans made the mistake of trying to turn Rover into a British version of BMW.'

    • 17 May: Rover pulls out of the Motor Show. The *Evening Mail* published details of an interview with Towers, after he visited our offices for a thorough debriefing by myself, business editor Jon Griffin and industrial correspondent Chris Morley on the whole Rover affair on 15 May. Editor Ian Dowell and Labour MP Richard Burden were also there. Griffin had asked: 'What models or ideas will Rover be revealing at this year's motor show in Birmingham?' Towers answer was succinct: 'None, because we won't be going.' Towers explained that the prestige biennial event at the National Exhibition Centre in October was the first casualty of budgetary cuts aimed at driving Rover

John Towers visits the Evening Mail to discuss exactly how his Phoenix bid succeeded. He is pictured with editor Ian Dowell (rear), Northfield MP Richard Burden and Stephen Dyson (right). *Picture by Phil Hitchman*

back into the black. He said: 'You do not sell cars at motor shows. You just think who goes to motor shows – motoring journalists who never buy a car in their lives. It just does not pay, it is an extremely expensive hobby…We are talking about millions of pounds on each show.' Rob Halloway, of the Society of Motor Manufacturers and Traders, said: 'It will be a real shame because … I am sure everyone would be delighted to see them there.' Alan Pulham, franchise director of the Retail Motor Industry Federation, which represents most of Rover's 300-strong dealer network, said the move was 'very disappointing' and urged Towers to find the money.' But Towers was unequivocal. Further cost cuts are also planned, he added, as 'it is a very important area. Our position is that you do not spend a pound until that pound returns something better in terms of what it gives you.'

• 1 June: Kevin Howe became Rover's new chief executive, following three weeks of rumours. Some workers said this choice was unpopular as Howe was not liked on the shopfloor, but others said Towers had proved his mettle by giving the job to the person he judged to be best for the business. Howe, aged 39, was managing director of Rover under BMW in 1999 before going to aero-engine maker Rolls Royce in Derby. He is known as a determined, hard driver who once helped increase productivity at Longbridge.

John Towers with newly appointed chief executive Kevin Howe and the new Rover 75 estate.
Picture courtesy of Rover

• 5 June: Rover unveiled across-the-board UK price cuts of 10 per cent, knocking more than £2,000 off a Rover 75, and more than £1,000 off the 25 and 45 models. Some observers said this was to help cut the company's stock of unsold cars, then numbering some 60,000. On the same day, Towers revealed a new subtle marketing plan with a campaign to give the guests of Posthouse hotels the chance to win one of 12 Rover 75s, rather than blanket advertising costing tens of millions of pounds.

• 15 June: Towers revealed that a 13-week schedule for relocating the Rover 75 from Cowley to Longbridge would start in late July, at the beginning of the summer shutdown.

John Towers launches his marketing alliance with Posthouse Hotels managing director Patrick Dempsey (right) with a Rover 75 Summer give-away on 5 June.
Picture by James Morgan

• 30 June: Rob Oldaker arrived as product development director, impressing industry observers. Once managing director of engine specialists Cosworth Engineering, Oldaker was also closely involved with the launch of the famed Rolls-Royce Silver Seraph.

• 2 July: A *Sunday Times* article, by Andrew Lorenz and David Parsley, suggested that Rover's production was about to plummet. It quoted a leaked supplier's letter sent by Rover, which said the company 'intended to cut output by 60 per cent from previous levels'. It also quoted one supplier, anonymously, as saying 'they will struggle to make and sell profitably more than 100,000 cars a year, and the total could be a good deal less.' The *Sunday Times* certainly hadn't given Phoenix much of a honeymoon period, virtually ignoring official explanations that the scaling down of production was to allow for the new Rover 75 and 75 estate production lines to be built.

• 4 July: A company spokesman revealed that Phoenix's Rover cars now had about 7,000 employees, and that its planned programme of up to 1,000 voluntary redundancies was proving more difficult than expected. Around 200 individual terms had been agreed, but with the future of Longbridge looking more secure, fewer people want to go.

• 7 July: Rover appointed motoring guru Peter Stevens as product design director. Stevens was once behind the McLaren F1 supercar, the elegant Lotus Elan and the prestige Jaguar XJR15.

New Rover directors, pictured from left: Nick Stephenson, deputy chairman; John Towers, chairman; Peter Stevens, product design director; Rob Oldaker, product development director; and Chris Lee, engineering director. *Picture courtesy of Rover*

• 14 July: Rover began its first big marketing drive since its change of ownership with the promotion of limited edition Rover 25 and 45 models to mark the Sydney Olympics. Rover became the official car supplier to the British Olympic Team. The result was pictures in many newspapers of famous athletes like Ashia Hansen posed next to Rover cars.

Rover sponsors the British Olympic team in one of its first new marketing plans. Pictured from left with John Towers are athletes Dwain Chambers, Dean Macey and Ashia Hansen. *Picture by Matt Dickens*

• 17 July: Thousands of workers at Longbridge were to enjoy an extra week's summer holiday to provide more time for the major revamp of the plant, with the vast majority of line workers given a three-week break instead of the normal fortnight. (It sounded good, although some workers told me they feared this would mean much longer hours, with fewer days off, once production was increased under Rover's flexible working deal, based on the banking of hours.)

• 21 July: Four months after 5,000 or more faced compulsory redundancy at Longbridge, Rover axes just 10 workers. Nearly 1,000 had volunteered for redundancy, as planned by Phoenix, but only ten compulsory redundancies are to be made after management and unions were unable to find them work within the new company.

• 24 July: Rover revealed that a 'serious player' had expressed interest in sharing platforms for the production of future models at Longbridge. Some observers were later to say that this 'serious player' was Malaysian car maker Proton, although Rover never confirmed this.

• 25 July: Rover revealed plans to produce up to 75,000 MGs a year at Longbridge, with around 60,000 new three, four and five-door variants to be added to the current 14,000 MGFs in the Spring of 2001.

• 31 July: *The Times* revealed that two key government departments had snubbed Rover, buying around 12,000 mostly foreign fleet cars. The news sparked anger from unions and politicians, although it was then revealed that earlier in the year the then BMW-owned Rover had not put in a bid for the contracts.

On the same day, the editor of the UK's used car price 'bible', Glass's Guide, revealed that Rover was set to produce one of the 'biggest design shocks ever' by introducing 'truly outrageous' high performance models. Bill Carter, autoprovision editor of Glass's, made his comments after a meeting with Towers and said the re-sale value of Rover cars had now 'dramatically increased' as a result. He added: 'We are now far more upbeat about Rover.'

• 3 August: Rover revealed plans to launch its 75 model and the MGF in South Africa and Australia, where it was felt there were 'great opportunities'. Gordon Poynter, now Rover's director of corporate affairs, added that the transfer of the 75 from Cowley to Longbridge was 'going to plan' with production still due in October.

• 8 August: Just days before I sent the final draft of this book to the publisher, I called Poynter for a last check on one or two details. I asked him, for the record, how many workers Phoenix now employed at Rover, a figure that was not easy to calculate, given that Land Rover, Powertrain, the body panel factory at Swindon, the Cowley plant and Gaydon were no longer part of the group. Poynter told me the figure at Longbridge, now that nearly 1,000 workers had taken redundancy, was 'around 6,000', although he stressed that Rover still had future options on Powertrain (around 1,500 workers) and Swindon (around 2,700).

He then said that in the near future the company was set to advertise for up to 40 skilled engineers for specific future projects. What a turnaround. Rover, set for possible closure with thousands of jobs at risk just five months previously, was now considering taking more staff on. Phoenix was flying.

• 25 August: As the book was going to press, it was revealed that Rover's MG was to compete in the Le Mans 24-hour race in 2001 for the first time in 35 years. Nick Stephenson, speaking as deputy chairman of Rover Group and director of Lola Cars, said: 'We are serious about developing the MG brand which previously has been under developed. A return to international motor racing is a major part of injecting excitement and performance into the brand.'

- 11 September: Rover announced that it had renamed itself as 'MG Rover', reflecting the elevation of the MG marque within the group.
- 12 September: In his first major interview since he was appointed, MG Rover's managing director Kevin Howe revealed that the company was enjoying a two-year high in retail sales. Howe also said the group was on course to sell a total of more than 200,000 in the year 2000. He added that production of the Rover 75 at Longbridge would be ready to start on October 4 2000, the same day as the last old Mini was due to roll off the line.

★ ★ ★ ★ ★

INDEX

Note: for ease of reference, some sub-sections are listed chronologically.